HUNTSVILLE

More Pictures from the Past

A Committee of Heritage Huntsville

© Copyright Heritage Huntsville, 1998

Published in 1998 by
Boston Mills Press
132 Main Street
Erin, Ontario
N0B 1T0
www.boston-mills.on.ca

An affiliate of Stoddart Publishing Co. Limited
34 Lesmill Road
Toronto, Ontario, Canada
M3B 2T6

Distributed in Canada by
General Distribution Services Limited
30 Lesmill Road
Toronto, Canada M3B 2T6
Tel 416-445-3333
Fax 416-445-5967
Canadian Telebook S1150391
e-mail gdsinc@genpub.com

Distributed in the United States by
General Distribution Services Inc.
85 River Rock Drive, Suite 202
Buffalo, New York 14207-2170
Toll-free 1-800-805-1083
Toll-free fax 1-800-481-6207
PUBNET 6307949
e-mail gdsinc.genpub.com

02 01 00 99 98   1 2 3 4 5

Cataloging in Publication Data
Huntsville : more pictures from the past

Includes bibliographical references.
ISBN 1-55046-231-8

1. Huntsville (Ont.) - History - Pictorial works. 2. Huntsville (Ont.) - History.
I. Heritage Huntsville (Association).

FC3099.H85H85 1998   917.3´16   C98-931133-3
F1059.5.H85H85 1998

Cover design by Gillian Stead

Design by Mary Firth

Printed in Canada

CONTENTS

ACKNOWLEDGMENTS

THE MEMBERS of the Heritage Huntsville (LACAC) Committee gratefully acknowledge the assistance of the following people who most generously have made both information and photographs available to us:

Jessie Adamson
Keith Alderson
Margaret Allen
★Roy and Dorothy Armstrong
Mac Avery
Susan Baird
Reta Baker
Floyd Bartlett
Roxy and Ken Beelby
Arvina Bennett
Diane Bickley
Mr. and Mrs. Wm. Billingsley
Ruth Binks
Dr. Stanley Birch
Frank Booth
Eva Boothby
Frances Botham
Iris Bray
Mary Buktenica
★Vera Cameron
Reverend Frank Carey
Pat Carnachan
Mary Carpenter
Diane Charlton
Bill Clarke
Mel Clarke
Terry Clarke Sr.
Jean Contant
Beth Cope
Judy Craik
Mary Crawford
Kenneth Curzon
June Dadswell
Mary Dubois

Stephen Dubois
★Walter Dubois
John and Kathy Earl
Gregg Evans
★Agnes Eybers
William Firth
Barbara Firth-Brown
Janet Fisher
Donna Flotron
Elaine Foster
Helen French
Larry French
Evelyn Gilchrist
Donald and Joanne Gilroy
Norman Goodwin
★Margaret Govan
William Grierson
John and Barbara Groves
Rose and Edward Hamblin
Laura Harper
Dwayne Hayes
Gwen Herbison
June Higgs
Robert Hill
Elspeth Hogg
★Anthony Hole
James Honderich
Barbara Hopcraft
Vaughn Hope
Roxie Hosking
Jack Hubbel
Daisy Hughes
Harvey Hughes
Viola Hunt

Tanis Hunter
Dennis Hutcheson
★Jane Hutcheson
Paul and Carol Johnson
Kenneth and June Jones
Joy Julian
★Jessie Kay
Catherine Kealy
Cheryl Keeter
Nona Keevil
Rick Keevil
Joan Mary Kell
Tim Kelly
Connie Kelso
Cindy Knappett
★Pat Lamon
Susan Larsen
Jack Laycock
Opal Magladry
Bruce May
Frank May
Helen May
Peter McBirnie
Joy McCaskill
Betty McConnell
Gil McFarland
★Myrtle McKenney
Donna Miglin
Douglas and Doris Millikin
Lawrence Morgan
Dr. Michael and Judith
   Morison
Frances Morrison
Reverend Edna Murdy

Muskoka Pioneer Village
Jack Newton
Bill Nickalls
Donal and Patricia Nickalls
★Ernie Norris
Stina Nyquist
Kenneth Oben
Mary Olan
Mern Parker
Barbara Paterson
Bruce Payne
Dennis Payne
Vera Peacock
Zetta Pells
Boa Quan
Jean Reynolds
Laverne Reynolds
Elizabeth Rice-Aben
John Riviere-Anderson
Jan Roberts
Miriam Robinson
Olive Robinson
Bill Rogers
Ted Rogers
Judith Ruan
Mr. and Mrs. Philip Rumney
Mary Schamehorn
Marlene Schell
Bert Schuch
Bernice and J.R. Scott
Shannon Shea
Reverend Eric and Mary Sisel
★George and Helen Snowden
Donald Snowden

Wanda Somerset
Esther Spencer
Don and Mary Spring
Eloise Stevens
Reverend Norman Strongman
Olive Stroud
Gail Stupka
Owen Swann
Grant Taylor
Craig and Mary Louise Teakle
Ed Terziano
Lyle Thompson
Doris Troth
Irene Turner
Evert Van Duuren
Nora Vincent
Margaret and Ronald
   Wallbank
Paul Walmsley
Clara Watson
Martha Briggs Watson
Mr. and Mrs. Murray Watson
William Weber
David White
Marion White
Don Wilson
Joan Woodcock
Beth Wright
Jack Young
Margaret Young
Hanna Zmuda

★Deceased

6

We have tried to include everyone who assisted us in any way. If, by mistake, we have omitted any names, we apologize.

We are extremely grateful to all those who have lent us old photographs. We know they are very valuable, and extremely difficult to find. We have not found as many as we would have liked, so have had to substitute more recent photos.

Many local citizens have helped us so much with this project. We would not have been able to proceed without the approval and support of Heritage Huntsville's competent Chairperson, Gail Moser. Another member of the LACAC Committee, Elspeth Hogg, has contributed greatly to our efforts with the research and articles on Port Sydney.

Barbara Paterson did the majority of the research for this book. We have been fortunate to have her assistance, as she is undoubtedly Huntsville's best researcher.

Beth Cope and Helen May produced a volume of photographs and information on many places on Lake Vernon, about which they are extremely knowledgeable. This has been very much appreciated. Some of their efforts have been included in this publication.

Without a doubt the person who has worked the hardest is Lisa Smith, the LACAC secretary and a Town of Huntsville employee. She keyed all of the articles, often presented to her in a jumbled form. She voluntarily did all of this in her own free time. That the whole book made it from manuscript to computer disk is due to her efforts. Lisa has also done many other odd jobs for us, always with a pleasant manner and a smile on her face.

Most of the newer photographs have been taken by Dr. Norris Hunt and Barbara Paterson. In all kinds of situations, they have shot pictures of all kinds of places. We cannot thank them enough.

The architectural descriptions for some articles have been written by Sharon McKenzie, Stephen Carter and Stephen Short, who have all been members at various times of Heritage Huntsville. We are grateful for their expertise.

We were fortunate to have the help of Mary Crawford, who volunteered to edit each article. It was a time-consuming job.

I wish to thank the many people I pressured into finding local information and writing articles. Sometimes it is not fun.

The staff of the Huntsville Public Library have always been most helpful and courteous. And to the planners of the new Huntsville Public Library, we cannot thank you enough for your foresight in including the Muskoka Room.

John Denison of Boston Mills Press encouraged us from the start to put together a second *Pictures from the Past*. If he had not done so, this book would not have been forthcoming.

To every last person who assisted us, our heartfelt thanks.

Heritage Huntsville (LACAC Committee)

HERITAGE HUNTSVILLE (LACAC COMMITTEE)

Chairperson

Maureen Hunt

Members and Researchers

Diane Bickley

Frances Botham

Diane Charlton

Beth Cope

Mary Crawford

Elaine Foster

Elspeth Hogg

Connie Kelso

Helen May

Joy McCaskill

Douglas and Doris Millikin

Barbara Paterson

Jean Reynolds

Shannon Shea

Evert Van Duuren

David White

Marion White

Architectural Descriptions

Stephen Carter, B.E.S (Arch), B.Arch.

Sharon McKenzie, B.Arch.

Stephen Short, Dip. Arch. Technology

Editor

Mary Crawford

Typist

Lisa Smith

Photography

Dr. Norris Hunt

Barbara Paterson

FOREWORD

IN 1989 THE HERITAGE HUNTSVILLE Local Conservation Advisory Committee (LACAC) decided to produce an inventory of buildings in Huntsville that were of historical or architectural interest. Sharon McKenzie, an architect on the committee at the time, made the initial selection of the buildings and then photographs were taken.

The committee then decided to learn something of the history of these buildings and the people who had lived in them. Barbara Paterson, an excellent local historical researcher, was hired for this assignment. Information and photos began to be accumulated by Heritage Huntsville. Committee members Stephen Carter and Sharon McKenzie, both architects, and Stephen Short, an architectural technologist, wrote brief architectural descriptions of some of the properties. Beth Cope and Helen May, also very good researchers and very familiar with Lake Vernon, produced a volume of photographs and information on places on Lake Vernon.

In the fall of 1997 Maureen Hunt, vice chairperson of Heritage Huntsville, thought that this information should be published to share with Huntsville citizens. The previous book *Pictures from the Past: Huntsville and Lake of Bays* (Boston Mills Press, 1986) written by the research committee of the Muskoka Pioneer Village, had been successful. John Denison of Boston Mills Press agreed to publish this project too.

Main Street, Huntsville, 1938.

A committee was assembled of people who had shown interest in local history, and projects were assigned to each researcher and writer. As time went on, other buildings and photos were added to the original Heritage Huntsville inventory.

So that is the story of how this book developed. It has taken a lot of effort on the part of many people. We hope you enjoy it.

Maureen Hunt
Chairperson

8

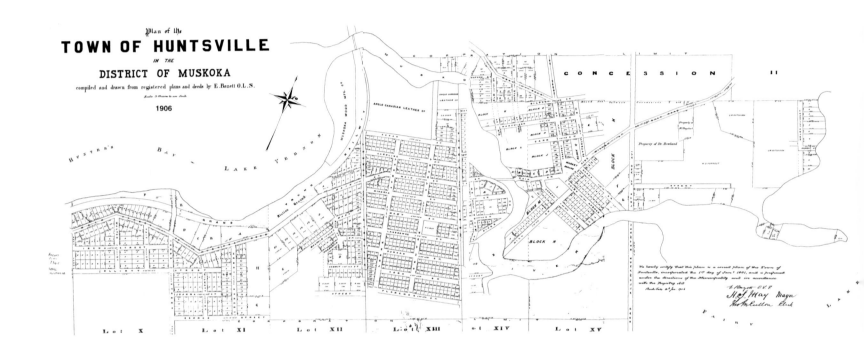

Plan of the
TOWN OF HUNTSVILLE
IN THE
DISTRICT OF MUSKOKA
compiled and drawn from registered plans and deeds by E. Bazett O.L.S.

1906

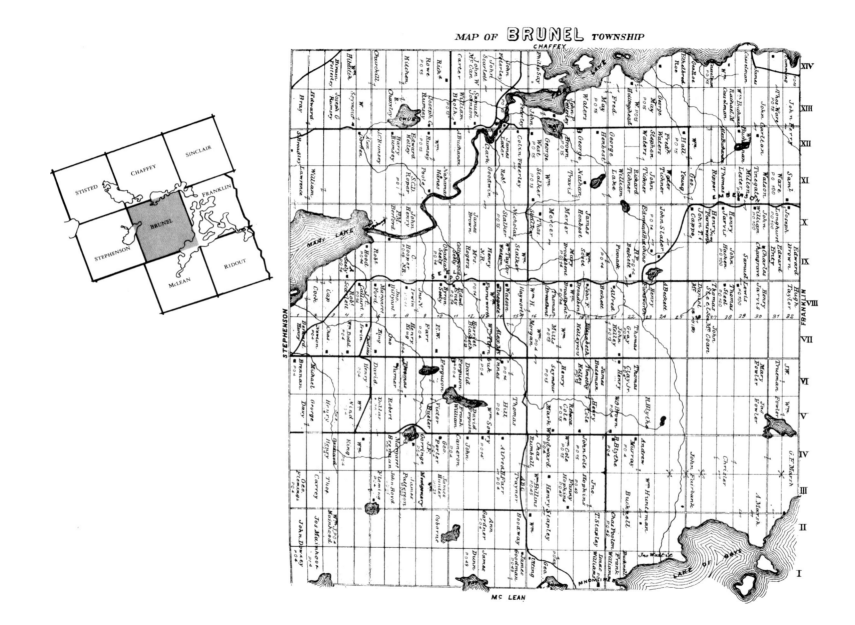

MAP OF BRUNEL TOWNSHIP

10

MAP OF **CHAFFEY** TOWNSHIP

11

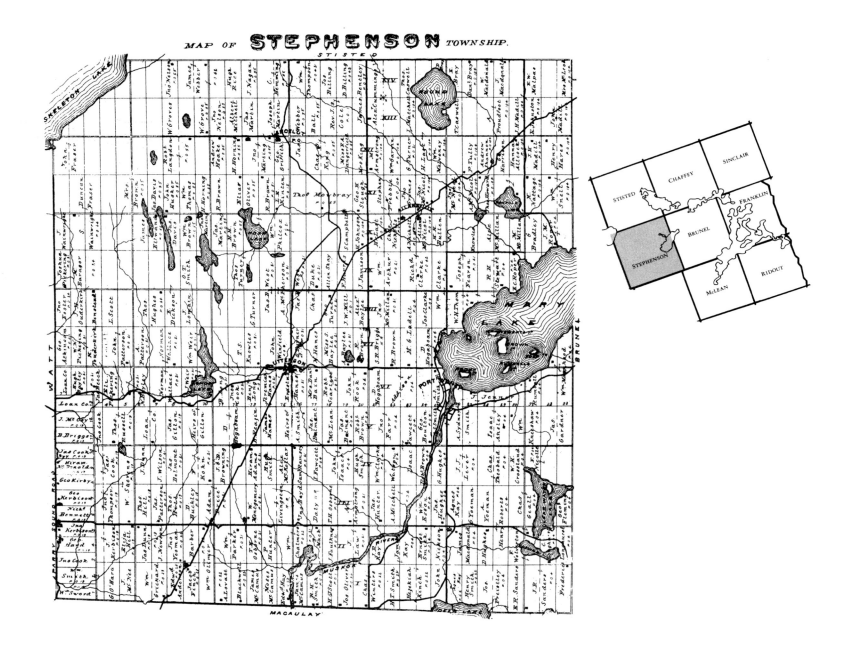

MAP OF **STEPHENSON** TOWNSHIP.

12

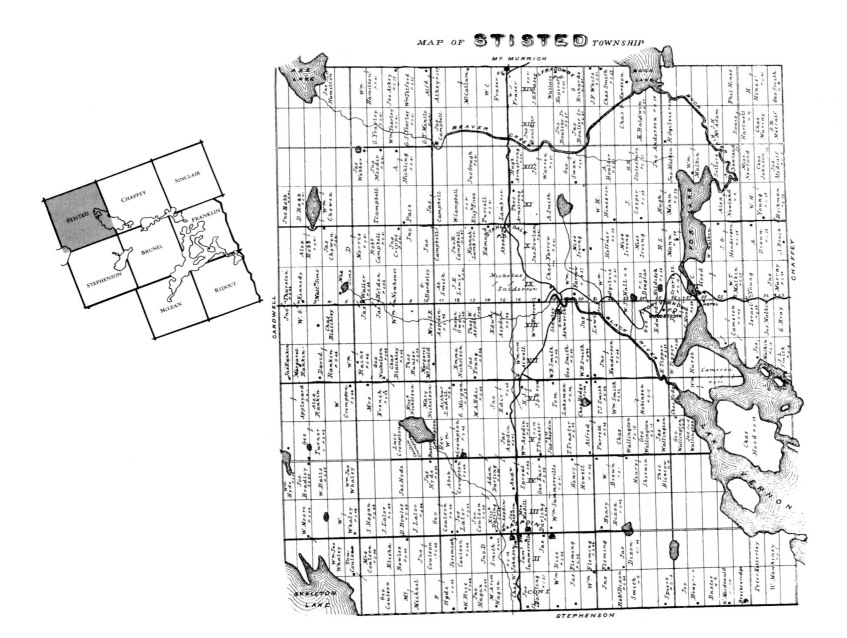

MAP OF STISTED TOWNSHIP

13

NOTICE
TO
Immigrants and Settlers.

DEPARTMENT OF CROWN LANDS,
TORONTO, 18th April, 1868.

NOTICE is hereby given, that the Lands in the Townships of HUMPHREY, CARDWELL, WATT, STEPHENSON, BRUNEL, MACAULAY, McLEAN, MUSKOKA and DRAPER, in the Territorial District of Muskoka, and in the Townships of McDOUGALL and FOLEY, on Parry Sound, (Georgian Bay,) are open for location under "The Free Grants and Homestead Act of 1868."

Applications for locations in the Townships of McDougall, Foley, Humphrey and Cardwell, are to be made to N. P. WAKEFIELD, Esq., Crown Lands Agent, at the Village of Parry Sound ; and for locations in the Townships of Watt, Stephenson, Brunel, Macaulay, McLean, Muskoka and Draper, applications are to be made to C. W. LOUNT, Esq., Crown Lands Agent at Bracebridge, in the Township of Macaulay.

Locatees, in addition to obtaining the Free Grant of 100 acres, will be allowed to purchase an additional 100 acres, at 50 cents an acre, cash, subject to the same reservations and conditions, and the performance of the same settlement duties as are provided in respect of free grant locations by the 9th and 10th sections of the Free Grants Act, except that actual residence and building on the land purchased will not be required.

For further information respecting the conditions on which the lands will be granted, apply to the above named Crown Lands Agents, or to the Department at Toronto.

S. RICHARDS,
Commissioner of Crown Lands.

The Free Grant Act of 1868 entitled any settler, eighteen years of age and over, to select 100 acres in a surveyed township and any head of a family could select 200 acres. This did not include the mineral rights or pine trees on the property.

Within the five years following selection, the locatee was required to have at least fifteen acres of cleared land under cultivation ("whereof at least two acres shall be cleared and cultivated annually"); to have built a house fit for habitation at least sixteen feet by twenty feet; and to have actually and continuously resided upon and cultivated the land, not being absent for more than six months in any one year. On the fulfillment of these conditions, the patent would be issued, and the settler would hold his or her estate in fee simple (that is, inheritable without limitation).

DOMINION OF CANADA.

EMIGRATION
TO THE
PROVINCE OF ONTARIO.

To Capitalists, Tenant Farmers, Agricultural Labourers, Mechanics, Day Labourers, and all parties desirous of improving their circumstances by Emigrating to a new country.

Attention is invited to the great advantages presented by the Province of Ontario, to various classes of new Settlers. Persons living on the interest of their money can easily get 8 per cent. on first class security in the Province of Ontario. Tenant Farmers, with limited capital, can buy and stock a freehold estate in Ontario with the money needed to carry on a small farm in Britain. Good cleared land, with a dwelling and barn on it, can be purchased in desirable localities at from 20 to 50 dollars, or £4 to £10 Stg., per acre. Farm hands can readily get work at good wages, with their board found.

INDUCEMENTS TO INTENDING EMIGRANTS.

FREE GRANTS OF LAND TO ACTUAL SETTLERS.

Land given away to all comers over 18 years of age. A family of several persons can secure a large block of land gratis.

The Government of Ontario offers as a Free Grant to any actual settler over 18 years of age, One Hundred Acres of Land in the Free Grant Districts.

THE FREE GRANT LANDS

Exhibited on the within Map are easy of access.

THERE ARE DAILY MAILS BETWEEN TORONTO AND THE FREE GRANT DISTRICTS.

Parties desirous of fuller information, concerning the Province of Ontario, will apply personally, or by letter, to WM. DIXON, Esq., Emigration Agent, 11 Adam Street, Adelphi, London ; or to any of the Imperial or Dominion Emigrant Agents in Europe ; or to the GRAND TRUNK RAILWAY OFFICES, No. 21 Old Broad Street, London ; or to the GREAT WESTERN of Canada RAILWAY OFFICE, 126 Gresham House, Old Broad Street, London, E. C. ; or to the NORTHERN RAILWAY OFFICE, Messrs. CUTBILL, SON & DeLUNGO, No. 13 Gresham Street, London, E. C. ; or to the CANADA COMPANY, No. 1 East India Avenue, Leadenhall Street, London ; or to ALLAN BROS. & CO., James Street, Liverpool ; JAMES and ALEXANDER ALLAN, Great Clyde Street, Glasgow ; ALLAN BROS. & CO., Foyle Sreet, Londonderry ; by whom Pamphlets, giving detailed information, maps, &c., will be supplied.

Emigrants bound for the Province of Ontario, will take vessel to Quebec, and proceed westward, either by Steamboat or Railway.

By reference to the Map, any desired point can be selected from which to look for a new home.

JOHN CARLING,
Commissioner of Agriculture and Public Works for the Province of Ontario.

Toronto, Ontario, March, 1869.

A BRIEF HISTORY OF EARLY HUNTSVILLE

NORTHERN RAILWAY

OF CANADA.

IN CONNECTION WITH THE

FREE GRANT DISTRICTS

or

PARRY SOUND AND MUSKOKA.

Land given away to all comers over 18 years of age. A family of several persons can secure a large block of land gratis.

The Government of Ontario offers as a Free Grant to any actual settler over 18 years of age, One Hundred Acres of Land in the Free Grant Districts.

Heads of Families get Two Hundred Acres as a Free Grant.

Locatees, in addition to obtaining the Free Grant of 100 acres, will be allowed to purchase an additional 100 acres at 50 cents an acre, cash.

TRAINS MOVING NORTH

Leave the Company's Stations. City Hall* and foot of Brock Street, Toronto, as follows :—

	A.M.	P.M.
City Hall	7.00	4.00
Brock Street	7.15	4.15

Fare from Toronto to Bracebridge, - - - **$3.75.**

CONNECTIONS.

BELL EWART—With Steamer *Emily May*, leaving Bell Ewart every morning, on arrival of Mail Train from Toronto, for Beaverton, Orillia and intermediate ports on Lake Simcoe, connecting with steamer for Washago: also stage for Gravenhurst, and steamer *Wenonah* for Bracebridge and ports on Lake Muskoka, and steamer *Wabamik* for ports on Lake Rosseau. With steamer *Simcoe*, leaving Bell Ewart every evening on arrival of Express Train from Toronto, for Orillia direct, returning to Bell Ewart connect with Morning Express Train for Toronto and Collingwood.

BARRIE—Daily stage to Penetanguishine. With steamer *Ida Burton*, leaving Barrie at 5.30 a.m. daily for Orillia and Washago, connecting with stage for Gravenhurst, and steamer *Wenonah* for Bracebridge and ports on Lake Muskoka, and steamer *Wabamik* for ports on Lake Rosseau.

COLLINGWOOD—The steamer *Waubuno* leaves Collingwood every Saturday morning for Parry Sound.

FRED. CUMBERLAND.

Managing Director.

Advertisement 1879, Rail and Steamer Service, Toronto - Bracebridge

HUNTSVILLE DERIVES its name from Captain George Hunt, who was really the first permanent settler of the village. He arrived with his wife and family in 1869 under the Ontario Free Grants and Homestead Act. The property on the east side of the Muskoka River, part of Lots 14 and 15, Concession 1, Chaffey Township, was his "location." He was responsible for having the Muskoka Road pushed farther north to Huntsville and for the bridge being built across the river. The first church services and school classes were held in his log cabin. A post office named after Captain Hunt was established.

With his temperance principles, he made it a condition in each deed issued on his original acreage that no intoxicating liquor ever be sold on the premises. Thus the hamlet grew more rapidly on the hilly, west side of the river where hotels had no restrictions. The building of the locks on the Muskoka River between Mary Lake and Fairy Lake in 1877 augmented the growth of the small settlement. Eight years later, the Northern and Pacific Junction Railway arrived in Huntsville. This was another great impetus for growth. The village of Huntsville was incorporated the following year, 1886.

With the decline of the farming experiment, many farmers left for the superior soil conditions of the western provinces. Others turned to the lumbering industry, which was flourishing, for jobs and to supplement their farm income. Many began to take summer tourists into their homes, and that was the beginning of the tourist industry in the area. The growth of the village was spurred on by the building of the tannery in the 1890s. Huntsville became a thriving little community with hotels, shops, newspapers, doctors and hospitals. A Main Street fire in 1894 was a severe setback, but the merchants confidently rebuilt their stores. By the turn of the century, the progressive village of Huntsville became incorporated as a town.

ON APRIL 18, 1894, A FIRE STARTED behind H.S. May's handsome hardware store at 65 Main Street East (where Pastimes Hobby Centre is now). All the buildings from the bridge to West Street were demolished with the exception of the original wooden Methodist church, 33 Main Street East, and its manse situated on the site of our present town hall.

The July 9, 1892, issue of the Toronto *Mail* featured an article on the village of Huntsville, calling it a promising summer resort and hunter's paradise. It described the "Lovely Lakes, Beautiful Scenery, Monster Lumber Industries" as well as the hunting and fishing, campsites and social advantages of the area.

William Cann, a hunter and trapper, built a shanty in 1862 on a hill in the centre of our pretty village nestled in the valley of the Muskoka River (on the site of All Saints Church, and the cabin was still standing in 1892). William disposed of his claims to R.J. Hilditch and George Hunt, who named the village and became its first postmaster and storekeeper. Progress in the development of the village site was slow — and it wasn't until 1871 that the Ontario Free Grants and Homestead Act of 1868 had much effect. Soon, Allan Shay, Fred Shay, George Lasseter and George and Nathan Norton settled in the village or on adjacent farms. In 1872 Scarlett Bros. of Utterson started a branch store in Huntsville. Dr. Francis Howland was induced by a bonus of $1,000 to move to Huntsville to administer to the medical needs of the eleven families, all told.

J. Stephenson and Co. started the first sawmill (where

Main Street, Huntsville, 1880s.

Blackburn's Landing is today) and for many years it was the only one. By 1878 Samuel Parish of Uxbridge had built a gristmill (situated near Vanity Fair, 84 Main Street East), but by 1892 it was known as A.N. Ingersoll's first mill.

The bridge was built across the Muskoka River in 1870, but by about 1880 it had been replaced by a "handsome swing bridge which constitutes so great an ornament to the village."

In 1885 the village presented little indication of ever becoming important, but the opening of the Northern and Pacific Junction Railway altered things. Huntsville, in 1892, ranked "in the volume of its traffic" the fourth station north of Toronto, and second only to one other in the District of Muskoka.

Steamers, all propellor driven but one, were the *Lady of the Lake*, the *Excelsior* (so badly damaged in the 1894 fire), the *Wiman* and the *Northern*. They were used on Lake Vernon, Peninsula Lake, Fairy Lake and Mary Lake, as well as the Muskoka River. The *Florence* and *Mary L* were on Trading Lake — otherwise known as Lake of Bays. One steamer went to Hoodstown at the far end of Lake Vernon, another through Fairy Lake and the canal to Peninsula Lake. (The article does not mention how travellers crossed between Peninsula Lake and Lake of Bays, but as it wasn't until 1903 that the Portage Railway was built, the crossing was likely made by horse and wagon.) The third route was southward through the locks (completed in 1878) down the Muskoka River to Mary Lake. The scenery along each of these routes was "magnificent" and surpassing anything the author had seen on this continent.

The hunting and fishing in the area made this a veritable hunter's paradise. Salmon weighing twenty pounds were easily caught, and there was an abundance of red deer and moose, thanks to a five-year hunting restriction made in 1889. Thirty bears were shot in the vicinity in 1891. The howl of wolves from the east and north of the village was said to be at times as familiar as the notes of the whippoorwill. Mink, otter and beaver were abundant, and trapping a lucrative occupation.

In describing the agricultural surroundings, the author of the 1892 article wondered: "How can one sow or reap on these crags? Where can one coat a scanty pasture for the hardiest goat?" However, he went on to say: "These rocky barriers which fringe the territory and frown upon the incomer are not true samples of Muskoka land; nor does the aggregate area of such rock constitute more than one-third of the land surface of the district." From the verandah of the hotel where the author was staying "not one rock or boulder" could be seen. The soil was a rich clay loam eighteen inches to two feet deep on the Fairy and Peninsula Lakes farms of Robert Ballantine, J.P., Mrs. John Taylor, William Castleman, Mrs. Hood, Hugh Taylor and Reverend Robert Norton Hill. These farms presented an advanced grade of husbandry.

Another area that was truly impressive was the marvelously picturesque and beautiful grounds of the Good Templars Fairy Lake Camp Association, now known as Memorial Park, comprising sixty acres of the western shore of Fairy Lake immediately joining the municipality. The area "constitutes prospectively one of the finest summer resorts in the dominion." The three rising hills behind the camp and the view from the top, our Lookout, were a "panoramic blending of nature and art, which once witnessed is not likely to be forgotten." In fact, the whole site was accorded the scientific "recommendation of the medical association of Muskoka, Parry Sound and Nipissing as a health and pleasure resort." The association was prepared to negotiate for the lease "on exceptionally favourable terms" of eligible building sites on the property through either the president, John E. Wilson, or the secretary, W.E. Hutcheson. We are happy this concept was not developed.

The development of churches was a very important issue for settlers throughout the new dominion, and Huntsville was no exception. It took only about fifteen years for the various congregations to be formed and churches built. The Bracebridge Methodist District was established in 1868 and mission services in Huntsville inaugurated in the Orange Hall (then on West Street, on the former Eaton's property). But it was not until 1874, under the pastorate of T.W. Hall and subsequently that of Reverend R. Toye, that the somewhat unpretentious church edifice was erected (the wooden church at the corner of West Street that did not burn in the Main Street fire of 1894). At the time of the article, the congregation was contemplating a new church (built in 1897).

By 1876 the adherents of the Presbyterian church were organized as a congregation by Reverend R. Moodie, clerk of the Barrie Presbytery, and placed in charge of M.H. Cameron, a popular young student of Queen's University. The membership at this time was only ten, "a mere handful it is true, and uphill work to face at that, but they were Scotch, and well, a church was erected and paid for before the end of the year." In 1884 Reverend James Sieveright, B.A., arrived, and a handsome stone manse erected for him (still standing at 8 Church Street).

The early Anglicans in Huntsville were an outpost of the Mary Lake

Mission, with headquarters in Port Sydney. The missionary in charge for some time was Reverend Edmund Cooper, who, it is related, once varied the service by boxing a boy's ears when he did not respond as devoutly as the minister thought he should.

In 1875–76 Bishop Fauquier visited, and through his influence a hall was erected (a wooden structure that was situated on the site between the present All Saints Church and Sutherland Hall). At the time of the article in 1892, under the ministry of Reverend Thomas Llwyd, a handsome new stone church was being erected, "which will be an ornament to Huntsville." The Roman Catholic Church of the Diocese of Peterborough had recently purchased a site and intended to erect a stone church (on Main Street West). There was a small congregation of Disciples, ministered to by Reverend W.M. Crewson, and the Salvation drum, with its following of "Army" recruits, was nightly "heard in the land."

The Huntsville Public School was erected five years before for $7,000, and was "commodious and well appointed." It had four departments, presided over by principal J.N. Shearer and three other teachers. Among the graduates a few had already made their mark in the world.

The Mechanics' Institute located in the Bettes Block, 38 Main Street East, had developed amazingly during the four years it had existed. It offered citizens a comfortable reading room, a library of over four hundred volumes, and the leading periodicals of the day — including always the *Mail* — from which readers could "select their mental pablum."

The Huntsville Hospital was founded in 1886 "to meet a long felt want in the neighbourhood of the lumber camps and sawmills of Muskoka." An insurance plan with a premium of five dollars per year entitled subscribers to all the benefits of the hospital, and casual patients were admitted at a normal charge. The institution was "laid out in approved ward style and amply supplied with hot and cold baths" and was in all respects a "model" surgical retreat. Dr. J.W. Hart, M.D., C.M, the proprietor and medical superintendent, had "acknowledged ability in his profession." And the staff of nurses ranked with the best-appointed hospitals in the Dominion. (This original hospital was on the east side of Chaffey Street).

Main Street, Huntsville, 1886.

The Huntsville Tannery was established in 1891 by D.W. Alexander of Toronto, and managed by R.J. Watson. It was the largest edifice of its kind in Muskoka and equal in capacity to any tannery in the Dominion. The weekly output was from 1,200 to 1,600 dressed hides, averaging twenty pounds each. The hides were all imported from the United States and the hemlock bark used in the tanning process reached 6,000 to 7,000 cords per annum, which at five dollars a cord represented $30,000 to $35,000. The number of hands employed was about forty and the business transacted "very large and extends not merely to the various provinces of the Dominion but likewise to Great Britain and other countries abroad. A visit to this mammoth establishment and a chat with the general manager will long be remembered."

The vast areas of standing timber, many of them untouched, made a tremendous impression: "Lumber is Huntsville's destiny. But since the coming of the railway in 1885 smoke stacks have been reared and sawmills now monopolize every navigable lake and stream." The Whalley Lumber Company was located at the outlet of Muskoka River from Hunters Bay, close to the railway. Its capacity was 30,000 to 35,000 feet of lumber,

35,000 shingles and 20,000 lath per day. This company employed forty hands and eventually became the Muskoka Wood Co. (today, Tembec Inc.).

Another mill on the bay was Heath Tait and Turnbull, with a capacity larger than the Whalley Co. and fifty-five employees. A feature of this mill was the electric light "by means of which it is illuminated when necessary throughout every department." There was also a well-stocked general store in connection with this plant (a building no longer standing at 118 Main Street West). The lumber mills of Brennen and Son (also on Hunters Bay) and J. Whiteside on the river are also mentioned.

Of all the hotels in early Huntsville by far the most impressive was Cook's Hotel (the Vernon House), now the Bayview. It was "the finest and most commodious structure of its class in the village and its proximity to the 'getting off place' (station) gives it an advantage. The accommodation is all that the most exacting ought to expect." The Dominion Hotel (Empire) was centrally located on Main Street and afforded accommodation "of all kinds second to that of no other house of entertainment in the village. Mr. McLean is a genial and obliging host." One of the best houses of entertainment "with an old time reputation" was the Gilchrist Hotel (Queen's), situated where the downtown A&P is. It was popular as a commercial resort and place of call. Thomas Birtch operated the Toronto and Nipissing Hotel near the bridge (southeast corner Brunel Road and Main Street).

In the "matter of temperance, benevolent and religious organizations," the village ranked high, with the AF and AM (the Masons), Foresters, Orange Order, Oddfellows, Templars, Sons of England, Sons of Scotland, as well as the Epworth League and Christian Endeavour and various church groups.

The village of Huntsville was incorporated as such in 1886 and the first reeve was L.E. Kinton, who retained the position until displaced by Dr. F. Howland in 1889, followed by Dr. J.W. Hart in 1891. The village officers in 1892 were reeve, Dr. Hart; councillors, Thos. Goldie, J.R. Reece, R.J. Watson, Wm. Wright; and clerk and treasurer, R.W. Godolphin. "A more level headed company of conservators of the interests of the rising municipality, such as Huntsville, it may justly be observed, would be difficult to duplicate in the district." The postmaster was James Hanes.

John Milne and Son was an "enterprising firm" manufacturing large quantities of "sash, doors, frames and mouldings, dressed lumber, also cant hooks. The factory has been greatly enlarged and a splendid new engine and boiler constitutes only a part of the increased equipment necessary to meet the growing demand. Tourists and others in quest of cottage buildings, or the erection of wooden buildings of any size or design, can realize all they desire and that too at an outlay which residents of the frontier may find marvellous." A planing mill owned by D. McCaffrey, the gristmill of Winnacott and Pugh and a cheese factory completed Huntsville's list of manufacturing concerns.

Three stores are mentioned in this 1892 article. Goldie and Fisher, and Hutcheson and Son were general merchants, selling everything, including groceries and dry goods. C.A. Wattson was a pharmacist who, besides drugs, sold stationery, fancy goods and wallpaper.

This completes this 1892 portrait of the developing village of Huntsville. Many of the institutions and buildings are still thriving, and new ones have been added. The town has progressed well over the past century, and now looks forward to the year 2000 and the twenty-first century.

HUNTSVILLE'S ORIGINAL COURTHOUSE AND LOCK-UP
HIGH STREET, HUNTSVILLE
1883

IN 1881 A GROUP of prominent Huntsville citizens, under the leadership of Louis Kinton, merchant, F.W. Clearwater, printer and publisher, and F.L. Howland, doctor, and editor of *The Forester*, petitioned the Ontario Department of Public Works "for a jail in this place." They understood that there was funding of $2,000 for such a project and they wanted to make sure that a local man got the contract. The group recommended John M. Forster, who was advertising in *The Forester* at that time: "John M. Forster — Architect, plans and specifications — estimates and bills of quantities prepared for all kinds of buildings. Charges Moderate."

The following year William Cann, a widower who had received part of Lots 14 and 15, Concession 1, Chaffey Township, from the Crown in 1875, donated an acre of land (Lot 41 in the Huntsville Plan 1) to Her Majesty Queen Victoria and to the Village of Huntsville for a public building. The lot was situated on High Street, with 280 feet of frontage, and ran through to Princess Street in the rear.

The records of the Ontario Department of Public Works for 1881 contains this entry: "A frame court room and lock-up is now under construction by J.M. Forster, his tender being the lowest. The work is under the supervision of the Permanent Clerk of the Works." The building nearly completely burned down on July 27, 1882. However, it was not occupied at the time and no workmen were present. Fortunately, the building was insured.

The Ontario Department of Public Works records for the following year show that "a settlement was reached with the

Huntsville's original town hall, south side of High Street. Also the courthouse, lock-up and jail.

insurance company and a new tender issued. Messrs. Proudfoot and Francis were the lowest bidders this time. The work is in progress. The building is roofed in and enclosed."

By September 1884 the courtroom and lock-up at Huntsville was completed and occupied, "the work having been done in a satisfactory manner. Furniture and furnishings were required...which were duly reported and approved, all having been completed."

The Georgian-style building was unusual for Huntsville

20

Huntsville's original Courthouse and Lock-up.

in 1883, and for future edifices in the town. Symmetrical in form, this two-storey building displayed an abundance of decorative wood detailing. The cladding consisted of a preponderance of narrow, horizontal wood siding extending from grade to the underside of the gable roof eaves. Vertical wood siding provided a contrasting element for the balance of the gable face. Wood trim, as evidenced in the base surround; door and window pilasters, corner blocks, lintels and sills; horizontal dental moulding; and gable and fascia trim were added features. High, multiple-paned double-hung windows, transom over the entrance door, vertical door panels, entrance steps and symmetrical brick chimneys on either side of the building accentuated the height.

The street level of the courthouse and lock-up consisted of a platform, a courtroom and the magistrates' room. From the centre hall, entrance stairs went down to the lower floor.

The lock-up occupied the whole lower section of the building. There was accommodation for the jailer — a main room, a bedroom and a kitchen, for his use and to prepare meals for the inmates. The prisoners who had committed minor violations, mainly inebriation, were held there — while more unruly inmates were taken to the jail in Parry Sound. There were cells for male prisoners leading off from a day room for the inmates. The female prisoners were provided with two cells and their own day room. An enclosed outdoor area to the west of the building contained an airing yard with a water closet in the centre. Another enclosed area had a cistern for water, plus a shed with an indoor water closet.

In his book *Heads and Tales* George Hutcheson relates that there was not enough room in the High Street building for the town clerk, Tom Cullon, so he had the office in his home for a while and later in the rear of a building on the south side of Main Street.

The upper floor served as Huntsville's town hall until the current impressive municipal building was built on Main Street East in 1926. The building was sold to the Loyal Orange Lodge at that time, which had previously had its headquarters in a log building on West Street, where Eaton's former store stands. George Hutcheson relates that the Orangemen erected a flagpole in front of the building with a metal replica at the top of King William, Prince of Orange, which had been made by Oscar Weiler, a well-known sheet-metal worker.

Fred Francis was caretaker of the early courthouse before he built his big red brick house across High Street in 1906.

George Pells and family took over the job until 1919. George was also the caretaker for All Saints Anglican Church. Zetta, his daughter, who lived on the lower floor of the building at one time, remembers very few prisoners — and most were "drunk and disorderly." George Olaveson then took over the job of custodian.

Unfortunately, in January 1939 fire broke out in the upper storey of the old courthouse, and it was completely destroyed. The Orange Lodge lost all its furniture and equipment, as well as all its records and regalia. Oscar Weiler's son, a fireman at the blaze, tried to save his father's handiwork at the top of the flagpole but was unable to do so. Fortunately, there was $2,000 insurance on the building.

The family of Silas Payne was living on the lower floor of the building in 1939. It was one of his sons who noticed the fire, which is thought to have started in the chimney of the huge box stove. Judge Bruce Payne, another son, was eleven at the time of the blaze. He remembers putting on an old pair of breeches to escape the fire — and later realized he let his new pair burn in the fire!

THE CANAL
C. 1889

PENINSULA AND FAIRY LAKES were originally connected by Peninsula Creek, a stream too small and narrow to be commercially navigable. In July 1886 the province of Ontario began construction of a channel by clearing the land of trees and stumps, stones, boulders, sunken logs and other debris from along the line of the proposed excavation. A cofferdam was also constructed across the outlet of Peninsula Lake, which enabled considerable material to be removed with scrapers drawn by teams of animals trained for that purpose.

Dredging commenced in early October and continued until the latter part of December, when a channel had been excavated for fully two-thirds the distance between the lakes. A roadway bridge, which interfered with the passage of the dredge, was removed and a temporary one was erected for the accommodation of the public. The progress of the canal was the main topic of discussion in the surrounding countryside.

In 1887 a two-hundred-foot bridge consisting of trestlework built on the "Queen Truss" principle, the whole resting upon framed bents constructed on top of cribwork piers, was completed. Strong and substantial, it was at a sufficient height above the water to enable steamboats to pass without any interference.

Three scows, each thirteen feet wide and forty-five feet long, were constructed. A large portion of the excavated material, which for various reasons could not be deposited by the dredge on the banks adjoining the cutting, was removed and disposed of in suitable positions in the lakes.

The canal was completed in 1889, running through low-lying land and marsh at the lower or Fairy Lake end, through high clay banks and finally through quicksand toward the upper or Peninsula Lake end.

The 4,612-foot canal was completed at a cost of over $19,000. The average depth was about six

The 1887 canal bridge.

22

The canal, looking towards Peninsula Lake (east).

feet at low water, and wooden retaining walls were installed where the material on the banks was likely to fall and reduce the depth. Portions of these retaining walls are still visible today.

The high bridge was rebuilt with steel in 1915 and was replaced again by the present structure in 1990.

In 1994 the Huntsville Chamber of Commerce and the Ministry of Natural Resources combined forces to spearhead a major cleanup of the canal, installed erosion-prevention measures, including signage, and encouraged property upgrades by private shoreline owners.

Heritage Huntsville, with the assistance of the Ontario Heritage Foundation, placed a historic plaque on a former bridge footing in 1995.

Today, the scenic waterway is well travelled during the navigable months by pleasure-crafters and admirers of the natural habitat and abundant wildlife.

MAIN STREET BRIDGES
C. 1870, 1884?, 1902, 1938

Since the earliest days of Huntsville, the focal point of the community, whether in its infancy during the 1870s or today, with a population nearing 18,000, has without a doubt been the Main Street Bridge. It still is an important landmark in Huntsville, adding much to the character and charm of our Main Street. Yet it is very difficult to ascertain for sure just how many bridges there have been across the North Branch of the Muskoka River at Huntsville — maybe three, maybe four!

When the first settlers arrived in this area in the late 1860s, there was no bridge across the river, but the water level of the river was lower than it is today. Local historians claim there were rapids at the site. When the Brunel Locks were built in 1873–1875 on the North Muskoka River, it raised the level of the river considerably. Captain George Hunt, who arrived in Huntsville in 1869, petitioned the provincial government to extend the Muskoka Road northward to Huntsville and to build a bridge across the river. The sessional papers of the Ontario Crown Lands Department of 1871 contains this report: "Muskoka Road — from Fetterley's at Vernon Lake, the road extends nearly due east, for the distance of nearly three miles, where it crosses the North Branch of the Muskoka River, between Vernon and Fairy Lakes. This portion of the road was partially made last year. Some additional improvements have been made this year, in the shape of under-brushing and clearing the track, but the road is still in rough and very unfinished condition. At the intersection of the river, at the end of the last described distance, a substantial pier bridge has been

The swing bridge, 1902.

erected, and it is here that the principal outlay has been made. The total expenditure upon the bridge and road this season is $1,701.44."

The same document reported that another excellent bridge had been constructed on the fourth mile, where the road crossed the north branch of the Muskoka River at the locks. The bridge exceeded four hundred feet in length, and its floor was made of "good sound" three-inch planks.

With the completion of the Brunel Locks in 1875 and the launching of the steamer the *Northern* at Port Sydney in 1877, navigation of Mary's Lake, the North Muskoka River

24

into Huntsville, Fairy Lake and Vernon Lake was now possible. As the rail-way did not reach Huntsville until 1885, lake and river transportation in summer was by far the easiest way to move settlers and their goods, plus supplies of all kinds.

The sessional papers of the Ontario Crown Lands Department of 1879 have this to report about the Huntsville Bridge: "Mary's and Fairy

Construction of the present swing bridge, Huntsville, Main Street East, 1938.

Lake Works: The bridge at Huntsville, under which the steamboat passes daily, was not originally constructed by this department, but was raised to admit the boat passing under. Complaint is made of the narrowness of the passages, 30 feet between the piers, being injurious to the boat during freshets, and this may require to be remedied by the construction of a centre span of 70 feet by the removal of one pier."

An 1885 report states: "Maintenance of Locks, Dams and Swing Bridges. The following improvements and repairs have been made out of this appropriation during the present year, 1884. Mary's and Fairy Lake Works. The piers and floor planking of the bridge in the village of Huntsville have been repaired."

Pictures of the Huntsville bridge in the 1890s show it to be a wooden structure set on squared timber piers, with a wooden superstructure in the centre of the bridge.

It is not until the report of the Commissioner of Public Works for 1901 that the problem of whether Huntsville has had three or four Main Street bridges arises. This is the entry: "Bridge at Huntsville — Provision was made in estimates for the present year for the construction of a new bridge across the North Branch of the Muskoka River in the Town of Huntsville, to take the place of one erected by the Department in 1884, which had become decayed to such an extent as to endanger the safety of the public…It will consist of one swinging span 135 feet in length, and fixed span 69 feet, 9 inches, for a total length along the centre line of 204 feet, 9 inches, all of which, except the joists and flooring, will be of steel." The report then describes the approaches and the pivot piers. So here is the question: Was there a new bridge in 1884, or was the bridge of 1870 just repaired?

Certainly the bridge of 1901 was an attractive structure, as shown in the picture on the previous page. The key lever to swing this bridge is now at the Muskoka Pioneer Village.

It appears that by 1937 Huntsville needed another bridge on the Main Street site. *The Forester* reports: "Construction work on Huntsville's new steel bridge is to commence immediately. The contract was let late last week to Atkin and McLachan of St. Catharines….The construction of a temporary bridge to provide for traffic during the construction period will be necessary and this will be built north of the present structure."

This bridge is one of the few remaining swing-style bridges in Ontario. Constructed and painted steel set on large concrete piers, the triangulated member, gussetted connector plates, exposed rivet heads and grated floor demonstrate conventional engineering techniques of the period. Pedestrian walkways flank each side, featuring a diamond grillage side railing enclosure. Tapered, part concrete, part steel, projected light standards illuminate the bridge at each end. Perched atop the bridge on the north span can be seen a wood-framed cottage-style roofed enclosure with the multiple-paned windows typical of the period — the bridge master's cabin. It is a steel arch truss swing bridge, with an overall span of 224 feet and a swing section of 170 feet. The swing mechanism was electric on this current bridge. The steel was from the Hamilton Bridge Company, the engineer in charge from the Department of Highways was A. Sedgwick. The sidewalks were two wooden planks with plywood on top.

Huntsville had opening ceremonies for the new bridge in 1938. In July of that year there is the following report in *The Forester*: "Huntsville's new steel bridge, reported to have cost over $150,000, was declared officially open for traffic by the Minister of Public Works, MPP Colin Campbell….A large crowd gathered for the occasion." A decorated motor truck, provided by Don Hanes as a mobile platform, was finally placed at the west entrance to the bridge. The Citizen's Band marched to the Dominion Hotel, where they headed the official cars, and played as they marched to the bridge."

Our current bridge has served us well for sixty years. There have been changes over the years. In April 1952 the timber was stripped off and a new deck constructed, followed by a complete resurfacing with creosited timber. A steel mesh deck was added for strength and durability later in the decade. As the last steamer had passed through the bridge in 1952, in the 1980s the swing mechanism was welded shut and the latch pier disappeared. New concrete sidewalks were also constructed.

The Huntsville Swing Bridge was placed on the province of Ontario's Heritage Board List in 1983, one of only eleven swing bridges left in the province.

THE VARIETY SHOP
7 MAIN STREET WEST, HUNTSVILLE
C. 1886

AT ONE TIME Huntsville's Main Street was lined with buildings similar to the one at 7 Main West. Now this little gem of a building is the only surviving wood-frame and wood-clad commercial building left. It is two storeys high with a "boom town" front that projects out at the upper story to cover the eave of the sloped roof behind. The building is clad in narrow shiplapped siding with wood trim at the corners. The entrance is recessed into the front elevation. The most notable features are the three original, tall, round-headed windows, in slender wooden frames, located on either side of the store entrance.

J. W. Gledhill arrived in Canada from the British Isles in 1879 and came to Huntsville six years later, reportedly on the first train into town on the new Northern and Pacific Junction Railway. He opened his store on Main Street West that year. The building is now the oldest commercial building in town.

The Variety Shop, 7 Main Street West, 1886.

Gledhill was a graduate of the Dominion School of Optics, and his store carried a full supply of optical goods. He also repaired watches and stocked every kind of fancy article usually carried in such a store in those times — watches, clocks, jewelry, fancy china, and so on. Here could be found handsome articles in old Japanese china, just the thing to make lovers of beautiful dishes happy. Here, too, school pupils could obtain every necessary book and supply; musicians might find violins, mandolins, guitars, banjos, gramophones, autoharps, concertinas and musical supplies of many sorts.

Gledhill was a member of the town council for many years and was one of the chief promoters of establishing an electric light plant in the town. Once the system was installed, he was practically the primary electrician for the town. He carried a stock of electrical fixtures and installed hundreds of services in stores, dwellings and public buildings. For seventeen years, Gledhill served as a provincial constable and was called upon many times for duty. He was a member of the Salvation Army and was instrumental in starting that group in Huntsville.

His first wife was Miss Orr of New Lowell, Ontario, whom he married in 1883. After her death in 1901, he married Mrs. Pink. Gledhill died fifteen years later, but his widow carried on the business for many years.

In the 1930s Norman Trickey opened a variety store at this location. He was well known for his kindness to young and old alike. In fact, the name "Trickey's" carried on for many years. Norman was also a member of the Salvation Army.

After his death in 1952 his daughter, Dorothy Sacken, ran the store. It was a great mecca for the schoolchildren to spend their few pennies, as it was very close to Huntsville Public School and later the theatre.

William Billingsley and his wife were the next owners of the business. School supplies and stationery were sold, as well as the previous stock. In 1971 Frank Booth acquired the store and sold it sixteen years later to Norman and Shirley Parker.

The store with the boom town front had a real transformation in 1994 when Catherine Kealey of Toronto purchased it. She moved to Huntsville for a lifestyle change. The business became an elegant coffee shop. The building was painted in bright colours, and the picket fence that had been there since the very early days was replaced. The interior was decorated in an attractive turn-of-the-century style. Except for the alteration in the upstairs window, the building retains its original style and character.

HUNTSVILLE TOWN HALL
37 MAIN STREET EAST, HUNTSVILLE
C. 1926

IN 1882 A BUILDING was constructed on High Street to accommodate a courthouse and lock-up. It was here that all municipal and federal business was conducted for the Town of Huntsville. By 1913 the town council and Board of Trade recognized the need for more space. They sent a delegation to Ottawa to request a new federal building. The delegation included Mayor H.E. Rice, Councillors Abraham, Ware and Cooper, as well as prominent citizens Hutcheson, Mayhew and Flaxman. They stressed the need for a public building to facilitate postal and other government services. The statistics presented at this time showed the rapid

development of the town in commerce, industry and tourism. The delegation was welcomed to Ottawa in great style by William Wright, M.P., the popular member for the District of Muskoka. The Minister of Public Works, the Honourable Robert Rogers, gave assurance to the delegation that the Huntsville desire for a federal building would be realized.

In a supplementary federal budget in May 1913, a grant of $5,000 was approved to purchase a site and build a new public building in Huntsville. Without consulting the local council or citizens, the federal government chose the present site on Main Street East. This property was owned by the Methodist church, and their manse was located on it. In spite of this difficulty, in February 1914, His Majesty King George V purchased the land from the Methodist church for $2,000. The church trustees who negotiated the sale were John M. Boyd, W. Irons and W. Mayhew. The manse was moved to the corner of Centre and Mary Streets, later torn down.

Huntsville Town Hall, 37 Main Street East, 1926.

28

In August 1914 World War I caused the cancellation of the construction, which was ready to begin. It wasn't until 1925, eleven years later, that the subject of a new federal building was raised again. By this time, the High Street courthouse was in deplorable condition. In his book *Heads and Tales* George Hutcheson writes that there wasn't room for the town clerk, Tom Cullon, to have an office there. He had to work from his home.

At a town council meeting J. Frank Kelly, chairman of the Property Committee, proposed a new petition to go to the government regarding the planned town hall. This proposal went through the local member of Parliament, W.J. Hammell.

In April 1925 another large delegation went to Ottawa, including prominent Huntsville citizens Mayor Dinsmore, A.A. Cooper, H.E. Rice, W.J. Moore, president of the Board of Trade, C.E. Paget, chairman of the Parks Commission, Dr. J.D. MacDonald, president of the District Liberal Association, J. Frank Kelly, T.W. Hutcheson, Major W.D. Forrest and Ernest F. Pechin, conductor of the Anglo-Canadian Concert Band.

They approached the current Minister of Public Works, the Honourable Dr. King. The group stressed the promising development of the whole Muskoka community, with special mention of its famous award-winning band and the presence of the finest resort in the country, Bigwin Inn.

In October of 1925 the federal government approved the public building to be erected on the previously purchased Main Street site. There were conditions attached to this contract:

(a) The municipality was to engage the services of an architect; the plans to be approved by the federal government's Department of Public Works.

(b) After completion, the municipality was to maintain the building.

(c) The government would pay an annual rent for its net space at the rate of 5 percent of the cost of the building (which was $68,250) and also the cost of maintenance and repairs, together with a yearly sinking fund to retire the investment at the end of thirty years.

In January 1926, under the guidance of councillor J. Frank Kelly, chairman of the Property Committee, the ratepayers of Huntsville agreed

Adding the clock tower from Toronto Union Station to the town hall, 1927.

to combine a municipal and federal building. This agreement was confirmed by a private act in the Ontario Legislature.

29

The architects were the firm of Ellis and Belfry of Toronto. The construction company, Williams Construction Company, was also from Toronto.

During Old Home Week, on August 3, 1926, the laying of the cornerstone for the new town hall took place. The Right Honourable McKenzie King, Prime Minister of Canada, did the honours. Many prominent people were present including Dr. King, Minister of Public Works for Canada, and the Honourable Howard Ferguson, Premier of Ontario. Among the local dignitaries were Mayor Dinsmore, Dr. Peter McGibbon, W.J. Hammell and J. Frank Kelly. The celebration included a baseball game, a band concert and fireworks.

R.H. Wright, chief architect of the federal Department of Public Works, came to Huntsville to confer with Mr. Dinsmore and the architects during the construction of the building. In January 1927 it was reported in *The Forester* that the building would be completed by the end of February. However, the project came to a halt pending a lawsuit served to the town by the construction company. In September the action against the Town of Huntsville was dismissed.

Business pertaining to the use of the new building appears in the minutes of the council and in the press. Rental charges for the use of the auditorium were listed: dances $20, concerts and political meetings $10, church events $12.50. There was to be no rental charge for meetings of the Memorial Park Commission, the I.O.D.E., the Board of Trade or the Women's Institute. *The Forester* at that time contains this statement: "The restroom was made available for the use of the Women's Institute under regulation." Just what that means is puzzling and one wonders how all the others managed! Rent charges for the Township of Chaffey were fixed at three dollars a meeting, with a maximum charge for the year of twenty-five dollars. Mr. Cullon, the town clerk, was authorized to collect the rent in advance.

On July 1, 1927, Huntsville celebrated the diamond jubilee of Canada's confederation and the opening of the new town hall. Two hundred pioneer citizens of Muskoka were invited for lunch and dinner in the new auditorium, catered by the Women's Institute. There was something for everyone in the program of festivities: a tug-of-war, music by the Yugoslav String Band, a tree planting and a parade.

A baseball game was planned, but the opposing team from South River failed to come. A local team was quickly assembled but after three innings the game was called off. The temperature that day was nearly one hundred degrees Fahrenheit. Many of the pioneers spoke about the early days in Huntsville and many old acquaintances were renewed. Telegrams were received from the premier of Ontario and from His Majesty King George V.

A month after the celebrations, the town sold the old courthouse to the Royal Orange Lodge No. 393. Unfortunately, it burned down in 1939.

The final glory for the new public building was the starting of the tower clock at 11 A.M. on October 11, 1927. More ceremonies were held.

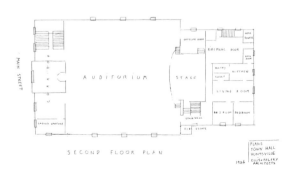

SECOND FLOOR PLAN

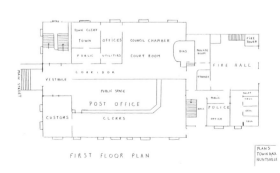

FIRST FLOOR PLAN

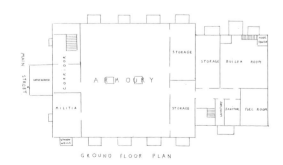

GROUND FLOOR PLAN

Peony bulbs presented to the town by His Royal Highness the Prince of Wales were planted on the west side of the building.

The story of the clock tower is a fascinating one. In 1926 Union Station in Toronto, built in 1871, was being torn down. Charles E. Paget of Huntsville thought that the new municipal building needed a clock tower. So in August 1927, Charles announced that he had purchased the old Union Station clock tower and would present it to the Huntsville town council. It was a master clock, built by E. Howard and Company of Boston, Massachusetts. The week after the purchase was announced, E.H. Briggs, a local jeweller and professional clock maker, councillor T. Millest and George Ralston, the town's electrical engineer, went to Toronto. They had the clock shipped to Huntsville, while Mr. Briggs transported the more intricate parts of the clock personally.

A base for the clock had to be added to the building. New parts, such as the dial hands and the three-hundred-pound motive power weights, had to be adjusted. Mr. Briggs had to make special tools to accomplish the reconstruction of the clock. An opening had to be cut in the floor of the tower to allow the eighty-pound pendulum to swing.

The town hall is an excellent example of the Georgian Revival style, popular during the 1920s but rarely seen in Muskoka. The clock tower, the large Georgian windows and classical stone pediment entry with transom above contribute to its architectural character.

The skillful integration of horizontal and vertical elements in the composition of the front east and west walls is achieved by the use of contrasting patterned brick and cut stone trim.

The red brick building is two storeys high, with a raised basement and a flat roof. The large panelled doors are monumental in size and very impressive. Above the entrance the large arched window dominates the two storeys and is surrounded by radiating bricks.

The hexagonal tin-roofed clock tower has a clock face on four sides and tall paned windows on the alternate faces. The tower is raised above the rectangular building on a short square base with three casement windows on each of its four walls.

The new town hall was designed as a multi-use building. The lower floor had a large armoury and an office for the militia. There were also three storage rooms, a boiler room, a janitor's room and a washroom. On the main floor were the custom's office, the post office, an office for the police and three cells for prisoners. Also on the main floor were offices for the town clerk, utility workers, the council chambers and courtroom. At the rear of the building was a garage for the fire trucks and hoses. On the third floor there was an auditorium, with a stage, a dressing room and a ladies washroom. Also on this floor was a two-bedroom apartment for the janitor and his family, as well as a fireman's room. A staircase led from the fireman's room to the fire trucks below.

There have been changes to the town hall over the years. In 1955 the arrangement with the federal government concluded and their departments moved out. The present post office was built that year. From 1959 to 1971 the Huntsville Library occupied the council chambers and the council met in a small back room. In 1971 regional government was established in Muskoka, and the jail and police moved to other quarters. In 1975 the Huntsville Senior Citizens Club 55 began their activities on the lower floor. In 1980 the Wilk Hoeglund Company renovated and redecorated the auditorium in an art deco style, which was greatly appreciated by the community.

In 1989 a major renovation of the sixty-two-year-old building was undertaken at a cost of $706,000. Cravit Ortred Architects of Toronto had the contract. The interior of the structurally sound building was gutted, insulation was added and new offices were built. Upstairs the apartment where the Woodcock family had lived as custodians of the building for thirty years was converted to new council chambers.

In 1996 a new fire hall was built on Centre Street North. The old one on High Street was remodelled for office space and storage.

Today our handsome town hall continues to serve the community well. Physically, it dominates the Main Street, bearing witness to the hard work and foresight of the early settlers and citizens who made Huntsville a great town.

Original Canadian Tire store, 1940.

CANADIAN TIRE STORE
15 MINERVA STREET, HUNTSVILLE
C. 1940

THE HUNTSVILLE CANADIAN TIRE STORE has been around for a long time and has been through a lot of necessary changes. Canadian Tire first opened its doors in Huntsville in 1940. It was a tiny store that supplied gas, oils, windshield washer fluid and such. Lorne and Archie McLennan operated the store at 15 Minerva Street until it moved in 1942.

For the next four years Frank and Maureen Hammond operated the Canadian Tire Store at 78 Main Street and Brunel Road. The store then supplied the town with mainly car parts and engine fluids. After leaving Canadian Tire in 1946 Frank and Maureen set up and ran Hammond's Well Drilling, which their son Tom took over when his parents retired.

After World War II money was not plentiful and the Canadian Tire Store did not reopen until 1952. Then it reopened at 7 King William Street under the ownership of Derrick Foreman. Bob Irwin was a business partner and his son, Casper, ran the garage. The store was then becoming larger and employed approximately thirty staff. It was divided into separate sections consisting of hardware, sporting goods, housewares and automotive. Bob and Casper left the partnership in 1960.

In 1967 Mel Taylor took over the location for two years before moving it to the corner of Cann and John Streets, at one end of the Brendale Square Mall. The site provided a larger store with plenty of parking. At that time the store was beginning to sell a larger variety of products from the different departments.

Mel Taylor ran the operation until William Weber from Windsor took over the store in 1974. The store's inventory was expanded and a propane filling station added. Profit sharing, which had always existed at the corporate level, was then extended to the store employees in most Canadian Tire stores. A computerized inventory system was also added. William Weber retired and sold the business to a Fort Frances associate dealer, Ken Moser, in 1990.

After purchasing the Huntsville store, Ken began planning to build a new store. The new building opened its doors at 77 King William Street in 1992. It was a spacious store with overhead storage racks to cut down on the amount of warehouse space required and put the products closer to the sales floor. Now, in 1998, Ken Moser runs the store at the same location.

The Huntsville Canadian Tire Store has had a number of loyal employees who have stayed with the company through many of the changes. Dennis Payne, who helped a great deal with this article, has been with the store since it was located at 7 King William Street in the early 1960s. Canadian Tire has been an asset to our community for many years.

Huntsville Planing Mills
8 King Street, Huntsville
c. 1880

Huntsville Planing Mill.

A PLANING AND MILL OPERATION existed in the hollow on the east side of King Street in Huntsville since the early 1880s. It appears that Thomas Birtch and later his son, Charles, both of Kearney, owned the establishment.

A fire destroyed the buildings around 1900, but a 1906 article in *The Forester* describes the business in glowing terms. A brick dry kiln and workshop, plus a new frame planing mill had been constructed. All manner of retail sash, doors, mouldings and dressed flooring were produced.

Duncan McCaffery ran the business originally, followed by Frank Irons and J.S. Winnacott. It was not until 1917 that Winnacott purchased the property. He in turn sold it to Gilbert Brooks.

Subsequently, Lewis Hill acquired the business, running it until incapacitated by a stroke. His son-in-law, Bob Robertson, carried on, but changing times had put the business in decline. Allan T. White had been casting about for a new business opportunity. In 1931, after arranging financial backing from his father, J.W. White, Allan left the Anglo-Canadian Leather Company in Huntsville and purchased the stock and premises from a willing Bob Robertson.

The new business got underway on March 1, 1931, under the trade name the Huntsville Planing Mills. Drawing on his experience in the hardware business, correspondence courses on the building trade and the expertise of his father-in-law, George Bushfield, in the lumber trade, Allan set out to achieve his goal of establishing a "comprehensive" industry.

By that summer a new office building replaced the ramshackle original one and by fall, a forty-eight-foot square warehouse was put up on the northwest corner of the lot. Stock was expanded to include gyproc, roofing materials and building hardware. By 1934 C.I.L. paint products were made available.

Allan had a connection with St. Mary's Cement and could then compete with Hern's, which had been the sole source through Canada Cement. Extra land for piling grounds was bought from the Dominion Bank in 1939, and a forklift truck made moving lumber simpler.

Bob Robertson had stayed on through the summer of 1931 to assist in the transition. At the beginning, Sandy Lewis, Horace Nelles and Gordon Hines joined the work force and Zetta Pells was engaged as bookkeeper/secretary. Allan's energy and driving determination combined with good salesmanship pushed the operation through the Depression and wartime. He was demanding of others as well as himself, but this was balanced by a sense of fair play. Local builders, resort owners, cottagers and townspeople responded.

In order to offset the winter slow-downs in the early days, the men kept busy replenishing stocks of sash and siding. Custom siding and furniture were made. By the time of the post-war boom, virtually all that might be required for any building job or repair was available.

Allan and his son David had long come to the conclusion that their disparate natures precluded any idea of a family partnership. Looking toward retirement, Allan found that Arnott Adamson was interested in managing the business. The operation was on a solid footing and changes were in the wind. Arnott came in sometime in 1956. Horace Nelles left in that year. Allan incorporated the business in April 1957 and his interest was bought out in the 1960s. Zetta Pells retired in 1961. Bill Nickalls, Arnott's nephew, had worked at the mill since 1958, except for a year's break. Bill took over from his uncle in 1971. A new showroom replaced warehousing on the east side of the street south of the original office building in 1978 and the Homecare Building Centre name was taken. Bill continues to serve the community with a business that has evolved dramatically over the past century.

THE HUNTSVILLE TRADING COMPANY
MAIN STREET, HUNTSVILLE
C. 1917

THE HUNTSVILLE TRADING COMPANY has a history of over eighty years in Huntsville — a long tradition!

In 1917 Max Ginsburg and his four sons, Maurice, Israel, Abraham and Samuel purchased property on Main Street West — Lot 154, Plan 12, beside the present Gospel Hall. There they opened their general store, the Huntsville Trading Company.

Max was born in Russia in 1861. For many years he was a grain merchant in Odessa, but he immigrated to Canada in 1913 with his wife, sons and two daughters. He bought a large farm in York County, where he re-entered the grain business. In 1917 the family moved to Huntsville and began their mercantile business at the Main Street West site.

Max Ginsberg had a keen business sense and a reputation for integrity, which he passed on to his sons. They were truly general merchants, selling oats, hay and seed grains, as well as groceries, clothes and household needs, and buying furs. They delivered, as most stores did then, and even paid the railway freight charge for expensive items specially ordered.

Max died in 1923, and the following year Maurice, Israel and Abraham made plans to take down the old wooden Johnson Block on Main Street East and the adjoining stores west of West Street. They proceeded to erect three new brick stores. The western section was the grocery store. A comment appeared in a 1924 *Forester*: "If their good example were followed by other owners of vacant property it would work out for the advantage of all." From their new premises Huntsville Trading Company began to advertise more sophisticated items such as evening and wedding gowns of the latest fashion.

Left: Interior, Huntsville Trading Co. (Connie Kelso) *Above: The log front store.* (Donna Miglin)

34

Looking for another challenge, Israel decided to run for mayor of Huntsville in 1929. He was elected and served for the year 1930.

The Ginsburgs hired Bob Ewing from Toronto as their general manager in 1938. He suggested adding a log front to cover their brick store, which they did. It was called The Log Front Store at that time. The interior was also remodelled. In 1943 the Ecclestone Block, now Huntsville Discount Drugs, and the Ginsburg's grocery section and general store were destroyed by fire, but all were rebuilt.

Israel entered the local political arena again in 1949. He ran for mayor, beating J. Frank Kelly with a decisive victory. Mayor Ginsburg stated that "he had expected to win by 150 votes, and he was only three out in his calculations." He served for the year 1950.

The grocery section of the store was sold to Loblaws ten years later.

The store with the log front continued to prosper throughout the years, but as the family members became older, Maurice and Israel decided to sell the business. Sky Flotron and his wife, Donna, purchased The Huntsville Trading Company in 1967 after a salesman told them about the enterprise, as Sky and his father were in the retail business in Toronto. By coincidence, the Flotron family had visited Huntsville in 1943 and had taken a snapshot of their two-year-old son Sky in front of the trading company with the log front on Main Street.

Donna and Sky made their merchandising more selective and changed the name of the store to Flotron's Huntsville Trading Company. They altered the store's front by making the two entrances into one and removing the centre window. They added the glass exterior wall at the back of the building and opened up the basement for merchandise. Under their guidance the store became very successful, with upscale fashions for men and women, plus sophisticated gifts and other wares.

The Flotrons sold the business in 1990 to Donna and Sven Miglin of Toronto who had initially been involved in the government retail concessions in Algonquin Park. They moved to Huntsville in 1983, and became partners in the Blackburn Landing complex by the Main Street Bridge. They opened a retail store, Traditions of Muskoka, there. When the Flotrons were looking for a buyer for their store, the Miglins seemed the

logical couple. They have carried on the style and ambience of the last thirty years of the Huntsville Trading Company, which is well known throughout Muskoka and beyond.

THE HUNTSVILLE FORESTER
72 MAIN STREET EAST, HUNTSVILLE
C. 1875

THERE IS NO BUSINESS in the community of Huntsville, Ontario, with a greater history than our local newspaper, *The Forester*. It all began very early in the life of the tiny village when in 1877 Floyd Clearwater, a weekly newspaper publisher in Whitby, Ontario, decided to head north, bringing with him his humble printing press. He discovered that Francis Howland, Huntsville's first doctor, had established a weekly paper in 1875 called the *Huntsville Liberal*. It was printed on the presses of the *Bracebridge Gazette*. The two men formed a partnership, but Dr. Howland withdrew from the newspaper shortly afterwards.

The name of the publication was changed to *The Forester* and Floyd Clearwater carried on the business. He was active in the community, and in politics he was a Liberal. For his family he built a handsome residence on High Street, part of which is the present Addison Funeral Home. After he withdrew from the business at the turn of the century, he became the local postmaster.

Early small community newspapers were very different than they are today. Before the Canadian Press wire service came into being, newspapers received news from telegraph companies, and expanded the newspaper by the use of "boilerplate" — one or two columns of news from private companies cast in stereo type and sent by express. In the early days of *The Forester*, 30 percent of its news consisted of boilerplate.

The Forester was published every Friday, and a December 6, 1878, issue states that the paper was "devoted to the material interest of the settlers, latest news, current politics, literature and miscellaneous matters." Subscriptions cost $1.25 a year, and rates for advertising ranged from sixty

35

dollars for a whole column per year to eight dollars for a quarter column for three months. Each issue had four pages: page 1 consisted of trivial items from international news; pages 2 and 3 contained local news; and page 4 consisted of a serialized novel — *The Red Court Farm* in this particular issue.

Of course there were many advertisements by local merchants and craftsmen, as well as businesses from the surrounding small communities. The church directory listed the Church of England, and the Methodist and Presbyterian churches. The Temperance Society held meetings, as did the L.O.L. 393 Huntsville. Patent medicines were advertised at great length — the cure-alls for every known complaint.

District news was a very important segment of the newspaper (as it is today). Every small community in the area had a column featuring local news and people. Births, marriages, deaths, school reports and travel plans were important features. There were very few pictures in early papers.

The Forester during all these years retained its fidelity to the Liberal party and strongly supported many issues that led to the growth of the town. Opposition to the original proposed route of the Grand Trunk Railway in the 1880s, along the shore of Lake Vernon to Hoodstown, was one of the most important issues in which *The Forester* took an active role.

The decision was finally made to accept Huntsville's plan, which resulted in the demise of Hoodstown and the growth of Huntsville.

It is not clear where the newspaper was originally situated, but by 1888 it was in the Bettes Block at the northwest corner of King Street and Main Street. After the 1894 fire on Main Street, until the present building was constructed, it was located just east of its present site, the east half of Lot 3, Main Street East, in a building owned by George May.

Incredibly, after the disastrous fire of April 18, 1894, *The Forester* managed to print a nine-by-thirteen-inch issue on April 20, 1894, just two days after the calamity. It was published on the presses of the *Bracebridge Gazette*.

In 1899 George Hutcheson Sr. took over the publication. He was born in Ireland of Scottish ancestry, and with his parents immigrated to Canada in 1847. The family settled in Tara, Ontario, where George learned the construction business and also operated a sawmill. In the 1870s he and his family of nine children moved to Gravenhurst where George operated a sawmill at Dee Bank, on the Dee River between Lake Rosseau and Three Mile Lake. Thirteen years later he moved the family to the small village of Huntsville, where he purchased the mercantile business of Smith and Culp, changing the name to Hutcheson and Son. At the northeast corner of Lorne

Forester office, 72 Main Street East.

36

Street and Main Street West he built the family home, Flora Villa, in 1887. After the Main Street fire of 1894, George Hutcheson returned to the construction business. He helped to build the Methodist church at Main and West Street in 1897, as well as other main street buildings. After purchasing *The Forester* in 1899 from Floyd Clearwater, he constructed the present Forester building in 1901.

The two-storey building was made of locally manufactured brick, the main floor having a door on either side, with a large window in between. All three were arched and had brick detailing above. The three windows on the second floor of the facade followed the same design.

In 1899 a young man named Harmon E. Rice married Harriet Hutcheson, a daughter of George Hutcheson. Rice was born in Lambton County, Ontario, in 1874 and left home at the age of sixteen to make his own way in the world. He joined a hardware firm run by William Craddock of Oil Springs, near his birthplace of Wyoming, Ontario. In 1895, William sent his young protégé to Huntsville to open a store in the thriving little community. At this time, Harmon became the correspondent for the Burks' Falls *Arrow*, which led to a lifetime career in newspaper work. Four years later, George Hutcheson invited him to join *The Forester*, and a partnership was formed. From that time on H.E, as he was known, was a fierce promoter of the newspaper and the town.

He told an interesting story concerning his early days with *The Forester* and its political affiliation. From its founding, the paper had been a Liberal supporter, but with the change of ownership to George Hutcheson, it announced its political independence. In 1901 a group of Liberals decided to establish a new paper, *The Huntsville Standard*. In 1902 a Conservative group offered to buy *The Forester*, to be political opposition to the *Standard*, with H.E. to stay on as editor. That year a legislative vacancy occurred in Muskoka due to the death of Dr. S. Bridgeland, the Liberal member. A Conservative, A.A. Mahaffey, was elected. The Conservative buyers of *The Forester* did not, however, have the finances to complete the purchase and *The Forester* reverted to its non-partisan policy.

In 1912 George Hutcheson retired and H.E. Rice became sole publisher. No man was better known nor gave more of his wisdom and service to the community than Harmon Rice. He served on the Huntsville town council for four years, before becoming mayor for eleven years between 1913 and 1945. He was the founder and first president of the Rotary Club in Huntsville. He also served as president of the Board of Trade, the Muskoka Children's Aid and the Muskoka Tourist Development Board, and as chairman of the Huntsville Hospital Board.

Harmon Rice was a staunch Methodist, and was active in promoting church union in 1925. With his wife and two other couples he helped to found the Huntsville Literary Club, which for fifty years filled a vital cultural void within what was a relatively isolated community.

Harmon and his wife travelled extensively in Europe and Canada, and in later years spent part of the winter in Florida. They could never understand why anyone would leave Muskoka in summer or during the glory of the fall colours. Always an active photographer, he had a large collection of photos of people, places and events.

At the newspaper office one of H.E.'s regular rituals was the coffee and gab session that took place every weekday around three o'clock. Various cronies and visitors joined to discuss matters large and small. He never lost the common touch.

Harmon Rice was also active in the Canadian Weekly Newspaper Association for many years and served as its president in 1942.

Seven years later the citizens of Huntsville gathered at a dinner to honour Harmon on the occasion of his fiftieth anniversary as editor of *The Forester* and to recognize his public service to Huntsville and vicinity. In 1964 he wrote a history of Huntsville.

On his death in 1967 Bruce West, a reporter for the *Globe and Mail* and former Huntsvillite, referred to H.E as Mr. Huntsville. No wonder!

By 1926 *The Forester* was advertising that it provided "Commercial Printing — best equipped job printing plant between Orillia and North Bay." That same year a newspaper-folding machine was installed (until then papers had been folded by hand). The newspaper advertised that "the operation of the press will be of interest to visitors to see the machines running." During this era H.E. Rice's son Paul became associated with the business.

The soft local red brick on the facade of the main street building did not stand up too well. The brick was painted white with some of the detailing in a darker contrasting colour. Further, technical changes occurred during the 1940s. A sheet-fed babock flat-bed press was acquired and the staff increased to fifteen. Later in the decade a seventy-five-foot addition was built onto the rear of the building to accommodate the expanding plant, which was now using intertype machines.

More changes took place during the 1950s. The press was changed to a rotary-roll-fed press in the enlarged basement. In 1952 the business was converted to a joint stock company with H.E. Rice as president and Paul Rice as vice president and managing editor. *The Forester* was advertising in these years for clean rags "minimum size 12 inches, no silk, satin or denim."

Also in this era, the facade of the paper's building was altered. The lower floor was covered with angel stone, the upper storey with glazed white brick. The attractive round-headed windows were made rectangular, as they appear today.

In 1962 an attempt was made to burn the building — a Molotov cocktail was tossed through the window of Paul Rice's office. Luckily two clerks noticed it and turned on the fire alarm.

Paul died in 1966 at the age of sixty-four, and one year later H.E. passed on, in his ninety-second year. The ownership of the local paper passed from Paul's widow to Francis Rice, H.E. Rice's other son, and Peter Rice, his grandson. Francis worked in Montreal as an executive for Canadian Industries Limited, but Peter and his wife, Jane, had moved to Huntsville.

In the 1970s *The Forester* expanded again with the grand opening of Ray Ball Printing and Stationery Supplies. Office supplies were sold in the front of the building (as they are today) and the newspaper offices were moved to the rear. The basement was used for assembling the news. In 1969 printing was changed to offset printing at Bayweb Press in Elmvale, and in 1975 moved to Muskoka Web in Bracebridge.

During the 1980s the newspaper was published twice a week — Wednesdays and Fridays. This venture lasted about a year.

Over its long history *The Forester* has had many editors. Heading the list, of course, was H.E. Rice, followed by son Paul. His successors were Bud Graham, Art Barton, Carl McLennan, Jack Kirkvaag, Hugh Clairmont, Charles Lawrence, Skip McLean, Joan Carter, Garth Thomas and Ev Van Duuren.

Well-known long-time employees were Bruce May, shop foreman from 1946 to 1993, and June Higgs, who was office manager for thirty-five years until 1995. As *The Forester* continued to modernize, some of the old hot presses were removed, and some of the old wood type fonts and equipment were sent to the Stephen Leacock Museum in Orillia where a printing museum was planned. For old time's sake one old linotype was kept. Editions of *The Forester* were photocopied and are available at the Ontario Archives and the Huntsville Public Library.

Peter Rice died in 1991, and the fourth generation of the Rice family took over the helm of the family newspaper. Elizabeth Rice-Aben, Peter's daughter, is following in her great-grandfather's tradition as editor and publisher.

Today, production staff typeset at the computers, design graphics, develop film and proofread the news gathered by reporters. The articles, columns and ads are pasted up onto flats, and then taken to McLaren Press in Bracebridge, where they are photographed and developed into film, which is assembled on mylar film before plate making. The plates are exposed photochemically or "burned" and then placed in the press for printing. The press is then fed newsprint by a huge web slicer. Following this process, the newsprint is cut, folded and bundled for transport or mail — a far cry from the original production of the newspaper by Floyd Clearwater!

In 1995 *The Forester* began publishing a Friday "Weekender" paper. The following year they bought Muskoka Publications of Bracebridge. They still publish the *Advance* weekly. Special publications are the *Vacation Guide* and the winter and summer *Passport* magazines.

Today the lower floor at the rear of the building is occupied by Colour Crazy, a separate entity owned by Elizabeth Rice and John Aben, Sr.

As a tribute to the long history of *The Forester*, on the wall of the office is a framed account dated June 12, 1891, and signed by F.W. Clearwater. The newspaper is without a doubt one of the bastions of the history of Huntsville, with its continuity of family and news.

TORONTO DOMINION BANK
34 MAIN STREET EAST, HUNTSVILLE, C. 1899
38 MAIN STREET EAST, HUNTSVILLE, C. 1925

ALTHOUGH THE COMMUNITY OF HUNTSVILLE was established in the early 1870s, it was not until twenty years later that William H. Matthews established the first bank, a private banking firm. His business lasted only a few years.

In 1899 the first chartered bank — the Dominion Bank — came to Huntsville. The bank had commenced in 1871 at 40 King Street East, Toronto, with staff, a manager and three clerks.

After the 1894 fire on Huntsville's Main Street, James W. Bettes built a handsome two-storey red brick building for the Dominion Bank. It still stands today at 34 Main Street East. Complementing the town hall across the street, this original bank building highlights numerous turn-of-the-century architectural features. With its design by local builder-architect William Proudfoot practically unaltered, it features classic vaulted Romanesque hooded windows with contrasting stone keystones and a cast-iron pediment with engraved relief. Extensive use of header, soldier and corbelled dental brickwork can be seen in combination with stone sills. The building remains one of the most prominent on Main Street.

James Bettes arrived in Huntsville before 1881. A year later, he was elected in a by-election to the Ontario Legislature for Muskoka–Parry Sound, but in 1883 he was defeated in a general election. He became sheriff of Muskoka in 1888 and moved to Bracebridge.

The Huntsville branch of the Dominion Bank opened in its prestigious building on January 1, 1899, with E.S. Anderson as manager. In 1906 *The Forester* mentions that F. Dallas was the genial manager and adds: "The bank has done much to aid and encourage industries of the town and district and has made it as easy as possible for farmers, business men and manufacturers to carry on their enterprises in a struggling community such as this was in past years."

In 1901 the post office moved into the eastern half of the Bettes Block (formerly Town Centre Sports, 36 Main Street East).

It needed larger premises, so in 1925 the Dominion Bank moved east to the corner of Main and King Streets at 38 Main Street East. The site had been the home of the White Bros. Hardware from as early as 1888, which in 1913 became known as Hern Hardware (Hern Hardware moved one store west to the old post office section of the Bettes Block) when the new bank building went up. The old Dominion Bank became the office of Dr. Edgar J. Evans, a family physician.

The new bank was an impressive building designed by John Lyle, one of Canada's foremost architects of the era. He studied at the Beaux-Arts

Toronto Dominion Bank, 38 Main Street East, 1925.

Dominion Bank, 34 Main Street East, 1899.

School in Paris for ten years before returning to Canada in 1906. He was responsible for designing the present Toronto Union Station, the Royal Alexandra Theatre in Toronto, the memorial arch at the Royal Military College in Kingston, and many banks throughout Canada. The builders of the Huntsville bank were Treagle and Sons.

This new bank, symmetrical in design, features a consistent rhythm of decorative masonry piers and large transomed windows focused around the glazed transomed entrance with its full stone jamb moulding and raised lintel moulding. The use of stone accents on the predominantly red brick facade is further seen at the continuous base capping, sills, continuous storefront raised dental molding cornice and coping on the raised parapet. Brick soldier coursing at the building base and bas–relief centred above the main entrance act as complementary detailing. Completing the facade is decorative cast-iron grillwork at the lower extent of all windows, sized equally to the transom above and globed cast-iron lights, mounted on the wall at either side of the entrance. The interior had eighteen-foot ceilings, was finished throughout in natural wood and had fine oak furnishings.

The Forester describes the opening of this new classical-style bank building in 1925: "At 10 A.M. Tuesday morning the handsome new premises of the Dominion Bank were opened to the public for business. The occasion was made notable by the presence of Mayor Dinsmore and members of Council, together with a large representation of businessmen and citizens."

In 1955 the Dominion Bank merged with the Toronto Bank, which was founded in 1856 by a group of flour merchants. By 1955 both banks were in the strongest position in their development with total assets of 1.13 million dollars. Amalgamation ensued and the new Toronto Dominion Bank had 450 branches, including one in London, England, and an office in New York.

John Lyle's beautiful classical red brick building was painted brown and the upper part of the facade was covered in the early 1960s (recently removed). An addition was made to the back of the building in 1979.

The TD Bank at 38 Main Street East serves the community well, and in 1999 looks forward to celebrating one hundred years in Huntsville.

VANITY FAIR
MAIN STREET EAST, HUNTSVILLE
C. 1950

BOB AND ZELMA EWING and their three daughters came to Huntsville from Toronto in 1938. Bob had been in the retail business before being hired by the Ginsburg brothers to manage their general store, The Huntsville Trading Company on Huntsville's Main Street. As the manager, it was Bob Ewing's idea to have a log front. He designed it and also made changes to the interior of the store. It became known as The Log Front Store.

In 1948 Bob opened his own business, Bob Ewing's Better Men's Wear. It was one of the first stores to open on the Main Street section of the newly renovated Empire Hotel. Two years later the Ewings opened Vanity Fair, a ladies' wear shop. They wanted to call it the Connie Shop, but daughter Connie was too embarrassed. Daughter Pat saved her by suggesting Vanity Fair. It was the title of the book she was reading at the time. The two stores sat side by side in the hotel block with an archway between them.

The success of Vanity Fair made it necessary to expand. The men's clothing store was closed, and Vanity Fair moved to 19 Main Street East. It was a large three-storey red brick building. To the west was the pool hall with apartments above. In 1962 the building was torn down and the present downtown A&P built. Fortunately, the Ewings were able to purchase the building where the store is now situated at 84 Main Street East.

In 1971, the year before he died, Bob Ewing sold the business to the Curzon family. Ken and Grace Curzon both had roots in Muskoka, having visited as children, and having had relatives in the area. Ken Curzon had a career in accounting and labour relations in various places in Ontario before moving to Huntsville.

They have owned Vanity Fairy for seventeen years and have changed their merchandise to keep in tune with the times. Daughter Barbara has played an active role in the business since the beginning. Vanity Fair has been a key part of Huntsville's Main Street for nearly fifty years.

Vanity Fair, Main Street East, 1950.

WARDELL AND COMPANY
86 MAIN STREET EAST, C. 1895
112 WEST ROAD, C. 1908

A BUSINESS THAT WAS WELL KNOWN and respected in Huntsville for over ninety years was Wardell and Company, "the Busy Merchants." It was founded by Matthew Wardell, who was born in Canada in 1843. During his early years he was very active in Toronto, describing himself in the city directory as an auctioneer, jobber and dry goods merchant at various locations in the downtown core.

In 1895, the year after Huntsville's Main Street fire, he decided to set up business in Huntsville. He rented premises at 77 Main Street East and in 1902 bought the building. A 1906 issue of *The Forester* has a description of the store: "The building is 40 x 62 feet in size.... The very large stock of goods carried might very well fill a store much larger. Every foot

41

of space obtainable is crowded with goods. There is a well-stocked dry goods department which contains practically everything usually comprised in the term 'dry goods.' There are ladies' ready-to-put-on skirts and blouses and white wear; men's clothing and furnishings; boots and shoes for both men and women, house furnishings in carpets, oil cloths, curtains, etc. All kinds of produce is bought from farmers, and considerable quantities of butter are shipped. Many tourists and campers are supplied from this store, for a gasoline launch is owned and used to deliver goods to Fairy Lake and Peninsula Lake resorts. It is a steady satisfactory business that is being done at the store and the years have brought a good measure of prosperity to its proprietor."

During the winter the family lived above the store, but in summer they used their lovely cottage called Bide-A-Wee on Fairy Lake. There were five children: Maude, Mary (Daisy), Claude, St. Clair and Annetta.

Tragedy struck on the morning of December 28, 1910, when a fire caused by an overheated box stove left the building in ruins. A staunch Methodist, Matthew Wardell had no insurance. However, his son Claude had purchased a small policy. The devastated family started over, moving across the street to a building at 86 Main Street East that had been occupied by Hanna and Hutcheson Bros. After paying rent of $600 a year and installing the hydro, in 1920 Claude and Maude bought the store for $6,000.

Faced predominantly in red brick with a fully glazed lower storefront, this commercial building highlighted a variety of architectural features. Divided vertically into bay divisions, masonry storefront piers of contrasting horizontal brick coursing and brick quoining are extended vertically for a full elevation height. The lower level focuses on a semi-arched main entrance, set between two piers and trimmed with bracketed corner mouldings and a centre keystone. Continuous canvas awnings extended over the full width of the storefront in summer. Punched single-hung windows at the second floor level featured stone sills and curved heads, accented by soldier-coursed hood moulding in contrasting brick tones, unified with horizontal soldier-coursed brick bands at the window level. Corbelled brick in a dental pattern accented the parapet line. The interior had a stone fireplace in the rear and originally a box stove for heat

Wardell and Company, 86 Main Street East, 1895–1986.

in the women's department. In 1939 the storefront was altered and new brick facing applied.

Claude and Maude (who married Donal Nickalls) were involved in the business all their lives. At one time, from approximately 1913 to 1917, the store was called Wardell, Boyd and Son; Annetta, Matthew's youngest daughter, had married Charles Boyd. His father established his own grocery store next door at 90 Main Street East in 1917, known as J.R. Boyd and Son. (Previously that establishment had been situated at the northeast corner of Main Street East and King Street.)

In 1957, Maude's son, Jack, and grandson, Donal Nickalls, took over Wardell's, and in 1973 Don Nickalls and his wife, Pat, were the proprietors.

Ernie Norris, who came to Canada as a Barnardo Boy, worked at Wardell's for over forty years, starting in 1929. He tells some interesting tales of the early days. Wardell's did bartering, for which tokens were used and some are still in existence today. The Wardells used to keep the store open until midnight on Saturdays and Christmas Eve. But Matthew Wardell wouldn't complete a sale at one minute past midnight on a Saturday because he didn't believe in Sunday shopping! When the tannery and Muskoka Wood Co. workers got paid on a Saturday night, banks were closed, so people came to Wardell's to cash their cheques. The store got in extra cash to handle the rush. Ernie even had a chauffeur's licence and he used to pick up Myrtle McKenny, another long-time employee, for work every day.

The store was famous for Scottish woollens, English Spode china and Hudson's Bay blankets. Ollie Knight, who worked for the Wardells, could make Hudson's Bay blanket coats, and Margaret Langford could make a man's suit. Miss Ganton worked at millinery upstairs in the store.

Maude Nickall's sons, Jack and Grenville, travelled all over Muskoka selling their attractive goods; they even went by boat to resorts on Lake Muskoka and the Lake of Bays. In the 1950s they had a store on Highway 11, and one summer a store at Bigwin Inn. During the late 1970s and early 1980s Don and Pat Nickalls had a branch store in Bracebridge catering to young people.

After the disastrous fire of 1910, the family moved to the house at 12 West Road, Huntsville. When this house was built is unclear, but Sam Quan, the present owner says that the year 1908 is etched into stone underneath the verandah. The house is situated prominently on an elevated site with an abundance of mature trees. The entrance is distinguished by the two flight steps commencing at the stone rubble lower retaining wall.

This unique home features a main roof, mansard in style, capped by a continuous projected parapet. Emerging from the second floor mansard is the sloped roof of the entrance porch, low in profile in contrast to the steep mansard above. A consistent pattern of round tapered columns supports the porch roof. Lattice wood screening encloses the open space below the porch projection. Large first-floor windows opening on to the porch assist in merging the enclosed home interior with the semi-enclosed porch area. Similar large second floor windows emerge from the slopped mansard with contrasting gable roofs.

Wardell House, 12 West Road, 1908.

Matthew Wardell died in 1934, his wife in 1937. The house passed on to Maude Nickalls. Then in 1944, St. Clair Wardell, who had been working in Buffalo, N.Y., returned to Huntsville and bought the pretty house at 12 West Road. A large addition was constructed at the back and it was turned into two apartments. The St. Clair Wardells lived upstairs and the lower apartment was rented out. Two years after St. Clair's death in 1980, the house was sold to the Quan family, who returned it to a single family dwelling.

Don and Pat Nickalls closed the Wardell store in 1986. It was a sad day for "Wardell and Company — the Busy Merchants, Dealers in Dry Goods, Furnishings, Clothing, Millinery, Boots and Shoes, Groceries, Flour and Feed." They had become a well-known institution in Huntsville and beyond. However, many of Matthew Wardell's descendants still live and work in and contribute to our community.

THE SCHOOL

CHAFFEY STONE SCHOOL
99 WEST ROAD, HUNTSVILLE
C. 1930

CHAFFEY TOWNSHIP'S FIRST SCHOOL was, in effect, a private school run in the 1870s by Captain George Hunt's mother at her home, a log building just east of the bridge. The first organized school was held at the Orange Hall located on West Street behind the former Eaton's store where, besides holding classes, the Orangemen met during the week and church services were held on Sundays. In 1878 the first school built with ratepayers money was built on Church Street.

In 1886 Huntsville became a village, but the students from outside the municipality continued to attend the village school until 1889 when it was decided to build a school for the Chaffey Township students in what was known as North Huntsville. A frame building was opened that year, with Miss Bonser as its first teacher. There were no desks and the students sat on benches. Built by J.P. Smith, the school was owned by Thomas Goldie, on whose land it was built.

In 1902 John Bildson, James Early and Uriah Hardy were elected as trustees and a new one-room frame school was built on property purchased from Sarah Toomes. Finished in rough pine, the interior was painted a glowing red. There were about twenty students, some of whom were of the Silver, Hanes, Bildson, Patterson, Norton, Cousins and Later families.

In 1930 increased population prompted trustees Forest McFarland, Colonel Lawlor and J. Robertson to have a new two-room stone school built. Forest McFarland was the builder. There seemed to be a problem heating the school, and within two years the trustees were persuaded to purchase storm windows to conserve heat. A cupboard was built in the basement to store the windows in the summer and the kindling in the winter as the caretaker complained that the principal was burning all his kindling. In 1938 the school was wired for electric lights. In 1940 the lawn was seeded, flower beds developed and the front walk built in an effort to beautify the school grounds. While Laverne Reynolds was the principal in 1945, the roof and front door received a coat of red paint; pail-a-day toilets were installed and the outhouses were torn down.

By 1947 there were eighty-three students and the school was overcrowded. In 1948 Evelyn Edwards of Aspdin was hired to teach grades three and four at the North Huntsville Community Hall. In September 1949 a room in the Huntsville Band Hall had to be rented to accommodate twenty-two additional students.

Work was begun on a new Chaffey Township School (Pine Glen) in April 1949, which was officially opened May 15, 1950, with about two hundred people in attendance. Ed Foster, chairman of the Chaffey Township School Board, chaired the proceedings. Speakers were Wilfred "Bucko" McDonald, M.P., D.R. McDonald, public school inspector, Harry Thornton, Huntsville High School principal and

44

Chaffey Stone School, 99 West Road, 1930.

Charles Percival. That year the students from the Band Hall and the Huntsville Community Hall were moved to the new school. Melissa, Ravenscliffe and Grassmere schools were closed and students transported to North Huntsville. Junior classes continued to be held at the stone school.

In recent years Community Living Huntsville purchased the stone school. This organization, formerly Huntsville and District Association for the Mentally Retarded, is a non-profit organization whose services are jointly funded by the Ministry of Community and Social Services and donations from private and corporate members. Community Living Huntsville is dedicated to providing services and support to people in our community with developmental delays and or disabilities. To achieve its goals, a variety of programs for both adults and children are offered at the old stone school on West Road.

CHURCHES

FIRST BAPTIST CHURCH
15 MAIN STREET WEST, HUNTSVILLE
C. 1906

THIS NICELY DETAILED BAPTIST CHURCH, situated prominently at the top of Main Street, was built in 1906 and became the sixth church building in Huntsville. It has a steeply pitched high gable roof with very shallow eaves and yellow brick detailing on the exterior red brick walls. The entrance is located in a small, enclosed vestibule facing the street. The windows along the side and the windows and door in the vestibule are decorated with an interesting continuous brick label or hood mould. The original purpose of this moulding was to throw rain away from the windows, although this hood mould is so shallow that its sole purpose is for decoration. Original interior features that have survived include the wainscot, stair rails and the interesting manual hardware that opens the window transoms. Over the years there have been at least three new ceilings.

In the early years of settlement of north Muskoka, there were few families of the Baptist faith, and they were scattered and busy clearing land and developing farms. The first Baptist missionary visited the area in 1879 and met with families in Brunel Township where the first service was held. It wasn't until the late 1890s, when Huntsville had grown and prospered due to a number of sawmills and the tannery offering employment, that a number of Baptist families gathered in Huntsville to worship.

In May 1902 the Baptist Home Mission sent Reverend Mr. Russell of Kingston to form a Huntsville congregation. The Orange Hall was rented for services that summer, but by the fall when Brother E.J. Bingham arrived, services were held at Snyder's Hall and the number of members increased. Brothers William Dickie and B. Beston were elected deacons, and Brothers P. Wells, John Wells and A. Smith were elected as trustees.

First Baptist Church, 15 Main Street West, 1906.

46

In April 1904 the lot on Main Street was purchased from Louis Ware for $200 and a persistent canvas of members was undertaken. Besides the money raised by local members, a $400 loan was obtained from the church board in Toronto. Lewis Hill, an owner of the Huntsville Planing Mill, agreed to supply most of the material on easy terms in addition to some badly needed labour. Volunteers including local bricklayers George Woodcock and James McFarland, who each gave one week to brick the church, did most of the work.

The church had a comfortable basement and auditorium that could seat about 250 people. Finally, with plank benches in place, a borrowed organ and a donated stove for heat, the opening service took place on December 16, 1906. The following evening there was a grand opening with pastors of Baptist churches in nearby communities in attendance. Reverend Norton of the Home Mission Board spoke words of praise and encouragement to the members. Member of Parliament William Wright, a prominent Huntsville resident, chaired the meeting. Soon a drive shed was built behind the new church. The Baptists in Brunel, who had been worshiping in schools and homes, found it difficult to attend church in Huntsville because of poor road conditions, and the pastor from Huntsville went to preach to them as time permitted.

The First Baptist Church, because of high mortgages and dwindling membership during World War I and the Depression, has occasionally experienced hard times. Between April 1916 and June 1917 the church was closed due to financial difficulties and lack of interest, but after the war membership increased with Baptists from Brunel filling the church. During the 1920s a parsonage at 26 Main Street West was purchased from Mr. Shay for $4,000.

The 1,200-square-foot Christian Education addition was made to the rear of the church in 1981.

Some of the prominent members who have contributed to this church are Tom Forbes, and James Cain, as well as the Stevens, Farnsworth, Crooks and Cryderman families.

HOLY TRINITY ANGLICAN CHURCH
NEWHOLM
C. 1889

IN 1870 DAVID FERGUSON, a United Empire Loyalist, obtained a land grant in the Township of Brunel. To get to his land, he and his wife, Annabelle Hamilton, travelled from southern Ontario by train to Washago, then by stagecoach to Port Sydney and by footpath through the forest to Lynx Lake, which was near their property.

Other pioneers came to settle in the area. By 1873 Annabelle Ferguson, a staunch Anglican, and other women began agitating for a church. In time, a log church was built on land donated by the Fergusons. In 1877, the first baptism took place. This early cabin church was known

Holy Trinity Anglican Church, Brunel Road, c. 1889.

47

simply as Trinity Anglican and was in use until 1888. It was replaced in 1889, closer to Newholm on Lot 15, Concession 5, Brunel Township, on land donated by the Rumball family. The frame structure, constructed by builder and master woodcarver William Morgan, was called Holy Trinity Church. Morgan carved the beautiful baptismal font as well. Alberta Howard, a teacher, raised money for the purchase of the church organ by going around the lumber camps seeking donations and also taking orders from the men to knit socks at twenty-five cents a pair. She later married Ernie Ferguson. In the early years the church was lit first by candles and then by coal oil lamps. Parishioners were asked to pay five cents a week for the upkeep of the church.

For many years Holy Trinity Newholm served and was supported by forty-three families as a mission church. Its parish church was initially Christ Church, Port Sydney, and later All Saints Church in Huntsville. By 1988 there were only ten people attending services and only four families helping with expenses and the church was closed. The building gradually deteriorated. It became prey to vandalism and precious artifacts disappeared.

In late 1993 concerned residents such as John and Barbara Groves and John Riviere Anderson initiated meetings with local historical groups, Muskoka Pioneer Village and the clergy of All Saints to investigate the options for its future. They were aided by Rae Marie Campbell, great-granddaughter of settlers David and Annabelle Ferguson, who kept the project alive by writing articles in *The Forester*, which generated a great deal of public interest.

Fortunately, this interest resulted in the church's revitalization by numerous volunteers who donated time, energy and money to replace joists, sills and roof, repair the windows with original glass and basically refurbish the church and cemetery. Summer services are now held at Holy Trinity and it is part of a totally new Anglican parish created in 1997, the North Muskoka Pioneer Parish, with the Reverend Edna Murdy as parish priest.

KNOX UNITED CHURCH
777 MUSKOKA ROAD 10, PORT SYDNEY
C. 1878

THE FIRST PRESBYTERIANS who took up land around the present village of Port Sydney in 1869 began to meet during that win-

48

Knox Presbyterian Church, Port Sydney, 1878.

ter in the small log house of James Kay and his wife and their family of five children. They would read the scriptures and sing the psalms and hymns. The services continued in 1871 in the home of the McFees, who had brought with them from Scotland a violin and a melodeon. As the settlement grew, the number of worshippers increased, and in the summers of 1873 and 1874 student ministers, who came as missionaries to the small scattered communities in Muskoka, included Port Sydney in their circuit. Soon it was necessary to meet in the schoolhouse in order to accommodate the number of people and discussions began about the possibility of building a church.

Albert Sydney Smith owned Lot 25, Concession 6, the land on the east side of the river opposite his mills. In 1877 James Kay, William Clarke and Alexander Mitchell, acting as trustees of the proposed Knox Presbyterian Church, negotiated with Albert Smith for Lot 33 of his plan for Port Sydney, registered in 1875. The Port Sydney congregation was united with St. Andrew's Church in Huntsville in 1880 to be served by an ordained missionary and when, in 1884, the Reverend J. Sieveright was appointed to the charge, the Home Mission Committee reported "His well-known building energy was soon apparent." The construction of the church was undertaken over the summer and fall of 1884, and that original structure forms the core of the present building.

The first services were held in the church early in 1885. The church was well built, with ten-by-ten hand-hewn beams around the perimeter, floor joists and studs mortized into these timbers, and the whole foundation constructed without nails. The rectangular building had a high gable roof. Six triangular-headed windows, three on each side, had eight lights in the bottom sash and thirteen lights in the upper sash. The floor was of pine boards, some twelve inches wide.

The pulpit, still in use today, was made by William Clarke and William Jarvis. James Kay's daughter, Agnes, came back from a trip to Toronto where, with the help of friends, she had procured an organ and money for pews. A box stove heated the church and the first addition to the building was a woodshed, constructed near the corner of the property in a convenient location for storing the contributions of wood. Then a drive shed was added at the rear of the building, with stalls for teams of horses and a single stall for the minister's buggy. A picket fence, shown in all the early pictures, helped to prevent grazing cows, who all wore a bell, from disturbing the service.

In 1909 it was decided to plant potatoes in a field belonging to Mr. Phippen. The proceeds from their sale were used to purchase a bell for the church.

The original woodshed was replaced by a shed adjoining the back of the church. In the 1920s this was improved for meeting use and by the 1930s was in use as a Sunday school room. Also in the 1930s electricity came to the village and the church was wired at a cost of forty-five dollars, donated by Phippen. Summer residents Jean Moodie and her father gave electric fixtures and a pulpit light. The Knox Church congregation expanded during the summer months with the arrival of the summer people, and this continues today.

49

During World War I, Knox Presbyterian Church joined with the Methodist church in Utterson, so that Church Union in 1925 was a fairly straightforward matter in Port Sydney. The church is presently part of the Locks Pastoral Charge, along with Locks United Church and Bethune United Church in Baysville.

In 1958 the congregation built a basement under the Sunday school and installed a furnace, later extending the space at the back of the church to include a kitchen, small storage room and a pail-a-day toilet. With no running water, the women of the church ran the kitchen using water brought in by Brodie Kay in large milk cans. Then in 1985 the congregation undertook extensive renovations and improvements in celebration of the church's centennial. A full basement was built underneath the church, including a kitchen and two washrooms, as well as a new porch with stairs to the basement. Water was piped into the building. The windows of the new porch were original, while a new stained-glass window designed and made by Norma McClure, a member of the congregation, was placed above the door.

The centennial celebrations began with a sod turning by Brodie Kay and Daisy Hughes, both grandchildren of people listed on the first Communion Roll in 1877. The original wood siding remains on the main structure while the new main doors, iron railings, concrete steps and basement entrance have been added. Knox United Church is still standing at the corner of Village Hill Road and District Road 10, looking very much as it did over a hundred years ago.

ST ANDREW'S PRESBYTERIAN CHURCH
HIGH STREET, HUNTSVILLE
C. 1897

THE FIRST PRESBYTERIAN CHURCH in Huntsville was built about 1884 on Church Street on land donated by George Hunt. The first elder was George Selkirk. Subsequent elders in the early years were

St. Andrew Presbyterian Church, High Street.

William Jones and Robert Aitcheson in 1886 and Hart Proudfoot in 1890.

By 1890 there was hint of a new church. It had become obvious that the village was developing on the west side of the river, and in 1894 the trustees resolved to dismantle the church and rebuild in a more central location. However, two years later a grass fire destroyed the old church, and the congregation met in Snyder's Hall until a new church could be built.

In August of 1897 the trustees purchased Lot 19 from William Randelson and an additional twenty-five feet of Lot 20 from William Wright at the corner of High and West Streets. Duncan McCaffery had operated a sawmill on this site from as early as 1884 but by 1893 had relinquished the property for unpaid taxes.

Later in 1897 trustees Hart Proudfoot, Samuel Smale, a tinsmith, and Charles Landell, a sawmill foreman, retired and by January of 1898 had been replaced by Captain George Marsh, a marine captain and seaman, and merchants Thomas Goldie and John Calderwood, all well-known residents of Huntsville. A $3,000 mortgage was arranged with William

50

St. Andrew Presbyterian Church, High Street.

Whitell of Huddersfield, England. Alex Corbett was the builder. Material, labour and services were provided by the Huntsville Lumber Company and Duncan McCaffery; Jacob Wardell and Frederick Cullon, carpenters; John Hoile, painter; John and Alfred Buckner, of Buckner Bros., plasterers and hardware merchants Wm. Butchart and White Bros.

The handsome brick church, built in a style reminiscent of European Romanesque architecture, was opened April 17, 1898. The style can be noted in the chunky weight of the building volume, the high stone foundation, the heavy corbelled eave at the tower, the brick arches and brick patterns, round-headed windows and four pinnacles surrounding an eight-sided spire. This church is a good example of a well-maintained building whose original architecture has been respected and preserved.

The first St. Andrew's Womens Missionary Society (W.M.S.) was formed in 1899 with Mrs. McVicar, the minister's wife, as the first president. In 1900 the Northern Lights Mission Band was formed. Other church organizations over the years have been the Excelsior Bible Class, Ruby Walker Evening Auxiliary, Ladies Aid Society and the St. Andrew's Club.

On record at St. Andrew's is a brief account of each of the many colourful and outstanding pastors who have ministered to this church over the years. Each has added a special event or moment to the church's history.

A significant memorial tree planting took place on May 15, 1920, at St. Andrew's when three maple trees were planted on the west slope of the church lawn and one at the front. The latter was planted in memory of World War I heroine, nurse Edith Cavell. A squad of local soldiers assisted in the work of planting. Their commanding officer, barrister and solicitor Colonel Donald M. Grant, was a long-time member of St. Andrew's Presbyterian Church. He was Sunday school superintendent for twenty-eight years and an elder from 1896 to 1925.

On Sunday, May 6, 1973, long-time members of St. Andrew's Mr. and Mrs. Findlay Whyte were honoured with the dedication of a memorial window. The chosen theme, Follow Me, was very appropriate for Mrs. Whyte, who was president of the Ladies Aid for many years and Findlay, who served the church for twenty-five years as secretary. From 1906 to

51

1925, Jenny (Abbott) Shaw, wife of C.O., conducted the St. Andrew's choir. Her fine contralto voice was recognized in music circles as far away as the United States. The many concerts the choir performed delighted Huntsville audiences and, although the proceeds were often for work within the church, many also benefited local charities.

In 1994 the electronic carillon was installed, providing warm and welcoming music to all the residents of Huntsville and carrying on St. Andrew's Presbyterian Church's musical tradition.

PRESBYTERIAN CHURCH MANSE
8 CHURCH STREET, HUNTSVILLE
C. 1885

CAPTAIN GEORGE HUNT envisioned Huntsville developing on the east side of the Muskoka River and he registered Subdivision 3 in March 1877. A one-and-one-quarter-acre lot, overlooking a proposed village square, was designated for the Presbyterian church site. That year a small house was built on the site where the first missionary, Joseph Andrews, lived for about eighteen months before he was tranferred to Magnetawan. It wasn't until the spring of 1884 that Reverend James Thirde, an uncle to Huntsville merchant William Strachan, arrived as the first resident pastor. Construction of a frame church was started about this time. Tragically, Reverend Thirde died suddenly, one month after his arrival. In July 1884 Reverend James Sieveright arrived, and contractors of the railway built the stone manse the following year. Reverend Sieveright was born in Aberdeen in 1833 and was ordained in 1857. Before coming to Huntsville he had been connected with eleven pres-byteries from Montreal to Winnipeg, the latter at that time the only pres-bytery west of Lake Superior.

Reverend Sieveright and his wife, Frances, had four children, all born in Quebec. Their eldest son, Archibald, a chemist, had a pharmacy on Main Street in Huntsville for many years before moving to Toronto. The

Presbyterian church manse, 8 Church Street, 1885.

family cow and a horse were kept in a stable on the property.

In 1886 Huntsville and Allenville became a pastoral charge and Reverend Sieveright was inducted at a stipend of $4,000, three-quarters

52

of which was Huntsville's share. In 1896 Reverend Sieveright resigned and moved to Burk's Falls where he was the editor of the *Arrow*. He died in 1916.

The manse remained empty for a time, as the wooden Presbyterian church on Church Street burned to the ground. Reverend Archibald McVicar, a young graduate of McGill University, who after three years in mission work in British Columbia, arrived with his wife, the former Mary MacLean, in 1899.

It was during Reverend McVicar's tenure that the new brick church was built at the corner of West and High Streets. Mary was the first president of the Women's Missionary Society formed in 1899. The three eldest McVicar children were born in this house before the family left in 1905. The next minister was the Reverend George McLennan, who was ordained and inducted on the same day, August 8, 1905. He was a member of the Canadian champion McGill football team that year! Two of his children were born at 8 Church Street. Reverend David H. Marshall came in 1912 and was destined to become one of the beloved of pastors at St. Andrew's. When World War I broke out he was asked to be chaplain of the local regiment by Colonel Grant, a prominent member of the Presbyterian congregation and in 1916 he resigned to go oversees. The congregation refused to accept his resignation and Reverend William Marrin and others filled in for him. Mrs. Marshall remained at the manse with their four small children, the youngest born in this house on April 16, 1915. Reverend Marshall returned safely in 1919 and on May 15, 1921, officiated at the planting of the Edith Cavell tree on the lawn the Presbyterian church on High Street. Shortly after this the congregation bid a reluctant farewell to Reverend Marshall.

By 1921 the manse was in need of major repairs and to cover expenses, William Watson, by then retired, gave the trustees a mortgage for $2,000 and moved into the parsonage. He was a member and liberal supporter of the church. His brother was Huntsville chief of police John G. Watson. Born in Ireland in about 1854, William came to Canada about 1884. Living in Collingwood for a few years, he came to Huntsville about 1888

and was associated with the Huntsville Lumber Company for thirty years, becoming a company director. William Watson was a municipal councillor for several years and a member of both the Orange Lodge 3993 and the Oddfellows. He was married in 1902 to Eva Murray of Huntsville. After a long period of ill-health William Watson died in February 1928 at his home where a private family service was held. Eva Watson seems to have continued to live in the manse until her death on June 11, 1932. Both are buried in the Presbyterian cemetery.

In 1938 the trustees of the Presbyterian church sold the property to the executors of Eva Watson's estate and in the fall of 1939 it was sold to William and Gladys Harkness.

Bill Harkness was an insurance agent with Sun Life Insurance Company. He was born in 1886 near Sundridge where his grandfather had come to homestead in 1881. He and his wife, the former Gladys Connor, lived in Huntsville during the 1920s but were transferred to Seaforth and then Strathroy before returning to Huntsville in 1935. During the 1930s and 1940s tourist cabins were popular and Bill built two cabins at a home they had on Chaffey Street. Gladys would often walk by the old manse on Church Street, which was almost hidden in an overgrown tangle of wild grapevines, and would comment that she was very glad she didn't live in the house on the hill. In 1939 the manse was for sale and Bill Harkness made the only offer that was received. The cabins were moved to the new site. Two additional cabins were built overlooking Fairy Avenue and named The Green Lyte Cabins. Bill died in 1942 and Gladys in 1983.

Bill Harkness had lost one arm in a hunting accident when he was eleven years old, but with determination he built the stone wall along Main Street and planted the hydrangea bushes we still enjoy.

Bill and Gladys Harkness's daughter Eloise and her husband, Nick Steven, a retired school teacher, purchased the property in 1963 and built the first phase of the apartment complex we see today. The Stevens replaced the front porch with an addition of two bedrooms, a bathroom and sun porch.

St. George's Anglican Church, Lancelot, c. 1880.

St. Mary's Anglican Church, Aspdin.

ST. GEORGE'S ANGLICAN CHURCH
LANCELOT
C. 1880

ST. GEORGE'S ANGLICAN CHURCH is situated close to a sharp bend in a gravel road that winds its way through the Muskoka woods as it reaches the small pioneer hamlet of Lancelot. It was built in 1880 to replace an earlier log church provided by the Reverend W.R. Crompton during his travelling ministry. The property, Lot 15, Concession 12, of Stephenson Township, was given to the diocese by Mr. Griffith, an English settler, and included room for a cemetery.

The white frame church remains much as it was then, although large cedar trees have grown up around the entry. The sides are of shiplapped lumber with barge-board trim at the base, on stone foundations. The roof is steep pitched with a four-sectioned hip roof over the nave and an open gable at one end, above which rises a simple belfry topped by a wooden cross. Slender windows with pointed tops and graceful mullion patterned banding complete the picture. A red Celtic cross of St. George is displayed on one of the exterior sides of the nave.

Recent interest in this historic church has resulted in funds being provided for maintenance of the building and its pioneer cemetery. St. George's is now open for summer services. Along with five other small mission churches St. George's is now part of a totally new Anglican parish created in 1997, the North Muskoka Pioneer Parish, with the Reverend Edna Murdy as parish priest.

ST. MARY'S ANGLICAN CHURCH
ASPDIN
C. 1885

ST. MARY'S IS THE OLDEST STONE CHURCH in Muskoka, its construction having commenced in 1885. It is located on a rise of land in what was the centre of the village of Aspdin, on a one-acre property donated by Charles William Johnson, the village storekeeper. He requested that it be called St. Mary's after a favourite daughter and asked that it not include a cemetery. (Upon his death, his widow donated an adjoining acre for the cemetery.)

It was built of local stone and has simple gothic windows, high gabled roofs and an enclosed belfry tower. The interior has a gently curved tongue-and-groove wooden ceiling and a handsomely carved wooden archway to the sanctuary. The seventy-four communicants who attended the opening service in 1886 were stirred by memories of their beloved parish churches in England and were pleased to be able to attend services in such a church in the backwoods of Canada. Other than the rebuilding

St. Mary's Anglican Church.

of the tower in 1911, the church today is little changed.

The church was brought into being through the efforts of William Crompton. He came to Muskoka to settle in Aspdin from England, where he had been a lay reader in the Church of England. Shortly after locating here, he was ordained a deacon and then in 1879 was ordained as a priest. As a travelling priest, he saw a need for churches in the settlements he visited in North Muskoka, and through letters and visits with his contacts back in England, he was able to raise funds for the construction and furnishing of more than twenty churches in the area. He was St. Mary's first priest.

He saw a need for community recreation so a meeting hall, sponsored by Lady Clifton, was built beside the church. It was called Clifton Hall. It boasted a stage and a library and strict rules for behaviour. Library privileges were twenty-five cents per year.

At one time St. Mary's Church had a congregation of 250, but over the years the numbers dwindled. For a time during the Depression it was part of the mission of the Cowley Fathers of Bracebridge, then it became inactive and neglected. Finally it reached such a state of disrepair that there were serious doubts as to its future.

Fortunately, recently a local support group from within the community searched for a plan of action with the Anglican Diocese of Algoma. Bit by bit, in true pioneer spirit and with donations of labour and home-grown materials, the church has been restored so that summer services are now being held and St. Mary's is now part of a totally new Anglican parish created in 1997, the North Muskoka Pioneer Parish, with the Reverend Edna Murdy as parish priest.

TRINITY UNITED CHURCH
33 MAIN STREET EAST, HUNTSVILLE
C. 1897

IT WAS FORTUITOUS FOR THE EARLY SETTLERS in North Muskoka that Reverend Robert Norton Hill settled on Peninsula Lake in 1869. He had given the first church service in the area at the home of Ira Fetterly in 1868, the year he was beginning to clear his land. The next year he began services at George Hunt's cabin on the east side of the Muskoka River at what became Huntsville. Although Robert had recently resigned as a minister with the New Connexion Methodists to take up farming, the need for a missionary to the settlers in the area soon persuaded him to again serve his church in what was called the New Connexion Methodist Lake Vernon Mission. Reverend Hill preached often, as did John Webster and ministers of the Bracebridge Mission of the Wesleyan Methodist church.

In August 1872 the Huntsville Mission was organized and services were held in the Orange Hall, a log building on the corner of Main and West Streets. By 1875 the New Connexion Methodists and the Wesleyan Methodists united, and plans were made to build a church in the growing hamlet of Huntsville. William Cann donated a one-acre lot in March of 1874, which became Lot A on Huntsville's first plan registered in September 1875.

In 1876 trustees John Fetterly, Fred May, Edward Bray, James F. Hanes, George Lasseter, William E. McDonald, John Silverwood and Robert N. Hill proceeded to build the first church in Huntsville, followed by a parsonage and large drive shed. The Methodist cemetery was located on this site until 1877, when John Fetterly offered a piece of property on his land for the Methodist Cemetery, now known as the Lock's Cemetery.

The church was spared in the Main Street fire of 1894, although there was some damage to the parsonage, which was settled with the adjuster for $186. By 1896 the congregation had outgrown the building and the decision was made to replace it. The building was put on rollers and moved to a lot on High Street and sold to the Free Methodist congregation for $210. It cost $85 to move it.

The board was beset with difficulties when the insurance company requested a personal bond from every member of the board. Reverend Joseph Wilson was successful in obtaining a resignation from those who were unwilling. Those remaining were William Wright, George Hutcheson, John R. Boyd, Maxwell Hall, Matthew Wardell, Frederick May, John R. Reece, Henry Warren, Harry L. Heath, William H.

Matthews, Jacob H. Johnson and William E. Hutcheson.

Excavation began during the winter of 1896 and construction began in the spring of 1897. George W. Miller of Toronto drew up the plans, and George Hutcheson submitted the lowest tender and was allotted the contract to build the church. Alex Corbett had charge of the brick and stone work. Mrs. Bettes of Bracebridge laid the cornerstone on June 28, 1897.

Trinity United Church has many architectural elements from the Victorian Gothic Revival style that was popular during the later part of the nineteenth century. Among the interesting features is the small porch entrance to the left side of the elevation, which mirrors the bell tower and main entrance to the right. These two forms of unequal mass frame the front facade that is rich in medieval detail. Four rectangular, small-pane stained-glass windows with stone lintels rest on a continuous heavy tim-

Trinity United Church, 33 Main Street East.

ber sill, diffusing light into the first floor lobby. Higher up (above three panels of brick parquetry) four lancet windows with acute brick arches rest on stone sills, illuminating the sanctuary balcony. The north face of the bell tower has a slender lancet window directing light onto the tower stairs leading to the balcony. Three lancet windows illuminate the upper stair landing. Three more lancet windows also illuminate the landing at the top of the tower stairs. Brick spires rise above the roof at each corner of the tower. The four spires, as well as the central roof of the tower, are topped with metal pyramidal cap flashings and finials. The longer, east and west elevations of the sanctuary are divided into four equal bays by brick buttresses with brick weathering. A single, large pointed-arch stained-glass window is centred in each bay. The large addition at the rear of the church has obscured a trio of lancet windows with trefoil tracery located high above the choir.

In 1913 William Wright, M.P., requested that the church sell eighty-five feet of its property to the east in preparation for the building of a new post office (it was not built until 1926). The property was sold and a new parsonage was built in 1914 on the corner of West and High Streets, now the offices of Hutcheson Sand and Gravel Company.

There have been many beloved pastors at Trinity, each contributing his talents to assist the congregation in the issues of his time and in the formation of a variety of church groups. A unique and very popular organization, the Fortnightly Club, was formed in 1942. A club for the young married people of Trinity, it held a meeting for discussion of topics of both community and national interest and a social evening each month. The annual lumber-camp suppers held at Frank Hubbel's mill at Oxtongue Lake were a highlight.

On February 11, 1948, a fire broke out in a cleaning cupboard in the furnace room, destroying the south end of the church including the choir loft and the pipe organ donated in 1926 by former church board member William H. Matthews of Tennessee. The Anglican, Salvation Army, Presbyterian and Baptist churches all made offers of the use of their premises during the emergency. For a short time services were held at the parish hall, but with the arrival of warm weather, the congregation returned to Trinity and worshiped in the basement until cold weather arrived. Arrangements were then made with Joe Giaschi to worship in the old Capitol Theatre. There was no charge, but the board agreed to fill his coal bin with coal! The damaged part of the church was constructed on an entirely new plan, including the chancel, church parlour, kitchen, choir-room and minister's vestry. It was at this time that the gallery was constructed to add seating for forty people. The church was opened in November 1949.

The newly constructed "gymnatorium" was officially named Trinity Hall on October 26, 1964. This Christian Education addition has provided a suitable site not only for church group activities, but also for Red Cross blood donor clinics and some very enjoyable theatre productions.

After one hundred years, Trinity Church continues to hold a prominent place in Huntsville's town centre.

COMMUNITY CENTRES

ALLENSVILLE HALL
ALLENSVILLE
C. 1901

THE MCNICHOL FAMILY came from Scotland to Canada in 1863. They acquired from the Crown four 100-acre lots in Concession 11, Lots 24, 25, 26 and 27, Stephenson Township. The village of Allensville is named after Allan McNichol. He settled on Lot 26. In 1871 he became the postmaster.

Lot 25 was the property of James McNichol. He died in 1891 and left his land to his nephew, James Hood McNichol, the son of Allan. In 1901 James gave a portion of Lot 25 to the village. James stipulated that the land was to be used for a community centre and that it was always to be a public place.

In May 27, 1902, the Union Hall Society was formed. A group of citizens became its first members: Daniel Bray, John W. Madill, James H. McNichol, John Johnson, Richard W. Amphlett and William H. Seymour. The committee had to manage and maintain the new public hall at Allensville. The society stated that it was to be used for church, Benevolent Society, public meetings and entertainment. The committee minutes stated that the Presbyterian, Methodist and Episcopal churches in Allensville "shall be entitled to free use of the hall for church business. For all other meetings and entertainments there shall be charged such fees as may be settled by the Executive Committee."

In December 1902 the Union Hall Society was incorpo- rated. Lawyer W.C. Mahaffy of Bracebridge certified that the name conformed to the act respecting benevolent providential and other such societies in Ontario.

The "Allensville News" section in *The Forester* of those days reports how hard everyone worked to erect the hall. William Proudfoot, a local builder, provided the plans. The people gathered stones for the foundation by hand. They organized work bees. Tea was available in the schoolhouse for the volunteers. Pledges were made to do certain jobs: William Seymour gave a week's work and F.W. Amphlett offered to dig ditches.

Allensville Hall.

58

By September 1901 the simple frame rectangular building was up. In October villagers celebrated the opening of the Allensville Union Hall. They held a hot supper and a free dance for all who had worked so hard on the project. The Allensville Hall continued to be the centre of the thriving farming community for many years.

In the 1950s plans were made to update the community hall. In 1960 the inside walls were covered with Masonite and gyproc, aluminum foil was added to the existing insulation and the roof was repaired. In the 1970s the exterior of the building was painted and stained and an auction was held to raise money to install running water and electricity. A new oil stove was purchased and a washroom added to the original structure. The fixed stage was replaced with a smaller, moveable one, and the frame windows replaced with aluminum ones.

In the 1980s special events were held to raise money for more painting and repairs: a walkathon, "You Fetch It" auction and "Paint the Hall" dance were held.

The history of the ownership of the hall has an interesting twist: Two Barnardo children — Anthony Hole and his brother — came to live with the McNichol family in 1920. When James McNichol died in 1948, Anthony purchased some land from the estate, which included the Allensville Hall. Apparently, the title to the land had never been transferred, although the community had used it for fifty years. In 1973 Anthony and his wife, Mabel, sold the property to the Allensville Community Centre Inc. Some fourteen years later the ownership was transferred to the Huntsville Kinsmen Club.

For over eighty years the Allensville Hall vibrated with the life of the community. Here, local people celebrated the important occasions, special events and good times of their lives.

Brunel Community Centre, Mary Lake Road.

BRUNEL COMMUNITY CENTRE
THE LOCKS
C. 1939

BUILT IN 1939, the building housing this community centre was once the first two-room school to serve S.S. 6, Brunel Township. Located on Mary Lake Road on the southeast corner of Lot 11, Concession 13, it was known as the Locks' School. Of frame construction (later covered with Insul brick) on a full concrete basement, it had tall ceilings and windows, a main centre door and a separate entry to the basement. An attractive bell tower on the roof completed the structure.

The original school for the pioneer families was a log building constructed in 1890 on the southwest corner of Lot 11. In 1906 a one-room red brick school was constructed down the hill on the southeast corner of the same lot, and in 1939 the present structure was erected immediately behind the red brick school.

This two-room school was in use until 1952, when the Riverside School on Brunel Road came into being with more space for the growing population. A new school was built on this site in 1993.

No longer needed for education purposes, the old school became the municipal offices for the Township of Brunel until 1971, when regional government made that redundant.

Since then this sturdy building has been greatly enhanced and upgraded with fresh paint, soft beige aluminum siding and a new porch and railing. The separate entry to the basement has been closed and the building made wheelchair accessible. The original school bell tower gleams above the entry, completing this attractive structure. Just as the schools once served the community in so many ways, the Brunel Community Centre is a focus for the people within the area.

Port Sydney Community Centre, Muskoka Road 10, Port Sydney.

PORT SYDNEY COMMUNITY HALL
MUSKOKA ROAD 10, PORT SYDNEY
C. 1925

THIS COMMUNITY HALL was built by public subscription in 1925. It was the third hall in the village. The first had been up the hill and to the east of the present building, near the end of the dam. It was destroyed by fire about 1902. The second floor of the former cheese factory, on the river at the end of Morgan Street, was then used as a community hall. It was, however, a dangerous location due to the possibility of a fire.

The property on which this building stands was used for years as a picnic ground. A young people's club in the village was very keen to have a new hall and carried on many fund-raising activities in order to raise the money necessary to build one. In 1921 George Cadieux, Arthur Clarke, Colin Crawford, Martin Hoth and James Jenner went to Albert Sydney-Smith, who owned the three lots, which were being used as a picnic ground, to ask whether he would sell the land for a new community hall.

When Albert hesitated, they offered $1,000 in payment for the lots. Albert finally settled on a price of $800.

The foundation stone for the new hall was laid on May 4, 1925. Arthur Clarke was in charge of the building. He had said it could be constructed for $5,000 and, with much help from Port Sydney residents, he had the job completed by July 1 for a total cost of $4,300.

The hall was formerly opened with a grand march led by Albert Sydney-Smith and Mrs. James Jenner of Clyffe House. George Johnson in his book Port Sydney Past notes: "Alfred Kay, who was present at both events, recalled the similar grand march led by Mr. Smith and Mrs. Ladell that opened the original hall nearly fifty years before." This was the last public event in which Albert Sydney-Smith participated. He died three months later on October 2.

This large, green, barn-like structure looking out over Mary Lake is built into the hill, so that the north side is two storeys while the south side, with a door to the kitchen, has an entrance directly to the second floor.

It is a long rectangular building with a steeply sloping hipped roof, clad in tin. The main entrance is located at the east end through a small vestibule and there is another entrance in the foundation at the west side of the building. Notable features are the exposed rafters and the main floor windows facing the lake. The main floor has a large hall and well-appointed kitchen, which has been modernized in recent years. The space below the main floor was used for many years as the station for the volunteer fire department. It now houses the community policing office.

The hall is a well-used and important feature of the Village of Port Sydney. The senior citizens' group, the Merry Mary Lakers, meets there weekly, except during the summer months when the space is taken over for a children's afternoon crafts and play time. The annual turkey dinner put on by the Chamber of Commerce, with turkey and pies cooked in almost every kitchen in the village, is held during the Cavalcade of Colour and immediately prior to a giant fireworks display on Rocky Island. The hall used to be the site of a weekly Saturday square dance and is still used for dances on special occasions and by local groups such as the Hill and Gully Snowmobile club. And it is used for public meetings of all kinds.

In 1996 the Community Hall was the recipient of a generous gift from Port Sydney residents Campbell and Evelyn McKean. The six paintings that now decorate the walls are copies of early photographs of the village painted by local artist Virginia Zandi. Albert Sydney-Smith's picture hangs above the platform and early scenes of the village adorn the walls.

STISTED AGRICULTURAL SOCIETY BUILDING, 1890–
STISTED TOWNSHIP HALL, 1890–1971
CONCESSION 9, PART LOT 15, STISTED TOWNSHIP, HUNTSVILLE

STISTED TOWNSHIP WAS NAMED for Major General Henry William Stisted, who was a senior military officer of the province and acted as

lieutenant governor of Ontario for several months prior to the appointment of Sir William Howland as lieutenant governor in 1867. The township has 46,860 acres and is approximately nine miles square. It was surveyed by Colonel John S. Dennis, land surveyor, and his assistant was Vernon Wadsworth, after whom Lake Vernon was named. In 1869 the Stisted Road was opened up, practically through the centre of the township, travelling northward.

After the establishment of the Ontario Free Grants and Homestead Act of 1868, townships in Muskoka were opened up for settlement and

Stisted Agricultural Society Building. Stisted Township Hall.

seekers of the free hundred-acre lots poured in. Stisted Township in North Muskoka was no exception.

The new settlers were anxious for some form of government, and in March 1874 they gathered at the residence of James Darling (now the Darling home at the Muskoka Pioneer Village) to elect a council. The reeve was John Darling and the four councillors were Henry Job, Jeremiah

Coulson, William McDonald and John Flemming. Joseph Lalor was the clerk and treasurer at a salary of twenty-three dollars a year. The returning officer, assessor and tax collector was Andrew Sproat. Each resident was allowed to keep one dog free of tax — any more than that were two dollars. No pigs, sheep, bulls, stallions or cattle were to run at large. Fences were to be five feet high. Every landowner was to do statutory labour on the roads for two days each year under the supervision of the pathmaster.

After meeting in various locations over the years, in 1890 the council bought four acres of land, which were almost in the centre of the township, from John Nicholas Schneider, Jr. William Quinn, of Yearly, erected the frame building — the Stisted Township Hall. It sits in one corner of a large field surrounded by forest on three sides and gravel road at the front. The simple thirty-by-twenty-foot rectangular structure with gable roof is roughly constructed of wood, and clad with unstained weathered siding. Some of the siding is vertical board and batten, although this is not consistent. The lean-to at the rear of the building is of horizontal boards. On each side are rectangular windows. Cedar shingles were originally on the roof, which has a small red brick chimney located in the centre ridge. Stisted Township council meetings were held in this unassuming building right up until 1971, when regional government came to Muskoka.

Marjorie Demaine in her book *Stories of Early Muskoka Days* describes a council meeting in the old hall. It was held at noon, probably the most suitable time, as there was no electricity in the building. The kettle sang merrily on the box stove for the proverbial pot of tea. Nearly everyone brought his own lunch. The ratepayers' meetings were often looked upon as the gala day of the year, and there were fiery speeches and hot debates. The settlers wanted to participate.

Marjorie also describes parties held there. In 1933 there was a fancy dress one for Halloween, with the participants dancing to the harmonious Schottische. Another time ninety guests attended a Hard Time party to aid the Stisted School Fair, and in 1935 a play, *The Country Minister*, was presented. The Etwell Operetta and Dance was held in 1940 in the Township Hall, with local talent. Such a good time was had by all that the crowd didn't disperse until two in the morning.

Besides being a municipal building, in 1890 the Stisted Township Hall was leased for ninety-nine years to the Stisted Agricultural Society. Its exhibitions and fairs have been held at the site ever since. It is interesting to note how much livestock there was in early Muskoka. The statistics from the Department of Agriculture indicate there were 4,903 horses, 9,439 milk cows, 8,602 other horned cattle, 11,325 sheep, 5,593 swine, 1,363 turkeys, 419 geese, 838 ducks and 78,966 hens and chickens. The settlers did come to farm!

There were changes to the building over the years, as the society's needs changed. In 1897 side desks for interior display were added. With the help of the Ashworth Women's Institute, a raised platform, kitchen and restroom were added in 1914, as well as a drive shed for horses and a grandstand. The year 1925 saw the addition of cattle pens. By 1946 the fair was so successful it was held for two days.

On the eightieth anniversary of the event in 1965 a portable electric plant was brought in and electric lights were used for the first time. The new era musicians also needed the hydro.

In 1998 the Stisted Agricultural Society will hold its 113th fair at the picturesque site in Stisted Township. This annual celebration of rural life in Stisted Township shows there is still an awful lot that hasn't changed.

FORMER BANDSTAND OF THE ANGLO-CANADIAN LEATHER COMPANY CONCERT BAND
12 SUSAN STREET, HUNTSVILLE
C. 1913

THE ANGLO-CANADIAN LEATHER COMPANY Concert Band was the outgrowth of an early Huntsville band composed of immigrant Italian workers at the leather company. Charles Orlando Shaw, manager of the tannery and a musician himself, was impressed with their talent. He became the founder and patron of the concert band. He hired George Simmons of Bracebridge in 1915 to teach and direct the members of the band. New instruments and uniforms were purchased. C.O., as he was known, imported talented musicians from all over North America, found them jobs in the tannery and supplied them with fine houses to live in.

In 1918 C.O. hired Herbert L. Clarke, a pupil of John Philip Sousa, to conduct the band, which soared to new heights under his leadership. That same year, the band was co-featured at the Canadian National Exhibition in Toronto. This was the ultimate achievement in musical circles, and was repeated for six of the following seven years, a record that was never equalled even by the great concert bands of the world. The famous Anglo-Canadian Leather Company Concert Band was disbanded in 1926, but the memory of its days of glory live on to this day.

Former Bandstand of Anglo-Canadian Leather Co. Concert Band, now a house, 12 Susan Street.

The former bandshell, built in 1913, is an octagonal-shaped building centrally situated on a generous lot, which slopes to the north. The roof, supported by eight concrete columns resting on a concrete foundation, has a medium-pitched slope and is clad with asphalt shingles. Each column is stepped at the bottom and top, roughly articulating a capitol and base. The soffit, which extends about eighteen inches beyond the columns, is constructed of painted wood.

63

The bandshell sits on a full basement, which can be entered through a door on the north, where the basement level is exposed. Windows provide light into the basement, which was used for storage and as a workshop for the tannery.

Diagonally across from the bandstand, to the east, was the Continuation School (Centre and Caroline Streets) and diagonally to the west was the Band Hall (Caroline and Lorne Streets). It was on the grassed slopes behind both these structures, and the lawn around the bandstand, extending to the Richard Sullivan home to the east (15 Centre Street), that the townspeople gathered by the hundreds whenever the band gave an outdoor concert.

John (Giovanni) Pesando, a long-time employee of the company and a member of the early Italian band that prompted the formation of the later concert band, purchased the bandstand from the Anglo-Canadian Leather Company in 1955. John installed the necessary plumbing and

electrical work around the bandstand and in the large room underneath. The conversion of the bandstand into a home was a big job — the railings had to be removed without damaging the structure. First a false ceiling had to be put in, but this made it easy to install insulation in the new home. John himself drew the plans for his home, and from inside the new house no one was aware of the octagonal shape. The ready-made concrete slabs for the sides of the new building were produced in Emsdale, Ontario.

It took many years for John to make satisfactory arrangements to purchase the right-of-way through the west side of his property. This was a well-worn path, used for many long years by Anglo-Canadian employees going to and from work. It was a great day for the Pesandos when the property could finally be fenced on the north side, and lawns and shrubs planted on the west side. Since John Pesando's death, the house has changed hands several times and a deck has been added.

Over the years scores of summer visitors come to Susan Street to view this bandstand home and to take photographs of this very vital part of the early twentieth century when Huntsville became so very well known because of its remarkable concert band.

ARMSTRONG-BICKLEY FARM
580 OLD NORTH ROAD, HUNTSVILLE
C. 1896

JOHN ARMSTRONG WAS BORN in Cardinal, Ontario. He originally left his home there looking for work, and travelled the Eagle Lake, South River and Manitoulin area of Ontario, where he made a living as a cheesemaker until he came to Huntsville in 1907. He learned that a butcher shop was for sale and, after making a thorough investigation of the possibilities of the business, he bought the store. His father had been a butcher, so he was familiar with the trade. His sons James, Harold and Frank, and later Roy, gave him plenty of help. The butcher shop was very successful. John Armstrong carried on until 1923, when he retired.

Anglo-Canadian Leather Company Concert Band in bandstand, c. 1920.

His shop was located at 57 Main Street East, where Ron Henry Jewellers is now located.

In 1920 John purchased a farm (Part Lots 16 and 17, Concession 7, Chaffey Township) on the Old North Road where he raised cattle, pigs and horses. Being an enthusiast of harness racing, he acquired the adjoining flatter land near the farm along the Big East River (now Ballantrae Heights subdivision). This purchase increased his holdings in the area to 188 acres and gave him ample space to train his racehorses.

In his book *Early Footsteps in Muskoka* Joe Cookson remembers when racing was held on the ice on Hunters Bay. A circular track was plowed wide enough to allow six horses to compete in each heat. The spectators

Right: Armstrong's Meat Market, 32 Main Street East, 1926. Below: Armstrong-Bickley Farm, 580 Old North Road.

stood around the track knee deep in snow, cheering their favourites. Horses and their owners came from many parts of Ontario to compete.

In 1926 John and his two eldest sons decided to go back into the butchering business, purchasing a shop at 32 Main Street East, where The Great Vine is now situated. Many resorts were opening up in the area, and butchering was a profitable business.

John moved into town in 1937 but retained the farm, barns and abattoir. His youngest son, Roy, and his wife, Dorothy, moved to the farm at that time, where they resided until 1967. Altogether, the premises and land on the Old North Road were owned and occupied by the Armstrong family for forty-seven years, from 1920 to 1967.

Originally, Charles Ambler obtained the timber rights in 1872, and 1881 was granted the one hundred acres as freehold land under the Ontario Free Grants and Homestead Act of 1868. Allen Gallately built the stone home located on part of the land in 1896. The present front of the house was originally the back of the house, as the Old North Road was what is now a portion of Fowler Road, veering off in a northerly direction a few yards past the house. In the 1920s the Ferguson Highway (now known as the Old North Road) was built, making the back door the front entrance.

The original stone front of the house, including a window casement, now forms an interesting wall in the dining room of the home, which has been renovated and expanded over the years. In 1922 a board and batten addition doubled the size of the living space in the home.

James and Amelia Long purchased the farm from Roy Armstrong in 1967 and subsequently subdivided the land, leaving the house and outbuildings and approximately thirty-three acres along the north side of the Old North Road. From 1969 on a series of short-term owners occupied the farm, until 1978 when Kenneth and Diane Bickley purchased it.

In 1981 a large and beautiful addition was constructed, once again doubling the living space. The house and property still retain the ambience of a rural Ontario farmhouse. The original spruce flooring, v-groove walls and ceilings, baseboards and doors have been retained wherever possible by the Bickleys.

BETTES-LAING-MAWHINNEY-TEAKLE HOUSE
9 RIVER STREET, HUNTSVILLE
C. 1884

9 River Street, before its restoration.

THIS DELIGHTFUL SITE along the west side of the Muskoka River as it runs through the town originally belonged to William Cann. He had obtained the land from the Crown under the Ontario Free Grants and Homestead Act of 1868. William sold the lots to Logan Davis, who later sold them to William H. Jones.

In 1884 Martha M. Bettes, wife of the sherriff, James Whitney Bettes, owned the property and built the charming clapboard house overlooking the river. The two-storey house has a predominant gable roof-shape to define its form. Exterior cladding includes asphalt shingles on the roof and narrow horizontal wood siding for the entire wall height. Decorative posts with upper strut bracings support the porch roof at both the front and rear. The shingle-hung windows are accentuated vertically with wide wood trim. The decorative head trim is both pointed and curved.

Martha and James, with a young daughter, came to Huntsville before 1881. In 1887 James bought Lot 14, Plan 1 on the Main Street, on which a building was constructed. He rented it to the White Brothers' Hardware. The whole area was known as the Bettes Block. In 1894 this part of Main Street was destroyed by fire. The hardware store was rebuilt, and later in 1900 the first Dominion Bank was erected to the west of the hardware store.

James Bettes had an active political life. In a by-election in 1882 he was elected to represent Muskoka–Parry Sound in the Ontario Legislature. In 1886 he was appointed sheriff of Muskoka, and in 1888 the family moved to Bracebridge, the county seat. Advertisements appeared in the local newspaper for the sale of the "very commodious" eight-room framed dwelling and barn.

During the next eighteen years Captain George Marsh, Edward Hurlburt, a carpenter, David Smith, a builder, and John Leckie, a minister. rented the house. In 1906 the house was sold to Peter Laing. The Laings came from Guelph, where they were in the wholesale butchering busi-

ness. In Huntsville their East End Meat Market employed five people. It had a large well-equipped shop and cold storage facility and supplied meat to the local resorts, the citizens of the town and the railway.

A 1910 issue of *The Forester* reported that Peter Laing left for the West with a load of horses. A year later an advertisement appears in the paper: "P. Laing and Son, Butchers and Livestock Dealer, Princess Street. Cash for Hides and Furs."

In 1920 the Laings sold their house to William Mawhinney, a merchant from Burk's Falls. William was married to Mary Valerie Wardell, known as Daisy, the daughter of a well-known Huntsville merchant, Mathew Wardell.

William had been in the retail business in Palmerston, Sturgeon Falls and Burk's Falls before retiring and moving to Huntsville. He used the large barn and garage on the property to store automobiles — people in those days "put their car up" for the winter. In the summer, he stored the cars of Bigwin Inn guests who travelled by steamer to the grand hotel on Lake of Bays. The barn collected a great many old licence plates.

Mr. Mawhinney died in 1930. The house was then rented to Lillie Braund. She was the widow of William Braund, a pharmacist who with his sons Edward and Pearson managed Braunds Drug Store. They served the citizens of Huntsville for over seventy years.

In later years, three Wardell sisters, all widows, lived together in the house by the river. The sisters were Annetta Wardell Boyd, Maud Wardell Nickalls and Daisy Wardell Mawhinney. During this time separate apartments were made in the house. Maud died in 1952. Daisy died twenty years later. The ownership of the house passed to the youngest sister, Annetta. She lived until 1985.

In 1986 Craig and Mary Louise Teakle bought the house. With good taste and much skill they have restored it to its original style and beauty. The apartments were removed and the porch opened. A new kitchen and family room were built and the bathrooms modernized. The barn was taken down and on that site a modern bungalow erected to house the senior Teakles.

The Teakle family love the old house in the heart of town, with its beautiful views of the curving Muskoka River.

CORBETT HOUSE
8 CAROLINE STREET, HUNTSVILLE
C. 1892

CLEARLY VISIBLE from Huntsville's busy town centre, this home is truly a centennial house. Alexander Corbett built this residence in 1892 and members of his family have lived there ever since.

Born in Rosshire, Scotland, in 1853, Alex came to Canada with his parents in 1873. The family settled at Embro, Ontario, for a few years before coming to Muskoka. At first they settled at Silverdale near Huntsville but by 1880 had located a free land grant in Franklin Township near Dwight. It was Alex's nephew, Harry Corbett, who operated Pine Grove Inn at Dwight for many years.

In 1889 Alex moved to Huntsville where he plied his trade as a mason. Working with William Proudfoot, he built many of the early brick homes in Huntsville, as well as both the Methodist church in 1897 and the Presbyterian church, of which he was a member, in 1898.

Alex Corbett's first wife, Isabella Munro, died in 1890 and he married Christina Ross in 1891. Christina and Alex had two children, William John Simon, born in 1892, and Mary Isabella, born in this house in 1893. William Proudfoot designed the house and lost his cane during the construction. Many years later the cane was discovered in a wall during renovations.

The Corbett house, with its covered wood verandah, has shallow arched openings and a diamond balustrade stretching along the main elevation. The upper floor windows are each marked by a gable that extends below the window head. The visible roof is shallow because a large section of the roof is flat. The gables extend from the roof ridge to the eaves and are uniform in size and shape.

Corbett House, 8 Caroline Street.

67

Following Mary's birth Christina was not well, and Sarah Ann Broughton came to care for her and the babies until Christina's death on July 10, 1894. Alex and Sarah were married in 1896. During the years after the Main Street fire in 1894 Alex laid the brickwork for many Main Street business blocks. He continued as a mason until he went into the implement business in 1904 as an agent for Frost and Wood, farm implement manufacturers.

About 1904 a large addition was built on to the back of the home to provide accommodation for up to five boarders. The addition had two open porches, which have been closed in and incorporated into the house. Otherwise the outward appearance of the house has changed little over the years. Joseph Santimour, who was conductor on the *Portage Flyer* for many years, lived with the Corbetts in the winter season when he worked at the tannery.

The interior of the home has changed to accommodate the lifestyle of each succeeding generation. In recent years the open staircase has been closed in for access to a second-floor apartment.

In early 1906 Alex Corbett was appointed bailiff of the local division court and in 1911 became the court clerk, a position he held for many years. At the time of his death in 1932 at the age of seventy-nine he was the oldest resident member of Unity Lodge, A.F. & A.M., having been initiated in 1889. He became master of the lodge ten years later.

Alex and Christina's son, William, became a researcher with General Motors in Oshawa and Toronto, and later moved to St. Catharines where he worked for a steel company. He was appointed to the Ontario Labour Relations Board and was recognized by his fellow members and Ontario industrialists as an authority in labour law. His younger sister, Mary, married Wilfred Beelby in February 14, 1917, and they lived at 8 Caroline Street all their married life.

Wilfred was an avid curler, a Rotarian, a long-time volunteer fireman, a member of the United Church choir and a volunteer for the Huntsville Red Cross, serving as president in the 1950s. He worked in the hardware business for thirty-seven years, twenty-three of which he was manager of the George E. Ecclestone Hardware Store. He continued as

office manager after being succeeded by his son, Kenneth, who had already been with the firm at that time for twenty-seven years.

Mary and Wilfred had two children: Florence Norrine, who married Bill Donaldson in 1946 and Kenneth, who married Roxie Archer on May 24, 1947. Ken and Roxie have one daughter, Valva.

Kenneth was commanding officer of the Huntsville Sea Cadets from 1949 to 1958, was a charter member of the Huntsville Lion's Club in 1941 and is a Rotarian. In 1984 Ken was honoured at a special Roast and Toast at the Constellation Hotel in Toronto. He was presented with a plaque from Stanley Tools Ltd. for fifty years of service to the hardware industry. Builders Hardware presented him with a golden key for this long service.

Today Alex Corbett's great-great-grandchildren visit the house on Caroline Street that he built so many years ago, which is truly remarkable.

CREWSON-CROOKS HOUSE
31 MAIN STREET WEST, HUNTSVILLE
C. 1891

THIS INTERESTING STONE HOUSE, built into the hillside of Main Street West, is situated on part of the original land grant to James Hanes under the Ontario Free Grants and Homestead Act of 1868. After James Hanes had subdivided his Main Street West lots, Lot 14 on the south side was sold in 1885 to Murdock Matheson, a hotelkeeper. Two years later it became the property of Albert Allen, a yeoman from McLean Township. In 1891 the lot was sold to William Morgan Crewson, who built the unusual stone house in the hilly terrain of Huntsville's Main Street.

William Crewson was born in Erin, Ontario, in 1825. He was an educated man, a minister of the Disciples of Christ. This Protestant denomination was characterized by a special concern for Christian unity and the New Testament. The elders served Communion, which was considered a memorial to the life of Christ, at the weekly church service. The sect was founded in Kentucky about 1801 and spread throughout North America. William Crewson was urged to spread the message in Muskoka and in 1885 he moved to Baysville. That first summer there were sixteen baptisms, as well as eight new converts, which caused quite a stir. By October a chapel had been built. The next year, over 132 people had been "brought to obedience of the gospel in the Muskoka–Parry Sound District." Evangelist Crewson received only his railway fare as remuneration, and was compelled to do manual labour to earn a living. Sometimes his only pay was farm produce. However, he did own several properties in Huntsville, one on Walter Street, another on Caroline Street, as well as the house on Main Street West.

In poor health resulting from hard work, in 1899 William gave his house to his son, Norman, under the condition that Norman look after him for the rest of his life. Norman was a tanner in New York State at that time, but he returned to Huntsville and worked at various occupations. William died later that year. Norman sold the stone house in 1907 and moved with his wife to Dorset to run a boarding house called the White House.

Crewson-Crooks House, 31 Main Street West.

John Gibbs owned the house for a year, then sold it to Morris Soskin, a merchant, and his wife, Rachel. A Russian, Morris and his family had immigrated to Canada about 1892. The idea of becoming a pedlar appealed to the young immigrant when he saw a pedlar on the streets of Ottawa. He bought supplies and walked from Ottawa to Huntsville, peddling along the route. On the trip he met a man with a horse and wagon, which he purchased. The name Soskin had already been painted on the side of the wagon — and it would cost five dollars to have the name repainted and only two to have his name changed, so he changed his Russian name to Soskin. Although he was a pedlar in the Muskoka area until World War II, Morris Soskin and his family lived in the stone house only for a short time.

The Crooks family, from Brunel Township, was the next owner of the house. According to the 1881 census, William Crooks, born in England, and his wife, Elizabeth were living at Concession 8, Lot 31, in Brunel, with their children — Francis, who was then twenty-four, James, Matilda Ann and David Ancel. The Crooks were also members of the Disciples of Christ. William came to Canada with a boatload of orphans from England when he was six years old. His mother thought he would have better opportunities in Canada. During the Atlantic crossing, he would stand on the ship's table to entertain the passengers.

Francis bought the stone house in 1911. He married Jane Lewis, daughter of Henry Lewis of Brunel Township. They had nine children — Martha (Howard), Louisa, Alma, Emma, Ancel, Arthur, Norman, Ethel (Richards) and Jessie (White). In the 1926 Huntsville Homecoming Booklet is a picture of five generations of the Crooks family — Francis with his father, daughter, granddaughter and great-granddaughter. When Francis died in 1941, his obituary described him as "one of Huntsville's most respected citizens, humble in his daily life and conduct, honest in his dealings with his fellow men, free from meanness, avarice and content to live simply and unostentatiously among his fellow citizens." Before his death Francis transferred the ownership of the house to three of his children as joint tenants — Ancel, Arthur and Martha.

Various members of the Crooks family have lived in the house for over fifty-seven years. Arthur and Ancel never married and Martha was an early widow. Norman Crooks and his wife, the former Edith Hunt, lived in part of the house when they were first married. Norman served with the 122nd Battalion during World War I. He and Edith had a large family — five daughters and four sons, many of whom remained in the Huntsville area.

Mary Olan, daughter of Norman and Edith, remembers an enamel sink and hand pump in the kitchen, and stairs leading from the entrance hall to the bedrooms on the third floor. There was an enclosed staircase to the lower floor, which became a separate apartment. She also remembers the deep windowsills, fluffy rag rugs on the floor, a player piano and Norman's lovely garden of muskmelons.

The architectural style of the house built into the hill illustrates many unique features. It has three storeys, each with its own entrance, with a flat roof construction enclosed by a three-sided third-floor mansard roof, clad in imitation shake asphalt shingles. A variety of dormer windows and unique mansard corner window cutouts at the third floor level allow natural light into the interior. Narrow horizontal siding surrounds the upper dormer windows. The first and second floors have prominent bay windows overlooking the street and Hunters Bay. The walls are made of rough mortar fieldstone to the underside of the roof. Built close to the street, this stone house is very visible.

In 1968 the Crooks sold the house to Robert and Dorothy Grady, who in 1983 moved to Georgetown, Ontario. The house was then purchased by Bruce and Julia Craik, the owners of Grandview Farm Inn on Highway 60 at the time. They completely gutted the inside of the building, making two modern apartments and adding a second floor exterior deck and solarium projection on the west side, as well as an enhanced entrance to the back on the third floor. After the Craiks left Huntsville in 1986, the property was transferred to Mr. and Mrs. Heinz Posedowski, who live in Magnetewan. This unusual stone house is still noticed by all who pass by on Main Street.

EARLY-MCFARLAND-CHARLTON HOUSE
113 WEST ROAD, HUNTSVILLE
C. 1875

JAMES AND MINERVA EARLY built the original two-storey home at 113 West Road. Minerva was the daughter of James Hanes, who in his later years was Huntsville's postmaster. She married Fred Shay, brother of Allen Shay. Unfortunately, Fred died a short time later as the result of an accident. In 1875, when she was thirty-six, Minerva obtained from the Crown Lot 13, Concession 2, Chaffey Township, eighty-two acres bordering on the north side of the village limits. Minerva married James Early and they sold most of the land to Thomas Gouldie. They did retain

Early McFarland-Charlton House, 113 West Road.

70

a small piece with frontage on the Muskoka River, where they built their large home and lived comfortably with their three children.

James, originally from Ireland, settled with his widowed mother in Carlton County near Ottawa before moving to Huntsville. He died in 1897 and Minerva sold her home in 1908 to her niece Millie Matheson, daughter of Allen Shay, and went to live with her brother, W.L. Hanes, for the last ten years of her life. Millie sold the house five years later to William Watson, the manager at the tannery. William in turn sold the house to James McFarland one year later in 1914.

James McFarland and his wife, Mary, came to Huntsville from Halton County in 1893. They had six children. Originally, James learned the blacksmith trade from his father but for several years did construction work for the Canadian Pacific Railway throughout Canada. In Huntsville, his skill as an accomplished stone and brick mason soon became widely known. The old stone Catholic church was one of his projects completed in 1899. Many private homes and a number of outstanding fireplaces at Bigwin Inn and in houses and cottages throughout Muskoka are still evidence of McFarland's art and handiwork. After 1930 he gave his own house its distinctive stone exterior on the lower portion with the help of his son Ross, and Herb McKenney, another well-known stonemason of the era.

The house was known locally as Flora Villa. In those days, the property was level with a large U-shaped driveway. The flower gardens in the middle were always quite an attraction, and James McFarland designed and built stone chairs and shelves on the side of the verandah overlooking a little pond. The old railway bridge on West Road was called Thunder Bridge because of the noise the traffic made when it crossed on the loose wooden planks. Eventually, it was replaced with a large concrete overpass, and the road, unfortunately, was raised in front of the house, obscuring the view. Trees were planted for privacy, and a new entrance off Winona Road was established.

Today, in the back yard, facing the river, stand five old walnut trees. It is unusual for walnut trees to grow this far north. One tree has a circumference of 132 inches and must have been planted when Minerva Early

lived there. They provide an umbrella of shade during the hot summer, keeping the house cool. The best swimming hole in town was under the railway bridge, above the tannery. The water was good with a sandy beach and a bridge to jump from.

During the Depression, many people lived and boarded in this home with Grandma and Grandpa Mac, as they were affectionately known.

James died at age seventy-seven in 1943, Mary died in 1955, and their daughter Dorothy, who never married, lived in the house on her own, becoming a recluse until her death in 1973. The bushes and trees became overgrown, and the home deteriorated during those years. Dorothy lived in one room and often only a single light could be seen. The house became known as the haunted house because it looked so spooky, and no one dared to go near on Halloween.

After being in the McFarland family for fifty-nine years, the home was sold to Ray Bubel and son. Major renovations began with new wiring, plumbing and roof. They were able to retain the Tudor-style design and the original ornate woodwork. The back porch was replaced with a bright sunroom with a brick fireplace. Despite all the fireplaces James McFarland had designed and built, his own house didn't have one. Did he purposely not have one because fireplaces are inefficient and lose a lot of heat of heat, or was it the old story of the shoemaker's family going without shoes?

Many people lived in the house during the next ten years while it was a rental property. In 1985 Bill and Diane Charlton fell in love with the old house, which was vacant and in need of tender loving care. They bought the house with its six acres fronting on the river, and continue to restore and retain all its original charm and character.

Harmony Hall, 27 Minerva Street.

HARMONY HALL
27 MINERVA STREET, HUNTSVILLE
C. 1903

WITHOUT A DOUBT, Harmony Hall is one of our most imposing older houses. It is majestically situated on the height of land overlooking Hunters Bay and the town. This area was part of Allan Shay's original hundred-acre land grant from the Crown. Lots 148 and 149 were sold to Lucy Isabel Carey in 1888 for the sum of eighty-six dollars. She in turn sold the property twelve years later to Jacob H. Johnson. On the early assessment rolls he called himself a builder. He was involved in the founding of the Huntsville Foundry, as well as owning a strategic wooden building on Main Street East at the northwest corner of West Street known as the Johnson Block.

A few months later, in 1900, Jacob Johnson sold the property on Minerva Street to his son, George, who operated a confectionery and china shop in his father's downtown building. It appears that the large house was built around 1903, while George Johnson owned the property.

In 1908 George sold the property to Telford S. Parkinson and his wife. He was an accountant with the Muskoka Wood Manufacturing Company. Four years later, the house changed hands again. It was sold to William Watson, another man involved in the lumbering business, namely the Huntsville Lumber Company. His brother was well-known Huntsville chief of police J.G. Watson, a local character of the era. Colonel W.D. Forrest, another Huntsville personage, bought the property in 1916. He served during World War I with the Grey-Simcoe Regiment. Captain William H. Elder of the Muskoka Lakes Navigation Company was the next owner.

Finally, in 1918 C.O. Shaw, president of Huntsville's Anglo-Canadian Leather Company, bought the imposing house for the famous conductor of his Anglo-Canadian Leather Company Band, Herbert L. Clarke. It is thought that the large library with its fieldstone fireplace was added at this time. With Herbert and his wife as the occupants of the home from 1918 to 1923, it became known as Harmony Hall.

The house is a fine example of the Italianate style of architecture that was popular around the turn of the century. The residence's character comes from its large size and its many verandahs and porches, bay windows and elaborate bracketing under the eaves. Originally, the exterior was constructed with narrow horizontal bevel siding with contrasting corner boards. This has been replaced with vinyl. The porch on the north side has been enclosed, and the decorative windows replaced. French doors lead from the living room to the lovely porch. The wooden columns between the windows and supporting the front porch have elaborate Ionic capitals and bases.

There are two bay windows on the west side of the house and one on the east. A large brick chimney is located along the exterior north wall. The fireplaces with wooden mantels and fine mouldings in the living room and dining room are still intact. The house has front and back stairs.

A very talented musician, Herbert Clarke was a cornetist, violinist and composer, as well as a bandmaster. He was born in Woburn, Massachusetts, in 1867. His father was organist and choirmaster at Jarvis Street Baptist Church in Toronto. At one time Herbert played in the Toronto Philharmonic Society, the Queen's Own Rifle Band and the Heinzman Piano Company Band. In 1888 Herbert was teaching and conducting at the newly formed Taylor Safe Works Band and the new Toronto College of Music. By 1890 Herbert was recognized as one of the leading cornetists of the era. He played under Victor Herbert with the famous U.S. Twenty-second Regiment Band, and later joined John Philip Sousa's Band, in which he was first a cornet soloist and eventually an assistant conductor. One of the incredible things about this whole story is that C.O. Shaw, himself a cornet player, was able to attract such a distinguished conductor to Huntsville. Under Herbert Clarke's direction, the Anglo-Canadian Leather Company Band soared to new heights.

One of the inducements C.O. Shaw used to attract musicians and others to Huntsville was his practice of buying some of the finest houses in Huntsville and allowing band members to live in them rent free. Herbert and his wife, who had her own music publishing company, occupied Harmony Hall from 1918 to 1923.

After the Clarkes left for the United States, the house on the hill was rented until C.O. Shaw sold it in 1926 to his daughter, Jennie Conway and family. She had married Charles Conway in 1913. Charles came to Huntsville as a bank manager with the Dominion Bank in 1910. He eventually became involved in the Anglo-Canadian Leather Company, where by the 1960s he was president and general manager. The Conway's three children, Abbott, Helen and Barbara, all have many wonderful reminiscences of growing up in the spacious home. The Conways were a driving force in the community. They were involved in local sports, the Red Cross, the Victorian Order of Nurses and All Saints Anglican Church.

In 1969 the house was sold to Paul and Maura Chisholm, both local high school teachers. Paul was of Scottish heritage and came from Nova Scotia, and Maura came from Ireland. This very social couple celebrated

both St. Andrew's Day and St. Patrick's Day with large parties at Harmony Hall. Unfortunately, Paul died in 1988, and Maura, two years later. The house was sold to Emilie Haarman-Viitkar of Utterson.

In 1993 Harmony Hall became a retirement residence. The large rambling house at the top of the hill has recently reverted to a private home.

HUTCHINS-HARNDEN-SNOWDEN-TAYLOR HOUSE
RAVENSCLIFFE ROAD, HUNTSVILLE
C. 1880

IN 1877 GEORGE HUTCHINS, a farmer of English descent, received the one hundred acres from the Crown in Chaffey Township — Lot 11, Concession 3. He had previously sold off the pine lumber rights on the land to W. Dyment. Selling lumber rights was a way for local farmers to raise some much-needed cash. George and his wife, Maria, built the attractive stone house on the Ravenscliffe Road and farmed the land. In 1901 he won prizes at the North Muskoka Agricultural Society Fair for his sheep and swine.

The Hutchins family belonged to the Salvation Army, and in 1897 they donated three-tenths of an acre of their land for a Salvation Army cemetery. Earlier, in 1879, another five acres were sold to the bishop of Algoma for an Anglican cemetery, which was enlarged to six acres in 1908. The Presbyterians also have an early cemetery there. These three cemeteries are still evident along the right side of the Ravenscliffe Road past the Hutchins homestead.

Rectangular in shape, this early two-storey farmhouse prominently displays an irregular, rough-mortared fieldstone wall construction featuring smooth, contrasting stone windowsills and enlarged lintels. A steep-pitched front roof gable accents the front entrance. Large rectangular double-hung windows have been symmetrically positioned on both the first and second floors. A shed-style asphalt-shingled porch roof on square, wooden columns with decorative wood-trimmed capitals extends closely to the underside of the main front gabled roof.

George Hutchins sold off the east half of his farm to Jacob Henry Johnson in 1887. When George died in 1909, he left his remaining property to his only surviving offspring, Elizabeth Louisa, who was married to John Keetch.

In 1913 Elizabeth Keetch sold the house and property to Perry and Ida Harnden. Perry is listed in the 1905 assessment rolls as a minister of the Free Methodist Church on High Street in Huntsville. In a June 1915 *Forester* Perry advertised that milk was available for delivery "to all parts of town twice daily, except Sunday," and in 1917 he was advertising for help at his Huntsville Dairy. After their son Willmot drowned in 1919, the Harndens decided to sell the farm. The purchaser was none other than C.O. Shaw, president of the Anglo-Canadian Leather Company in Huntsville and the builder of Bigwin Inn on Lake of Bays. At that time he was amassing farmland in the area to service the famous resort. The

Hutchins-Harnden-Snowden-Taylor House, 326 Ravenscliffe Road.

Bigwin Barn was built beside the Muskoka River across from the tannery complex and is still standing today, although greatly altered.

In 1922 C.O. Shaw sold the farmlands to his family — Charles George Shaw, Pauline Gill and Jennie Elizabeth Conway.

The house was used for farm workers on the Bigwin farm during the 1920s. Lance Watt, a worker who lived in the house for three years during that time, remembers the land being used to grow turnips and corn — and also for pasture.

In 1930 the Shaw family sold the west half of Lot 11, Concession 3, plus another eighty acres to Joseph and Ethel Snowden who had been renting the farm for a year. They lived in the house from 1930 to 1966. It originally had a centre staircase with a living and dining room on one side and a bedroom on the other side with a pantry behind it. The Snowdens added a wooden section across the back, which became the kitchen. There was a back set of stairs leading to three bedrooms on the second floor. In 1937 hydro was installed, and in 1945 the Snowdens added the side door and portico.

Joseph Snowden came from England. Before buying the farm he had worked in a mine in Cobalt, with the Canadian Pacific Railway and with his brother Harry farming in Brunel Township. His only son, Turner, remembers going to the stone school on West Road and herding cattle on the farm property. Joseph Snowden became the manager for the Bigwin dairy. After his death in 1962 his widow, Ethel, moved to North Bay and the house was sold to Les Adams, a Huntsville real estate agent. Since then there have been various owners, including the Brouses and Grahams. In 1972 the house was partially gutted by fire. One of the owners, Ross McLeod, converted the house into a triplex.

In 1988 the house was purchase by Grant Taylor and his wife. Today, nothing of the interior of the original house remains except the front door. The Taylors, who craft beautiful pine furniture, altered the inside of the house to suit their needs, with a large living room and dining room across the front, a corner staircase, a kitchen-family room, bathroom and showroom for furniture sales across the back.

The barn is gone and the land subdivided. But due to the work of the Taylors, the exterior of the house has been greatly restored and enhanced. It is an attractive example of an early Muskoka farmhouse.

THE HUTTENLOCHER FARM
MARKLE'S ROAD, HUNTSVILLE
C. 1880

IN 1879 JOSEPH PREBBLE and his wife, Ellen, received Lot 10, Concession 10, in Brunel Township from the Crown. It consisted of ninety-seven acres situated on the north branch of the Muskoka River about a mile above where it enters Mary Lake — a beautiful piece of property. The Prebbles likely built the very attractive farmhouse situated on the rise of land back from the river. Joseph sold the farm to Samuel Holinshead and his wife in 1907.

Hottenlocher House, Markle's Road.

The Holinsheads were very early settlers on the south side of Fairy Lake. In fact, descendants are still farming the original homestead. Samuel was raised there, but decided to try farming on his own on the Muskoka River site. However, nineteen years later he sold the property to Charles Rimmington and family.

The Rimmingtons had farmed a smaller farm at Newholm, Concession 2, Brunel Township, after immigrating from England. Mary Schamehorn (nee Rimmington) remembers moving to the Muskoka River property when she was sixteen. The farm had good land, and the Rimmingtons sold milk, butter and eggs. Mary remembers that her mother used to keep the cans of milk cool in the very productive spring. After selling the farm, Charles Rimmington worked for the Department of Highways.

Joseph Huttenlocher left Germany in the mid-1920s to settle in Toronto. He was twenty years old and left behind a very affluent lifestyle to seek his own path in a new country. When he stepped foot on Canadian soil he knew not one person nor spoke any English. In the mid-1930s he met and married Anastasia (Theresa) Lukowicz, who was born in Wilno, Ontario, to Polish parents. Although she spoke Polish and English fluently, she was not conversant in German. However, by that time Joseph had mastered the English language. They operated a rooming house close to Toronto's downtown core, but the Depression and their yearning for fresh air and the freedom of owning country property brought them north to Muskoka. They bought land and a small farm off the Port Sydney Road. However, they wanted more land and a bigger house and started looking for new premises.

They bought the Rimmington farm on the Muskoka River in 1950 and moved there with their children, Joe and Frances. Since the move from their previous homestead was only a few miles via a bush road, that was the route they chose for the move. They moved a complete household with a farm wagon and an exuberant team of horses. The countless trips back and forth caused a lot of stress to Theresa, who feared for the safety of her precious china and other treasures packed in barrels and wooden crates. The only catastrophe occurred when her Singer treadle sewing machine fell off the wagon on the steep ascent on the creek gully road. Although she continued to use it, it never worked perfectly after that fall.

The farmhouse was an example of the fine planning and construction indicative of its era. This two-storey red brick-clad house faced the Muskoka River. Three dormer windows and covered verandah extended across the front. Entrance was via a hand-carved heavy wooden door with its original bubbled glass. The entrance hallway extended the full length of the main floor and was wide enough to allow a stairway to the second floor. The stairway was flanked on one side by a hand-carved banister with lovely hand-carved spindles, which also extended across the main part of the second floor hall. The hall was at least four feet wide and the ceiling ten feet high, all panelled with narrow hardwood boards. The floors throughout the house were hardwood.

On either side of this main floor hall were two large rooms, a kitchen and living room, each with a chimney intended for a wood stove. The living room had not been painted, and when Theresa had finished spending days scrubbing the walls and ceiling, the result was incredible. The walls were made of alternating light and dark wood boards. She scrubbed the floors, then hand sanded and waxed them to a golden gleaming honey surface. The room was a place of extraordinary craftsmanship.

Three large bedrooms and a bathroom occupied the second floor. The three dormer windows facing the river had wide exterior windowsills and offered barn swallows a place to sunbathe on hot summer afternoons.

The full basement had fieldstone walls and a hard, packed-dirt floor. In the centre stood a large cast-iron wood furnace.

At the back of the house was a room two storeys high that was almost as large as the main house. It had its own chimney. It appeared as though the original builder had grand plans for this area as well but never completed the work. The area was referred to as the back porch and Joseph immediately claimed it for the first wood room.

Even though Theresa toiled from dawn to dusk with the daily chores of life on a farm, she managed to find time to plant and tend a large flower garden with dozens of different species ranging from a variety of roses to hollyhocks, gladiolas, poppies, tulips and so on. The summer profusion of colours in the yard was extraordinary, and boaters passing by on the river would come in to photograph her garden. And none departed without lemonade or a cup of tea. In addition Theresa tended a large vegetable garden, strawberry patch and raspberry bushes. She usually had such a prolific berry crop that she had to sell some each season, and that was after she had preserved and frozen all that the family could possibly consume in one winter. In the winter, whenever she had a free minute she designed and made patchwork quilts, each one unique and reminiscent of her beloved summer flower garden.

The property had a large barn with a stable underneath, which was eventually converted into a dairy farm operated by the family. Neighbours recall seeing the Huttenlochers take their milk to town in the early days. Joe Jr. decided to retire from this business just recently in 1996.

The view takes your breath away. Across the river from the farm is Hillcrest Lodge and housekeeping cottages. From the hill behind the house Mary Lake is visible.

Joe, his wife, Nancy, son Jacob and stepson, Darryl, live on the farm now. Theresa passed away in 1986 and Joseph in 1991. Daughter Frances married Al Botham and lives only a few miles from the farm. They live on Lynx Lake Road and operate B's Antiques.

THE KELLY-GILROY HOUSE
68 WEST STREET SOUTH, HUNTSVILLE
C. 1942

ONE OF THE MOST COLOURFUL PEOPLE in the life of Huntsville during the first half of this century was J. Frank Kelly. He was born in Bermuda in 1879 and was posted to our town by the Salvation Army as staff captain with the army's immigration branch. In this capacity he made several ocean crossings. In 1912 he just missed being a passenger on the ill-fated *Titanic*.

Frank Kelly had a marvelous baritone voice and was an accomplished bass player, so he was a tremendous addition to the Huntsville Salvation Army Band. However, when the army wanted to transfer him out of Huntsville, a town he had grown to love, he happily became a Methodist to avoid the move. Throughout his life he was very active in every facet of Trinity United Church's endeavours, both musical and otherwise.

When he arrived in Huntsville around 1909, he boarded with the W.H. Davis family, in their large home on the corner of Duncan and West Streets. William was a prominent citizen involved in real estate, cattle dealing and a delivery business. In 1912 Frank Kelly married Alice (Nellie), William's daughter. They moved to Calgary, where their only son, Terry, was born. Frank was involved in the real estate business there. Returning to Huntsville in 1915, the young family lived again with Davis Senior.

Frank became involved with the Canada Life Insurance Company. He was very successful in placing the first group insurance policy for the Anglo-Canadian Leather Company in Huntsville. For a time Frank was employed as purchasing agent for the company. When C.O. Shaw formed the Anglo-Canadian Company Band, Frank played a prominent role as premier bassist. Later, when Bigwin Inn on Lake of Bays was opened, he was featured in many musical events there both as a musician and singer.

Politics was another of Frank's passions. He was elected to the Huntsville town council in 1925 and was very active in pursuing the plans with the federal government for a new municipal building and post office, which materialized in 1926 with the construction of our

Kelly-Gilroy House, 68 West Street South.

Frank Kelly, Mayor of Huntsville 1932–35, Councillor of Huntsville 1925–31, MPP 1936–45, Mayor 1946–48.

handsome Georgian-style town hall at 37 Main Street East. He and George Paget were responsible for retrieving the clock from Toronto's Union Station and having it placed on top of the new local municipal building.

After serving as councillor from 1925 to 1931, he was mayor of Huntsville from 1932 to 1935. The following year he ran for the Liberal party and was elected to the Ontario Legislature with a landslide victory, serving as a provincial member until 1945. During the Depression years he was known to do his utmost to find jobs or help for many local residents. After his term at the Ontario Legislature, he returned to local politics and was Huntsville's mayor again from 1946 to 1948.

It wasn't until 1942 that Alice and Frank built their fine home at the top of the hill at 68 West Street South. That section of land had been part of the Crown grant in 1874 to William Cann. Eleanor Davis acquired some of the property in 1907, and Frank purchased some adjoining land in 1924. Architect Wendell P. Lawson of Leaside (Toronto), Ontario, drew the plans for the house. At that time, Huntsville homes designed by architects were very rare. Nothing but the finest materials were used. The home displays many of the stereotypical elements of a New England Colonial Revival style. The white painted siding boards, multi-paned windows with shutters and moulded cornices, front portico with classical detailing, panelled front-entrance door with narrow sidelights, side portico, returned eaves and circular attic windows in the gabled end-wall are all defining elements of this style.

The detailing is completed in the rear elevation with a two-storey bay window, a bulls-eye window on the main floor and an open verandah with segmental arches resting on square columns. The interior had a large double parlour and a fine classical staircase. The builder of this stylish house was George Yearley from Bracebridge.

It was during his years serving in Mitchell Hepburn's Liberal legislature that Frank Kelly became involved in promoting tourism for his beloved Muskoka. In fact, the late Joe Cookson called him the Snow Carnival King. Along with his friend H.E. Rice, Frank conceived the idea of promoting sports and vacations in Huntsville's winter wonderland. The Canadian National Railway was persuaded to run a Friday night "Ski Special" to Huntsville. When the train pulled into the station, Frank Kelly and the townspeople would be there to greet the passengers and then parade through the town carrying torches. His promotion of Huntsville as a winter and summer sports capital helped the community during the lean years of the 1930s and 1940s.

Frank Kelly was also a very active Rotarian. The pinnacle of his career came when he was nominated to the Canadian Hall of Fame for his contributions to his community.

Frank and his wife both died in 1971, and in 1973 the lovely house was sold to Donald Gilroy and his wife, Joanne. They owned an outstanding collection of early Canadian pine furniture and artifacts, which graced the charming home. They were a vital couple who contributed much to the community.

Donald and Anna MacKenzie, who purchased it in 1993, now own the house. They are enjoying living in one of Huntsville's finest examples of colonial architecture.

THE MADILL HOUSE
HIGHWAY 11 SOUTH, HUNTSVILLE
C. 1895

JOHN AND MATILDA MADILL came to Ontario from Northern Ireland. They originally settled near Port Hope, but in 1870 they decided to move to Muskoka with their two children, John H. and Fanny Ann. They located four 100-acre lots in Stephenson Township — Concession 12, Lot 31, and Concession 13, Lots 30, 32 and 33.

The pioneer settlers in the area were very anxious to have a church. A trustee board was formed and John Madill donated a section of Lot 33 for a place of worship. The log church was built by volunteer labour and each family donated two rounds of squared timbers. The Madills, Brays, Fetterleys, MacDonalds, Hogobaums and Proudfoots were involved. Construction of the church was completed in 1873 at a cost of six hundred dollars. Itinerant missionaries of the Wesleyan Methodist Church conducted the first services. Regular services were held until the 1940s, but now services are held twice yearly. The adjoining cemetery is one of the oldest in the area.

The church is one of the few remaining squared timber churches in the province. Both the church and cemetery are now administered and maintained by Trinity United Church, Huntsville.

John Madill died in 1888, and his wife ten years later. John H. Madill settled on Lot 31. There is a family photo of the original primitive house and log barn on that lot.

In 1895 the present, typical Ontario farmhouse, very visible off Highway 11 South, was built. Rectangular in shape, with a tail at the rear for the kitchen, it is built in the vernacular style of white narrow clapboard. The main floor consists of a large living room and two small bedrooms. Upstairs are three more bedrooms and a large room over the kitchen where quilting was done. Many of the rooms have dark wood wainscotting on the walls and panelled wood ceilings.

John H. Madill married Margaret Darling (daughter of another Stephenson Township pioneer family) in 1876. They had seven children,

Madill House, Highway 11 South.

Elfie, John, James, Agnes, Archie, Elizabeth and Margaret. John H. Madill died in 1900. His wife lived in the farmhouse until she died in 1948. John, Agnes and Archie never married, and carried on farming on the property. They were all very active in the Allensville Community and at the Madill Church. John died in 1962, Agnes in 1965 and Archie in 1973. It was the end of an era of Madill farmers in Stephenson Township.

The original Muskoka Road (Ferguson Highway) ran behind the Madill house, and its original long driveway was off Stephenson Road 12 East. But with the realignment of the road after World War II, the new Highway 11 passed in front of the house. In 1976 the highway was expanded to four lanes. The driveway is now off Stephenson Road 12 West.

In that year the property was purchased by Yvonne and Edward Cox, who continued to farm the property. According to Yvonne, they loved every minute of it.

In 1982 Vaughn Hope and his wife bought the old farmhouse and property. No matter what time of year you drive by you can usually see the Hopes' cattle grazing on the lovely farm fields.

McConachie-Walmsley-Cameron House

57 Main Street West, Huntsville
c. 1892

THE LOT ON WHICH THIS VICTORIAN-STYLE HOUSE is situated was originally two acres, being part of the land granted to James Hanes in 1868 under the Ontario Free Grants and Homestead Act of 1868.

In 1891, after having been owned by Bernard Phillips, the lot was sold to John McConachie, who built the large, attractive house overlooking Hunters Bay in 1892. John was a real old-time character, as related by Joe Cookson in his book *Roots in Muskoka*. He built and owned the first shingle mill in Huntsville on the site of what was the Tembec Inc. mill site on Hunters Bay.

His little mill was operated by horsepower — that is, a horse that walked around and around prodded by a boy with a stick! This turned the gears that operated the mill. At one time old John, or Mac as he was called, also ran a shingle mill and a grocery store at the Portage. Joe Cookson remembers him entertaining in the lumber camps during the long winter nights. He eventually became a log scaler for the Bethune Lumber Company. He was also a talented mechanic and millwright.

John was born in 1848 in Ancaster, Ontario, where he served as bailiff before coming to Huntsville. In 1870 he married Elizabeth Johnson, also of Ancaster. They had five children — three sons and two daughters. Cora, the elder daughter, was an opera singer. Lillian married Ernest Ware, grandson of Samuel Ware, a well-known early settler in Brunel Township. After the death of Elizabeth McConachie in 1915 John moved to the Dominion Hotel on Huntsville's Main Street. The house at 57 Main

McConachie-Walmsley-Cameron House, 57 Main Street.

Street was sold to Maggie and Robert Hartley, who four years later sold it to Henry I. Silk.

Henry was a scaler for the Huntsville Lumber Company. His wife ran one of the many private nursing homes in Huntsville in the house with its seven bedrooms. It is rumoured that even an amputation was performed there!

The Silks moved to Hamilton and the property was bought by Percival Walmsley and his wife, who lived there from 1923 to 1945. Percival came from England, where he was trained as a lawyer. He gave up the law because of poor health and immigrated to Canada where he farmed at Port Cunnington on Lake of Bays. In 1905 he married Gertrude Dew, who came out alone from England to marry him. In fact, their wedding was the first one to take place at St. John's Church at Fox Point, Lake of Bays. They called their farm at Port Cunnington Park Place. After producing six children, the Walmsleys moved into town to the Main Street West house, so that their children could complete their education at what was then called the Continuation School. In Huntsville, Percival assisted William Rumsey and lawyer Kenneth Mahaffy with their work. The family was active in All Saints Anglican Church, the Huntsville Literary Club and the British and Foreign Bible Society. After the death of the Walmsleys — a very community-oriented and friendly couple — the property was purchased by the Murray Cameron family in 1945.

The Camerons were Scottish stonemasons who came to Canada in the early 1800s. They settled in Strathroy, Ontario, where Murray was raised. He attended Queen's University before taking up a career as a schoolteacher. He first taught at Fort Francis, Ontario, where he met his future wife, Vera Staeder, a fellow teacher. Vera was from Iroquois, Ontario, where her ancestors had settled as United Empire Loyalists.

After their marriage, the couple moved to New Liskeard, where Murray taught until 1935. He also taught at Burk's Falls, Sundridge and Temiscaming, Quebec. But from 1937 to 1938 and 1944 to 1952, he was a science teacher at Huntsville High School. During these years the family bought a resort, Rockwynn, at Lake Cecebe, which they operated until 1972.

During her Huntsville years, Vera Cameron was active in Knox Presbyterian Church, and was elected the first woman elder. She was also involved in the Muskoka Pioneer Village, the Literary Society, the Canadian Institute for the Blind and the Queen's University Alumni. She was a friend, guide and teacher to all. She and Murray raised six children, all university educated. After Murray's death in 1965, Vera stayed on in the family home.

The house on Main Street West is built on a sloping heavily treed lot. The two-storey Insul brick-clad home on a roughly mortared fieldstone foundation illustrates many design features common in late nineteenth-century construction. Prominently placed, a one-storey bay window projection capped by a mansard-style roof dominates the front facade. The main gable-style roof rises above. Double-hung windows on each bay face provide an abundance of natural interior light into the front parlour. A complementary two-storey bay window projection exists at the east side elevation, illuminating the large panelled dining room and the bedroom above. Continuous perimeter wide wood trim and wood infill panels accent window locations. Large decorative bracket, wooden circular-edged shingles and moulding trim at the bay window and wooden finials and brackets fretwork at the gable peaks are added features.

Balancing the eastern bay projection at the first floor is a porch with a low-sloped roof, supported on equally spaced square columns. It wraps the corner of the building. Large windows open on to it. On the roof of the porch is a small balcony, above which is a steep-pitched gable roof peak with more bracket fretwork.

In 1986 the house was sold to Hugh and Betty MacConnell, who came from Scotland. They modernized some of the interior and in 1992 had the Insul brick covered with tongue-and-groove siding and some of the front of the building faced with red brick. In this roomy house the McConnells now run Betty's Bed and Breakfast. Undoubtedly, all the guests enjoy their stay at this charming Victorian house built over one hundred years ago.

MCMILLAN-SOMERSET-SNOWDEN FARMHOUSE

ROWANWOOD ROAD, HUNTSVILLE
C. 1875

ONE OF THE PRETTIEST EARLY FARMHOUSES in Muskoka is nestled among the rocks and trees beside Spider Creek. Its shining steel roof with three prominent gables can be seen above the flat farmland from Rowanwood Road.

The Malcolm McMillan family, who came from the Island of Islay, first settled in Grey-Bruce County. In 1871 two of Malcolm's sons, John and Alexander, came to Muskoka. Alexander received the Crown patent for the property on Rowanwood Road, while John took up land nearby in the village of Utterson.

McMillan-Somerset-Snowden Farmhouse, Rowanwood Road.

Alexander and his wife, Sarah, built the lovely red brick farmhouse. It features a conventional gabled roof. A steeper pitched front gable highlights the main entrance. There are gabled dormers in the second floor above the roof of the main floor porch. The double-hung windows are large and rectangular in shape. Square columns support the porch roof. The porch gives the house much charm with its intricate wooden fretwork, moulded stair railings and latticework. The foundation of the house is solid stone. It has an interior centre-hall plan with a wide staircase to the upper floor. There are also stairs from the kitchen to the five bedrooms. There is oak wainscotting on the main floor.

The house and farmlands were sold to William Francis Somerset in 1897. The Somerset family was listed in the Debrett Peerage in England. Frank, as he was known, descended from General Lord Charles Henry Somerset, M.P.

Two years after purchasing the Stephenson Township property Frank married Laura Thoms of Port Sydney. They had six children, William Vere, Helen Louise, Lionel Francis, Henry Fitzroy, Jessie Catherine and Lenora Mary. Jessie married Brodie Kay and remained in Port Sydney all her life.

It was the Somerset family who did much of the fine interior finishing to the house. Recently, the signature "Onyett and Hunt 1902" was found beneath many layers of wallpaper. Onyett and Hunt were prominent decorators in the early days of Huntsville. At this time the east corner of the basement was partitioned to make an iceroom with an outside hatch for loading the ice. A large wood furnace was installed to heat the house.

The farmhouse roof has eighteen-by-twelve-inch steel shingles embossed with a maple leaf design. Donald Snowden, who later lived in the house, remembers the shingles being painted.

There was a large barn on the property with stalls for thirty-six horses, which were imported from England. There were also sheep and chicken pens and an implement shed.

Jessie Somerset, who grew up on this prosperous farm, remembered the wonderful boxes of gifts they received from wealthy relatives in England.

In 1926 Frank Somerset's wife, Laura, died. In 1927 Ann Margaret Lawrence of Allensville became his second wife. She was the daughter of Charles T. Lawrence, who owned the farm where Gryffin Lodge on Mary Lake is situated. A few years after their marriage Frank and Ann went to England to visit the Somerset relatives there.

Frank Somerset died in 1942 at his Muskoka farm. His obituary states that he was one of the most industrious and capable farmers in the area. He had been president of the Stephenson and Watt Township Agricultural Society. Christ Church Cemetery in Port Sydney is the final resting place for him and his wives, Laura and Ann.

In his will Frank Somerset bequeathed all his silver and jewelry to Ann. The property was left to a Mr. and Mrs. Herman Peters of Durham County. They sold it to George and Helen Snowden.

George was the son of Harry Snowden, who came to Canada with his brother, Joseph, in 1908 from Lancashire, England. The two brothers farmed in Brunel Township. George married Helen Hanes, a descendant of one of the earliest Huntsville settlers. He became famous as a lacrosse player and later as a lacrosse coach. He farmed for thirty-seven years, from 1950 to 1987.

George Snowden's grandson Donald Snowden provided much of the following information regarding changes that were made to the farm buildings during the Snowdens' occupation.

The original buildings were in disrepair and the barn had fallen down. A new barn and milk house were built. The Snowdens installed an oil furnace but kept the old wood stove in the kitchen. The large pantry was converted into a bathroom. The original dining room became a living room and the former living room was turned into a family room. An enclosed porch with a low gable roof was constructed on the front of the house, replacing the open verandah.

The Snowdens kept milk cows and pigs. They used the fields for grazing and grew barley, wheat and oats. In 1960 George became a beef farmer. George and Helen had two children, Shirley and Harry. Shirley's children, Kevin and Donald, grew up on the farm.

In 1986 the farm was sold to Peter Tobias, a Huntsville lawyer. He used the flat farm fields as a runway for his airplane. In the sale transaction the Snowdens severed twelve acres along the road, where they built a retirement bungalow. George Snowden died in 1990. Today his daughter, Shirley, occupies the property.

Steven James Keeter bought the Snowden farm in 1987. He and his wife, Cheryl, restored the interior woodwork to its original luster and did extensive decorating. After a short residence in the area, the Keeters left and the house was up for rent.

This house has witnessed a great deal of country living in its many years and is still one of the most attractive old farmhouses in Muskoka.

MORLEY COLLEGE
THE GILCHRIST HOUSE
22 HANES STREET, HUNTSVILLE
C. 1896

ELIZABETH W. MORLEY, LLCM, who originally came from Saint John, New Brunswick, bought land on Hanes Street in Huntsville in

1896 to establish a school. A *Forester* of the era had this advertisement: "Morley College, Conservatory of Music and School of Art in union with London College of Music, London, England. Visitor: Venerable Archdeacon Llwyd. Principal: Miss E.W. Morley, LLCM."

It appears that the exams written by the students were sent to the London College of Music in England to be corrected. However, practical examinations were held locally. On June 10, 1898, the examiners were Albert Ham, Esq., and Miss Doe, organist at St. James' Church, Toronto. An article in *The Forester* of July 8, 1898, described the closing exercises of the school: "The second closing exercises of Morley College were held on the evening of June 5th. The Reverend Archdeacon Llwyd occupied the chair, and on the platform were Dr. Bridgland, MPP, Sheriff Bettes and Mrs. Bettes, of Bracebridge, Miss Morley, LLCM, and the teaching staff of the College. There were musical selections by the students, speeches and the giving out of proficiency awards. The event was well attended in the large school room and all present were pleased with how well the pupils had acquitted themselves."

Although it seems that the school was mostly for young ladies and for studying music and art, both the late Frank Hutcheson and Marjorie Hart obtained some of their general education there. Frank Hutcheson even mentioned formal dances for the students. Evidently there were boarders at the school, as well as day pupils.

A picture of the building appears in the 1926 *Souvenir Booklet of Huntsville*. Built on a rough exposed stone foundation, this large two-storey building is clad predominantly with brick, accented with stone windowsills and stone parapet capping complementing the foundation base. The elevation featured large two-storey bay window projections with an abundance of single-hung windows unique in their shape due to slightly curved heads.

Glazed transoms over the exterior doors in combination with glazed sidelights matched the height of the exterior windows in a uniform horizontal building line. The sign above the parapet read Morley Ladies College, Conservatory of Music.

After such sophistication and high standards in such a prestigious

Above: Morley College, 22 Hanes Street, 1896.
Right: Gilchrist House, 22 Hanes Street, 1902.

building for Huntsville at that time, tragedy struck. In April 1899 the school burned to the ground. It was not rebuilt. Some pupils transferred to another Huntsville private school on Duncan Street, run by Mrs. and the Misses Hayden.

The property changed hands in 1901, when John Thomas Fleming, a stonemason from Sinclair Township, bought it. He designed and built the present stone house at 22 Hanes Street overlooking the Muskoka River. The early photograph shows a rough-mortared stone facade cladding in combination with wood horizontal siding, deck and porch uniform gables at the second floor level and a combination sloped and flat roof. It typifies turn-of-the-century construction. Highlighting these base elements was an abundance of decorative fretwork popular during the period. Placed in a consistent fashion are the decorative porch railing balusters, post brackets and gingerbread trim, deck newel posts, as well as cresting at the roofline and decorative fascia brackets. A glazed transom over the exterior door, bay window projection, stone soldier coursing over the second-floor windows and the use of wide wood exterior trim at the bay projection are added accents. *The Forester* reported that John Fleming planned to convert a portion of his lovely house into a summer home for tourists. In 1907, when the house was sold to Mary Jane Clarke, a widow, for $1,450, she did take in boarders.

William Scott, who came from Eramosa, Ontario, bought the property in 1914. He was a teacher at Huntsville Public School from 1917 to 1929. He also grew vegetables, kept chickens and sold eggs, and had horses in a barn behind the house.

In 1931, the house changed hands again. Evelyn Gilchrist and her husband, Jack, a pharmacist, bought the property. Evelyn made many changes to the house over the years, removing the porch from the south side of the house and altering the use of the rooms.

She had the present living room panelled, and had a stone fireplace built by Herbert McKenney, a well-known local stonemason of the time. A tennis court was built, and in 1940 an apartment was made upstairs.

Evelyn is the granddaughter of Andrew Tait, of Orillia, who in 1886

organized the Heath, Tait and Turnbull Lumber Company. In 1892 this firm became the Huntsville Lumber Company with Andrew Tait as president.

WHITESIDE-CONWAY-WARDELL HOUSE
11 HIGH STREET, HUNTSVILLE
C. 1904

THE LOT ON WHICH JOHN WHITESIDE built his second home in 1904 was part of William Cann's land grant from the Crown under the Ontario Free Grants and Homestead Act of 1868.

John Whiteside was one of the most enterprising of Huntsville's early settlers. Arriving from Innisfil Township in 1879 he opened up a general store on Main Street between the bridge and King Street, on the north side. In 1885 he ventured into the lumbering business, forming the Riverside Lumber company. It was located on the river bend where Jake's Hoagie Heaven is now. Although the business was successful, the site had some disadvantages.

The narrowness of the river forced him to move his log boom every time a steamer went by. Also, his mill was not situated on the railway line, unlike some of his competitors. Fire seemed to be a problem in Mr. Whiteside's life. His mill burned in 1892 and his Main Street store burned in the great Main Street conflagration of 1894. He rebuilt the mill but not the store. Eight years later in 1902 his first residence at the corner of Brunel Road and Park Drive burned down. Not to be daunted, in 1903 he purchased Lot 23, on High Street, and commenced building another substantial home.

Two storeys in height, this handsome house is clad in red brick with wood accent trim. The roof shape is a simple cottage style. Originally a porch with a shed roof extended across the entire front and east side of the home. Uniformly spaced Colonial columns sitting on the wooden porch deck supported the porch roof. The 45-degree corner bay window, exterior balcony projection with its decorative railing and the square overhanging oriole window, faced in narrow clapboard set on the diagonal, add interest and profile to the front elevation. Various window styles are evident including single hung, used singly or in combination, and combination-style hung with multiple paned transoms.

Mr. John Whiteside died in 1911, but the Riverside Lumber Company carried on under the management of Richard and Charles Dinsmore, nephews of John Whiteside. They formed the Bethune Lumber company continuing to cut wood in Sinclair and Bethune Townships until 1936.

In 1918 Mrs. Emma Whiteside sold the house to C.O. Shaw, president of the Huntsville tannery, the Anglo-Canadian Leather Company. Mr. Shaw's daughter Jennie and son-in-law, C.W. Conway, moved into the house. Charles Conway (known as C.W.), from Uxbridge, Ontario, was born in 1886 and came to Huntsville as manger of the Dominion Bank in 1910. After a stint at the Moose Jaw, Saskatchewan, branch of the Dominion Bank, he returned to Huntsville and married Jennie Shaw. They had three children, Abbott, Barbara and Helen. In 1916 Conway

became assistant manager of the tannery, later becoming president and general manager when his father-in-law retired. The Conways, along with the Hutcheson family, founded the Huntsville Ski Club, which was situated south of town, off Highway 11. C.W. was also prominent in the development of the Huntsville Downs Golf Course. The three Conway offspring, all living in southern Ontario, still maintain cottages in the Huntsville area.

In 1927 the attractive red brick house at 11 High Street was sold to Claude and Mina Wardell. Claude Wardell was the eldest son of well-known Huntsville merchant Matthew Wardell who established a successful mercantile business in town in 1895: "Wardell and Company — the Busy Merchants." They maintained a strong presence at 86 Main Street East until 1986 — over ninety-one years!

Claude Wardell was born in Toronto in 1883 and came to Huntsville with his parents, brother and sisters in 1895. In 1917 he married Mina Harper, whose father, Reverend Dr. Henry Harper, was the minister at Trinity Methodist Church in Huntsville from 1900 to 1904.

Whiteside-Conway-Wardell House, today and in 1926.

85

Claude succeeded his father as president and general manager of Wardell's. From 1912 to 1917 the store was associated with J.E. Boyd and known as Wardell, Boyd & Company. The store originally sold groceries as well as dry goods, however, it eventually became famous for English bone china, Irish Belleek, linens, Hudson's bay blankets and coats and fine woollens. Other members of the Wardell family were involved in the business, especially Matthew Wardell's oldest daughter, Maude Nickalls, and her two sons, Grenville and Jack. In 1954 Claude Wardell gave up as general manager of the store, and two years later Jack Nickalls and his son Donal bought Claude's interest in the business.

Claude and Mina were very active in the community, especially with Trinity Methodist Church. They belonged to the Literary Society and Claude was involved with the Board of Education, the Rotary Club, the Unity Lodge, the Loyal Orange Lodge and the Independent Order of Oddfellows.

The Wardells had one daughter, Joan, who still lives in the family home. She was educated in Huntsville and at Branksome Hall in Toronto and graduated from the University of Toronto. In 1951 she married Jack Woodcock. Jack was Huntsville's fire chief for seventeen years, as well as serving in the Canadian Navy, working at the tannery, and the Canadian National Telegraph. Joan and Jack were very involved with the Huntsville Ski Club in the 1940s and 1950s when many provincial meets were held. Jack was a provincial ski champ in 1949 and the Woodcocks' daughter Jane was a Canadian ski champion in 1972. Joan served on the Huntsville School Board and then became Chair of the Muskoka Board of Education in 1969.

Joan Woodcock bought her parents' house that same year, 1969. Many changes have been made to it over the years. The porches that surrounded the house on the front and back were removed in the 1930s, but the east-facing porch was not taken down until 1976. The current, glassed-in front porch with classical columns was added in the late 1940s. An apartment was made upstairs in 1951 and the interior stairwell was removed and an outside stairwell built on the west side of the building. At that time the dining room and music room were made into bedrooms and the kitchen and pantry were altered.

The charm of the interior of the house has not changed. The high ceilings with dark wooden beams are still intact. The tile fireplace has a heavy wood surround, with a large, wood-framed mirror above. On each side of the fireplace are inset bookcases with glass doors. The early gold and glass bell-shaped ceiling light remains, as do matching wall sconces on each side of the fireplace.

This substantial home set on a large property still reflects a charm that was prevalent in the early days of Huntsville.

J.E. MOSLEY HOUSE
1 LANSDOWNE STREET WEST, HUNTSVILLE
C. 1920–21

JAMES EDWARD MOSLEY was born at the time of Canada's Confederation, in 1867. Maybe that is what made him such a concerned and loyal citizen. He grew up in Aurora, where he attended school. In 1891 he married a local girl, Eva Danbrook. They produced one son, Myrell, born in 1884. With some business experience under his belt, in 1901 James moved to Huntsville, where he found employment working as chief clerk in the hardware store at the corner of Brunel Road and Main Street East.

At that time William Mitchell owned the business. The former owner had been H.S. May, whose original hardware store was where the Main Street fire of downtown Huntsville in 1894 got started.

James Mosley advanced quickly in the hardware business, because in 1902 he bought the store from Mr. Mitchell. An ad in *The Forester* early in the century states "J.E. Mosley and Son — Lumbermen's and Bushmen's Supplies in Simonds x-cut saws, splitting wedges and mauls, handles and files. Horse blankets and stable supplies. Game traps in Victor, Hawley, Norton and Newhouse. Dealers in shelf and heavy hardware. Oils and Glass." Mosley's also sold hunting licences, and business was usually very brisk. All his life James was a keen lover of sports and an enthusias-

J.E. Mosley House, 1 Lansdowne Street West.

tic hunter and fisherman. At the same time, he was also one of our first local conservationists.

James was a devout supporter of the Conservative Party of Canada. In the famous federal Reciprocity election of 1911, "J.E" bet H.E. Rice, editor of *The Forester*, that the Liberals under Wilfrid Laurier would not be re-elected on the platform of Reciprocity. J.E. won the bet when Conservative Robert Borden became prime minister. In Huntsville there were great celebrations, parade and all.

But between Mosley and Rice there was more than a simple wager — because its public settlement was set for three o'clock on Main Street. J.E. produced a decorated wheelbarrow with a large banner across the front stating, "The Larger Markets R.I.P [rest in peace]."

In this conveyance H.E. Rice pushed Mosley, smoking his cigar of success, from the swing bridge to the post office and back to his store, while hundreds of citizens turned out to witness the pranks.

Dr. Hart produced a bunch of forget-me-nots for the mock grave of the Liberal party. The Grain Growers of Canada were even going to supply a simple and inexpensive gravestone. To finalize the event, Mosley and Rice each made a political speech from the back of a wagon on Main Street.

A couple of years after this humorous event, Mosley and Son decided to acquire the Ford Motor Car Agency for the territory from Severn Bridge to Powassan. The Fords were parked on the street in front of the hardware store in Huntsville, but the Mosleys operated a garage across the street at the lower level of a store, backing on the river. In 1913 J.E. Mosley Ford Agency advertised "Ford, the Universal Car — there are only two kinds of cars — the Fords and can't affords!" He ordered twenty cars in 1914 and citizens were sure he would never be able to get rid of them. Model T's sold for $650 that year. One of the cars was a runabout, which Mosley tested up and down Main Street.

He sold the hardware business to A.E. McGregor in 1919 and purchased Lot 203 and part of Lot 204, Plan 18, on Lansdowne Street, to build himself a fine house. Although there are plans by William Proudfoot, local builder and architect, for a house for J.E. Mosley, they do not match the layout of the actual house. Well-known stonemasons James MacFarland, his son, Ross, and Herb McKenney did the stone work of the house.

Stan Goodwin watched the house being built. Horse-drawn drays brought the stone from the Muskoka River. Carpenter for the house was James Field; painters and decorators were Oynett and Hunt.

Surrounded by a mortared, smooth cobblestone-style retaining wall with concrete capping complementary to the house facade, this home displays many unique features. Built on a rough mortared fieldstone foundation below grade, the stone features have been extended above grade through the exterior stone veneer of mortared smooth stone to the underside of the roof eave.

Stone chimneys at both sides further accentuate the use of stone, as do unusual stone accents in the form of large stone corner quoining, shaped stone sills and lintels at windows, raised porch column bases, arched lintels at basement windows and openings to ventilation space below the porch and inlaid stone patterns with contrasting coloured mortar. One of these stone patterns on the front porch is in the form of a snail.

Low in scale through the use of a conventional asphalt shingled gable roof incorporating the second-floor space within, the second floor has been expanded through the use of shed-style dormers on both front and rear elevations with a preponderance of window on the vertical dormer face. Smaller punched horizontal and vertical windows on the end elevations are set over a slightly flared roof projection that extends the main roof slope visually around the entire building on the vertical ends.

A recessed porch located on the north face features a consistent rhythm of tapered wood, full and half columns on the concrete-capped raised stone bases. A variety of window styles is evident, all of which feature traditional small pane divisions: eighter for the full window extent or upper portion only. Inside, the house has an unusual fieldstone fireplace and much fine woodwork.

James Mosley died in 1958, his wife having predeceased him in 1952. His obituary stated that he possessed a keen sense of humour but was also "resolute in his opinions on national matters. As a citizen of keen civic pride he never hesitated to express a good word for Huntsville." His son, Myrell, carried on the Ford dealership for some time.

For the next ten years the house belonged to Edgar and Vera Payne. It changed hands twice again before George and Elaine Foster bought it in 1978. George was a publisher for over twenty years. Unfortunately, he died in 1995. The Fosters made very few changes after they purchased the property, but they did enhance the beauty of this house with their exquisite taste and loving care. This is indeed a cherished home.

MOUNTAINVIEW
HOWLAND-SISEL HOUSE
17 CHURCH STREET, HUNTSVILLE
C. 1885

MOUNTAINVIEW, with its fine Gothic detailing, was built about 1885 for Dr. Francis Howland, Huntsville's first physician, on a large piece of land that stretched to the river. Surrounded by beautiful

Mountainview, Howland-Sisel House, 17 Church Street.

lawns, it featured a tennis court, which was offered for the use of village tennis enthusiasts. In 1898, *The Forester* mentions a garden party given by Dr. and Mrs. Howland for the Presbyterian Ladies Aid.

The doctor had his office at his residence and kept a small team of ponies, which he used to propel an ordinary buckboard when weather permitted and where roads were passable. He would drive as far as possible and ride one of the horses the balance of the journey, while the remaining animal, securely tied to the rear wheel, would eat from the bundle of hay that was invariably part of the doctor's equipment. Dr. Howland was a man of portly physique and there was anxiety that, as the sole occupant in a two-wheeled sulky, angles stressed to an alarming limit, he himself would return a patient.

He had a big dog, which seemed to have had the run of the village. In September 1895 *The Forester* reported that Dr. Howland's big dog "was shot on Sunday night for worrying sheep" belonging to the butcher, H. Metcalf, that were pasturing on Allan Hanes's farm at the other end of town. The dog killed four sheep and was after a fifth when it was discovered. The dog started for home with its load of lead, and when it arrived there the doctor gave him a dose of poison to put him out of his misery.

Immediately following his arrival in Huntsville in 1875, Dr. Howland established *The Liberal*, the forerunner of *The Forester*. He gave a good deal of time to the editorial work, and many changes in the attitude of the government to the needs of the growing community occurred as a result of his vigorous appeals. He was instrumental in having the courthouse and lock-up built on High Street in 1883 and in the decision to bring the railway through Huntsville two years later. Active in politics from the early years, he became mayor of Huntsville in 1904 and, a staunch Liberal, ran unsuccessfully in the provincial election in 1905.

Dr. Howland died at his home on November 8, 1916, and was buried in Barrie, Ontario.

A year later Lucy J. Howland sold the property to Charles O. Shaw of the Anglo-Canadian Leather Company. This house was one of the first of almost ninety homes C.O. Shaw purchased in Huntsville for employees and members of his band. From 1920 to 1927, John Thomas Collins, the flute and piccolo soloist in the Anglo-Canadian Leather Company band, lived here with his wife, Carolyn, and their children, John and Ethel. John became a championship chess player of international renown. He founded the Hawthorne Chess Club, named after the address of a modest home in Brooklyn, New York, that he shared with his sister Ethel. Among his seven chess prodigies is Bobby Fischer, just recently defeated in an exciting match with the computer, Big Blue.

In 1927 the Anglo-Canadian Leather Company band was disbanded and during the following years a number of families rented the house. During the mid-1930s, W.T. Sharpe, a music teacher and church organist, occupied the house, and in 1944 Mr. and Mrs. Abbott Conway lived there. Abbott Conway is C.O. Shaw's grandson.

Ted and Lorraine Finnigan purchased the house in 1963. Ted managed the General Motors dealership in Huntsville. It was Ted who pre-

sented the idea of a new school to the town council, which was built in 1967. It was during the Finnigan's ownership that the front entrance was partitioned to make an entrance to a second floor apartment. The apartment was rented during the late 1970s to Ivan Gondos, a pianist and composer, who played at Deerhurst for a number of years. He had a grand piano in the living room. It was Ivan Gondos who, from his deathbed, sued Haygood Hardy for plagiarism of his composition "The Homecoming." Although the suit was defeated, Ivan Gondos died before the decision. The Finnigans moved to Burlington in 1981.

The new owner, Reverend Eric Sisel, formerly a newspaper reporter and editor, was ordained in 1969 by the Toronto Conference of the United Church of Canada and that same year was appointed minister of Lake of Bays Pastoral Charge. After a dispute with the United Church of Canada, Eric founded the Lake of Bays Mission Church in 1978.

The Howland House is a good example of nineteenth-century Ontario farmhouse vernacular architecture. The home is well preserved considering its age and type of construction.

The home sits on a small corner lot facing Church and Mill Streets. The two-storey woodframe structure has a generous verandah that wraps around the east, north and west elevations. Wooden Doric-style columns that rest on red brick piers support the roof of the verandah. A pair of french doors lead from the parlour to the east side of the porch.

The steeply sloping gable roof has a large dormer on the east and west side. A Gothic window sits in each of these dormers. A bay, with five windows, adorns the east elevation. The upper sash of each window is divided into four lights that have a decorative Gothic pattern. The rest of the windows, with the exception of a second-storey sunroom at the back of the house, are double-hung and have four equal lights. The tongue-and-groove horizontal siding has corner board trim and a wooden water table board.

The interior of the home has a beautiful wooden staircase leading from the main entry to the second floor. Two balusters on each tread support a fine wood handrail. Unfortunately, the original open stairwell has been enclosed by walls that were added at a later date. The interior of this charming house has retained most of its original wood baseboards and door mouldings.

Eric and Mary Sisel raised five children in this home and, although they have all left to make lives of their own, the house continues to be a busy one. Weddings are held at the house from time to time and weekly Bible study meetings and choir practices continue the musical traditions of the house.

OSCAR WEILER HOUSE
2 WALPOLE STREET, HUNTSVILLE
C. 1899

IN 1898 JAMES AND ELIZABETH HANES sold Lots 43 and 44 on Walpole Street to Oscar and Ada Wieler. The Hanes had received a hundred acres in the west section of Huntsville under the Ontario Free Grants and Homestead Act of 1868. It was the Wielers who built the attractive clapboard house on Walpole Street. This two-storey home, with its conventional gable roof style features an abundance of wood detail. Accent wood banding at the gable eaves and second floor, and continuous wood trim at the perimeter of windows and doors compliment the narrow horizontal siding. The large front deck at the first and second floors provides an extension of the wood trim accents. These are highlighted by the use of large, capped deck railing posts at both decks and consistent structural support posts to the upper deck. A latticed closure below the lower deck is also evident. A variety of window shapes, ranging from predominant rectangular double-hung to the uppermost attic circle head have been incorporated.

Oscar Wieler, of Pennsylvania, was a tinsmith and plumber who came to Huntsville around 1890 from near Hanover, Ontario. He worked for White Bros. Hardware before setting up his own business at 86 Main Street East. An 1894 Huntsville *Forester* advertised "Oscar Wieler, Main Street, manufacturer of cheap tin ware, creamers, sap buckets, stoves for

sale." Oscar later moved his business to 30 Main Street East, where Treasures and Trophies is presently situated. He married a local girl, Ada Ullman, whose father, Jacob, was the stage coach driver between Bracebridge and Huntsville. The Wielers were active in All Saints Church. Oscar made a lantern for the Reverend Lawrence Sinclair, an early minister of the church, to use when he travelled to his various churches.

In 1908, the Wielers sold the house to Arthur Paget. He came to Canada in 1898. His father, George, had immigrated from England nearly twenty years earlier. George and Arthur worked together in the Huntsville Syndicate and the Paget Grain Door Company. A patent was issued to them in 1923 for a special railway car grain door. By 1925 Arthur was president of the Paget Car Cooperage Company. They were involved with the Croft Lumber Company as well.

Arthur Paget married Edith Phillips of Huntsville in 1902. They were very active in the social life of the town. Arthur was mayor in 1919 and 1920.

In 1919, the Pagets sold the house to Claude and Lillian Fowler. Two years later they sold it to Kenneth and Lulu Rose.

Oscar Weiler House, 2 Walpole Street.

Kenneth was an engineer, a graduate of the University of Toronto. Before coming to Huntsville, he had worked in railway construction in Central and South America. In 1923 he came to Huntsville as district engineer for the Department of Highways. He supervised the first government-improved roads in Muskoka.

Lulu died in 1931. Kenneth married Beatrice Ireland and the house became hers when he died in 1940. Some seven years later the house became the property of Bob and Jane Hutcheson. Bob came from a well-known Huntsville family. His father, Frank, was president of the Muskoka Wood Company.

The Hutchesons resided in the house for ten years and made many changes. They modernized the kitchen, changed the wood stove to an oil furnace, and replaced the softwood flooring with hardwood.

The house was sold to Robert S. Claus in 1961. He was a school inspector for the District of Muskoka. The Claus family lived in the house for nineteen years and was probably responsible for the additions on the north and back of the house. In 1982 Robert's widow sold the house to Robert Roper and Margaret Armstrong, who three years later sold it to Giselind and Herbert A. Fuesor.

Thomas and Janet Roberts of Hillside bought the house in 1987 and made it into a duplex. They renovated the exterior in keeping with its original style, maintaining the charm of this turn-of-the-century home.

PAGET HOUSE
75 MAIN STREET WEST, HUNTSVILLE
C. 1903

IN 1903 GEORGE PAGET commissioned William Proudfoot, a local master builder, to draw plans for this handsome Victorian-style home overlooking Hunters Bay.

The house reflects the boldness with which Canadians viewed themselves in the first few years of the century. It is evident in the embellished picturesque profile created by the Queen Anne styling and the variety of materials that are cleverly integrated into its design.

The twin three-sided pavilions on either side of the front porch are the most notable features of the Paget house. Their steeply pitched shingled roofs rise to filials at the top, surmounted by crenellated crestings. The effect is enhanced by the massing of the front porch and the hall dormer between the pavilions, giving a complex interplay of angles with upward pointing shapes. The house retains its original windows with the main pane surrounded by small lights. The materials, shingles on the upper floors and narrow clapboard lower down, plus the ashlar of the foundation, all help to create the opulent decorated effect of this style.

The interior, with its centre hall plan, still has most of its original features, including a fireplace of fieldstone surrounded by fine wooden moulding, with a mirror above in the library, and a fine staircase and newel post. Lath and plaster, as well as some of the original wallpaper are evident inside the house.

The Paget family occupied this house for almost fifty years, and was active in the community and the district for some seventy years.

George Paget, a native of Bristol, England, came to Huntsville in 1879. Upon his arrival in Canada, he first lived in the London, Ontario, area where he and his brother, Henry, worked with a pork packing company reputed to have been the first company to ship Canadian bacon to Britain.

George had four children. His three sons all came to Canada at some time: George Vosper lived in British Columbia and later returned to England where he worked as a confectioner; Alfred Percy lived in Winnipeg where he was the secretary of the Bureau of Charities; and Arthur Edward, who joined his father in Huntsville about 1898. The only daughter, Florence Mary, married Hedley Jenkins, an agent for Bibbey's Confectioners, and they lived in Bristol, England.

George Paget was forty years old when he came to the growing hamlet of Huntsville as a grain merchant. Within a few years he was working as a government timber inspector, becoming well known throughout the Muskoka and Parry Sound districts. He was active in connection with a

Paget House, 75 Main Street West, c. 1903.

number of industrial enterprises including the Sturgeon Falls Pulp Company, which was later transferred to the Imperial Pulp and Paper Company. In the early 1890s George saw the possibilities of development

in New Ontario, and located the site upon which the town of New Liskeard was built. He sold much of this property in 1906. In 1899 George formed a partnership with Dr. Jacob W. Hart and John Whiteside to carry on the "trade and business of lumbering manufacturing; and dealing with lumber, timber, wood and wood products in Huntsville," under the name the Huntsville Syndicate. Three years later, this partnership dissolved and George formed a new partnership with his son Arthur and his nephew Charles Paget, which was carried on under the same name. This same year, George received a charter to purchase and carry on a sawmill and lumbering business. The Croft Lumber Company was built on the Magnetawan River near Ahmic Harbour. George was president and Arthur, his nephews Charles and Alfred, and James Rae of Croft Township were major shareholders. Alfred Paget managed the mill, which seems to have operated until about 1920. In 1926, Alfred built and operated the Knoepfli Inn near Magnetawan, which is still in business.

George Paget was a councillor on the first Huntsville town council in 1901, serving as assessment commissioner. His active interest in both municipal and district politics never flagged and he was well known in political circles in Toronto. George was a member of the Unity Lodge for many years. At the time of his death, on June 17, 1912, at the age of seventy-three, he was president of the Paget Grain Door Company, the Croft Lumber Company and the Huntsville Syndicate.

After his father's death, Arthur and his family continued to live in the house. Arthur had married in England, and after the birth of his son, James Alan, his wife died. He joined his father in Huntsville about 1898 and in 1902 married Edith Phillips, a daughter of early pioneer Bernard Phillips. Arthur and Edith had two children, Dorothy and Bernard Arthur. Arthur carried on the family business. A patent for Arthur and Charles Paget's grain door invention was issued by the Canadian Patent Office in 1923. With the end of the Croft Lumber Company about 1920, it seems that the Paget Grain Door Company was expanded and established as Paget Cooperage Company in Buffalo, New York. The 1921 Buffalo Directory listed Arthur's old friend from Huntsville, A. James Reece, as secretary.

By 1925 the Paget Car Cooperage Company, manufacturers of grain doors, named Arthur E. Paget of Huntsville, president, J.A. Campbell, vice-president and Charles E. Paget of Huntsville, general manager. They had three cooper yards in the Buffalo area. Annual meetings of the company were held in New York City. Charles Paget died in 1940, and the Paget family seems to have withdrawn from this business after 1942.

Arthur and his wife were active in the community. Arthur served as chairman of the Utilities Commission for some years and in 1919–20 was mayor of Huntsville. He was president of the Huntsville Social Club and the Huntsville Downs Golf and Country Club. The Pagets were active members of All Saints Anglican Church. Mrs. Paget was particularly interested in patriotic services during the two world wars and worked with the Red Cross. The family belonged to the Huntsville Literary Club and often entertained in their home. One occasion was described in the February 15, 1934, *Forester*. "'The Literary Club' met at the home of Mr. and Mrs. A.E. Paget. The subject of the address was 'Edgerton Ryerson and Education in Upper Canada' and was delivered by H.E. Rice. The musical included violin selections by Reverend F.J. Baine, M.A., with Mr. Freeman at the piano. G.F. Hutcheson conveyed thanks to the club, speaker, program artists and Mr. and Mrs. Paget and Miss Eva Phillips for their hospitality."

Arthur and Edith's daughter, Dorothy, married to Lieutenant-Colonel Kenneth Mahaffy, died suddenly in 1936, leaving Ken with four children. Bernard Arthur, known as Bun, became a well-known bush pilot. During the early years of World War II, he served in the Fairy Command. He was killed in a plane crash near Baie Comeau, Quebec. He left his wife, the former Jean Lawrason of Hamilton, and a daughter, Sandra.

Arthur Paget died July 5, 1948, in his eighty-second year, at his home in Huntsville. He left the house and property to his son, James Alan, his only surviving heir, with the provision that Eva Phillips, his wife's spinster sister, who had lived with Arthur and Edith for many years, could stay in the house for as long as she lived. Eva lived there until her death in 1952.

From 1952 to 1954 Arthur's nephew, Norman Paget (son of Charles), manager of the Highland Inn in Algonquin Park, rented the house with its original furnishings. The fireplace wall of the library was lined with books to the ceiling. A huge oak desk and chair faced the street. A prickly horsehair sofa was vividly remembered by Norman's daughter. It was during the Paget's tenure that the front porch of the house was enclosed.

The property was sold to George and Irmgard Schmidt in 1956. George built the motel next door, and the house was used as a rooming house. A kitchen was put in upstairs and wash basins in each bedroom on the second floor. George Schmidt was said to have entertained the idea of using the house for a distillery — using the spring water from the hill behind the house.

William Earl and Mary Carpenter bought the house in 1961, and lived there for twenty-seven years. The Carpenters made very few changes to the house during their stay. They did make the pantry into a washroom, and put a doorway between the kitchen and the library. The Carpenter family remembers that in the spring the grounds were covered with the daffodils planted haphazardly on the property. There was a perennial garden in front of the house and schilla grew profusely along the driveway.

In 1989 Larry French, a local builder, bought the property. He demolished a frame garage on the property that had deteriorated over the years. The town of Huntsville is most fortunate that Larry restored this unique and historical home to its original grandeur for all to enjoy. It is now a prestigious office building overlooking Hunters Bay.

PROUDFOOT-BOLEY-WALMSLEY HOUSE
2 CAROLINE STREET, HUNTSVILLE
C. 1901

THE HOUSE THAT HART PROUDFOOT BUILT for himself in 1901 at the corner of Caroline and Centre Streets is unusual for Huntsville. Rare in style due to its flat roof construction, this home illustrates a strong Italianate influence. The exterior facade is clad in narrow horizontal wood siding. Roughly square in shape, it has some interesting features.

Left: Proudfoot-Boley-Walmsley House, 2 Caroline Street. Above: Boley's Bakery, 27 Main Street East.

It has projected dental fascia mouldings, regularly spaced intermediate brackets and lower plain horizontal banding, with protruding accent strips. There is a large bay window projection on both the first and second floors. Wide wood trim painted in a contrasting colour adds accents to all the doors and windows. The gable roof canopy with its vertical accents around the door, and circle headed windows above, give an elegant finishing touch.

The four lots, 91, 92, 109 and 110, that Hart Proudfoot bought in 1897 were part of the Shay plan. Alexander and Jane Proudfoot settled on Lots 28 and 29, Concession 13, Stephenson Township in 1868. Alexander was one of the men who helped to build the historic Madill Church in Stephenson Township. The Proudfoots had four children: Mary Isabella, who taught school in Allensville for many years; William, who became a well-known builder and architect in the Huntsville area; Hart and Alexander Jr.

After leaving the family farm, Hart's first job was clerking in Scarlett's store in Utterson, at that time a settlement more developed than Huntsville. By 1878 he was in Huntsville working with his brother, William. An ad in the July 11 *Forester* of that year states "Huntsville Carriage Works, Buggies, Waggons, Cutters, Sleighs, All kinds of repairing neatly and promptly attended to. A number of first class pumps on hand. H. Proudfoot." He also did general contracting and carpentry work over many years along with William.

In 1887, following the incorporation of Huntsville as a village, Hart Proudfoot was appointed assessor. He performed this important job for more than forty years and served the town in one public capacity or another for fifty years. He was secretary of the Board of Education. He was also a member of the Presbyterian church, and with amalgamation, moved to the United church in 1925. He was a charter member of the Huntsville Sons of Scotland Lodge. In politics, he was a Liberal. In his later years, Hart Proudfoot engaged in the insurance business.

His first marriage was to Alma Shay, daughter of pioneer Allan Shay.

They had three children. After Alma's death in 1888, he married Alice Godolphin, daughter of Richard Godolphin of Huntsville in 1901. They had one son — Douglas.

When Hart Proudfoot died in 1941 at the age of eighty-seven, his obituary praised him as "one who enjoyed universal respect among our citizens. He led a clean life, was the soul of honour, and earned deep respect through his conscientiousness and honest dealing with his fellow citizens. His passing is a severe loss to Huntsville."

In 1942, the house at the corner was sold to Albert B. Boley and his brother Baptiste "Ting" Boley. Their father, Peter R. Boley had come from Italy and worked in the Huntsville tannery. Peter Boley and Louie Rowe returned to Italy in the early 1900s to recruit more workers for the Anglo-Canadian Leather Company.

The Boleys were involved with the famous bands of the tannery — Peter played in the original Italian workers' band, and Albert played the drums in the famous Anglo-Canadian Leather Company Concert Band.

In the 1930s Albert and Ting opened a bakery on Huntsville's Main Street (where the present Bank of Nova Scotia is). It was well known in the community, and included a restaurant. At the back of the bakeshop there was an open kitchen where locals used to gather to catch up on the town news.

A postcard of the era describes the business: "Boley's Bakery and Dairy Lunch provides a combination Bakery, Dairy and Lunch Service to the travelling public in Huntsville, Ontario. You will be welcome here." The photo shows the interior of a very modern 1940s-style establishment. "Excellent Food Served Here" is the caption.

In 1958 the Boleys sold the northern part, on Susan Street, of their four lots to the Roman Catholic Episcopal Diocese of Peterborough. St. Mary's Roman Catholic Church stands on the site now.

Albert and his wife, Antoinette, lived in the house on Caroline Street. Albert died in 1964 and the bakery was sold. His widow stayed on in the house until her death in 1984.

In 1986 the house was sold to Paul Walmsley, originally of Hamilton, Ontario, who is running an insurance adjusting business from the premis-es. According to Paul, the original house was practically unaltered when he purchased it, but he has made the main floor into offices, with living quarters above. However, the exterior of the flat-roofed house built in 1901 in the snowbelt town of Huntsville remains unchanged and adds architectural interest to our downtown core.

RIVERSIDE
31 PRINCESS STREET, HUNTSVILLE
C. 1896

THE HOUSE ON THE RIVER at the foot of Princess Street was the home of William and Jemima McGregor. William was born in Bangor, Maine, in 1849, a descendent of a Scottish family whose roots in North America began in Connecticut in the late 1600s. His father, Josiah, seems to have built sawmills throughout the state of Maine until he immigrated to Brougham, Ontario, in 1865 with his wife, Ann Barbara Folkins, and their three eldest children, William, Louantha and George.

In 1872 younger William married Jemima Barnes at Unionville and in 1881 they were living in Bracebridge with their four small children, Lillie, Freddie, Bertie and Minnie. Two more boys, Percy and Arthur, were born before the family moved to a farm at the mouth of the Muskoka River on Fairy Lake. Their youngest child, Eva Laura, was born there in October 1889. Just four months later Lillie died and was buried at the Lock's Cemetery.

William McGregor seems to have been a man of action. *The Herald Gazette* reported the following incident in September 1891: "In Brunel, near the Lock's last week, a bull belonging to Mr. G. Brown got into Mr. McGregor's Field. The latter sent his son to drive the animal out and the bull refused to be disturbed. The boy left and informed his father who started for the field with his rifle determined to bring the animal out dead or alive. When he got there the bull was of the same opinion as when the son attempted to molest him and turned on the intruder. Mr. McGregor, however, drew a bead on his bullship and dropped him in his tracks pre-

95

Riverside, 31 Princess Street, 1896.

ferring this mode of settlement to being gored to death by the vicious beast. Whether Mr. McGregor would pay for the animal or not is the disputed question."

Perhaps as a result of the great Main Street fire in 1894 William decided to again go into the lumbering business, and in July 1895, with $120 in cash and a $565 mortgage, he purchased three town lots on the Muskoka River at the foot of Princess Street. He purchased the machinery from Mr. Stephenson's mill a short distance up the river (where Blackburn's Landing is now) and moved it to his property, where he and his sons built and operated a small saw and planing mill.

The following year he and Jemima arranged a $1,750 mortgage with Jemima's brother, George Barnes of St. Catharines. George was the owner of Barnes Wine Company, founded by his uncle and reputed to be the oldest wine company in Canada. We have to assume that the money was for his handsome new home built adjacent to the mill.

The business did not go well and in November 1901 the Leckie brothers purchased the mill. Within a month *The Forester* reported that "Mr. Leckie lost part of his thumb while operating one of the machines. It is a rather unpleasant introduction but we hope Mr. Leckie may soon be able to go again." By March 1902 Irons and Winnacott had purchased the mill and moved it to their factory on King Street. The machinery had been moved earlier, which suggests that the Leckie brothers had given up on the sawmill business following the accident!

About this time William left the family and worked as an agent for several companies, including the Watrous Engines Company. It is unknown where or when he died, but he may be buried in the family plot in Brougham.

To support herself and her family Jemima began taking boarders. In October 1902 there appeared in *The Forester* the following ad: "Preparing for the Tourist Trade — Some very extensive improvements have been made to in and around the McGregor property on the shore of the river at the foot of Princess Street. The object is to go more in the tourist trade for next year. A verandah has been placed on the south and west side and the interior thoroughly overhauled. Mr. Fred McGregor is doing the work." In the June 26, 1906, *Forester*, accompanied with a photo, is the following description: "Riverside, the home of Mrs. McGregor, has been given the above name because it is close to the river's edge. Mrs. McGregor began catering to summer visitors about five years ago. Her home is splendidly adapted for the purpose. A wide verandah extends along the side and end nearest the river and a balcony above affords a beautiful survey of an animated scene, for the Muskoka River at this point is always busy with some form of life. Canoes, rowboats, gasoline launches, passenger boats and steam tugs towing large rafts pass the door daily. In the distance a sawmill's cheerful hum sounds on the ear and the smell of new sawn lumber is wafted in the breeze. All but one of the bedrooms of Riverside open on the river. They are neatly and cleanly furnished, the sitting rooms cozy and comfortable. The cuisine is prepared with much care and skill and here right in town may be enjoyed the privacy of a restful holiday near to nature's heart and yet in touch with the throbbing pulse of the town." Jemima could accommodate twenty guests and from the first of June until the end of September this was a "delightful restful home for those who do not relish the more bustling life of the large resorts." The rates were from five to seven dollars per week and every modern conve-

nience was provided "for the comfort of the guests."

In 1915 Frank Paterson, the first resident agricultural representative for the Muskoka and Parry Sound districts, was stationed in Huntsville and boarded at Riverside. In 1917 Eva McGregor and Frank were married at Riverside.

Jemima ran her boarding house until the early 1920s. She died September 20, 1923, at Eva's home in Port Hope.

Arthur McGregor, after serving during World War I, operated a hardware business at the corner of Main Street and Brunel Road and he and his wife, Pearl Bonser, owned the house until the early 1930s. During the 1940s it was Clarkes Funeral Home and more recently was owned by Emil Jensen, who turned it into apartments.

It has been one hundred years since Eva McGregor was spanked and sent to bed for running logs on the Muskoka River at the foot of Princess Street — she couldn't swim!

RUMBALL-MORISON COTTAGE
11 DAIRY LANE, HUNTSVILLE
C. 1930

THIS QUAINT FIELDSTONE HOUSE sits well back from the street on a large, well-treed lot. The most notable feature of the house is the exterior walls constructed of fieldstone in many different hues, shapes and sizes. The masonry joints are quite narrow and deeply raked to emphasize the stone. The proportions of this building are pleasant, being roughly square with a deeply pitched, cedar-shingled roof that covers the upper storey and extends down to the first storey. Cedar-clad dormers are located in the roof. There is a large fieldstone chimney at the side of the house.

In 1930, when he was sixty-three, James McFarland built this home for Reg and Ellen Rumball. Herb McKenney was his right-hand man and James's son, Forrest, also helped.

Reg Rumball was born at Petersville (now part of London, Ontario) in 1865. The family came to Port Sydney in 1871 along with the Morgans

Rumball-Morison House, 11 Dairy Lane, 1930.

and other related families including Albert Sydney-Smith. His mother, Catherine Rumball, died in 1878 and his father, Charles, married Florence Moody, who had come to care for the six small children. Four more children were born before Florence and two of the children died in a diphtheria epidemic in 1887. The following year, Charles moved to Newholm to farm and in 1897 married Frances Ellen Morgan, the daughter of William Henry and Matilda Wiles Morgan. William Henry built the first hotel in Port Sydney, which burned in 1885.

Reg worked in lumber camps as a cook until he became manager of the Britannia Hotel on Lake of Bays from 1905 to 1910. That year he moved to Huntsville and purchased a farmhouse and barns on Dairy Lane, where he founded the Huntsville Dairy. He added to the farmhouse and purchased the Knott farm (where Roger's Cove Retirement Home is now) as pasture for the cattle. Members of the family were sent each day to get the cattle, using a trail that we know as the Highway 60 by-pass. In 1930 the dairy was sold to Bert Horton and the lot severed for his retirement home. Ellen died in 1939 and Reg in 1941.

The house was left to their daughter, Alma Kate Rumball. Alma never married but taught in country schools before she became unwell and spent time in a sanatorium. She lived at 11 Dairy Lane from 1941 until 1948 when she sold the house to William John Cecil Lawrence. Alma moved to Toronto where she had a successful ceramics business on Spadina Avenue. Her business was sold to the University of Toronto and in 1950 she returned to Huntsville to live at a cottage on Fairy Lake where she painted. York University owns Alma's collection of lovely drawings.

William was the eldest son of Charles Lawrence and his wife, Lucy Crompton, daughter of Reverend William Crompton. William Lawrence attended school at Allensville and after his father's death in 1937 continued to farm the family farm at the site of Gryffin Lodge. In 1942 he married Lillian Blanchard in Weston. The stone cottage became William Lawrence's retirement home until his death on February 3, 1966.

Later that year Janet Fisher, daughter of Arthur and Edna Hutcheson, moved to 11 Dairy Lane. At this time the house was decorated with paint and wallpaper and pine kitchen cabinets were installed. The hardwood floors were refinished, a bathroom built upstairs and a very large steel bathtub removed to make way for a downstairs coat closet. The garage was built at this time. Janet's two children, to commemorate Canada's centennial in 1967, planted the two, now very large blue spruce trees on the property.

Dr. Michael Morison spent all his childhood summers at his grandparents' summer cottage on Lake of Bays and it was his life-long dream to make his home in Huntsville. After graduating from Queen's University in 1968, he spent a year in Edmonton followed by three years in England doing post-graduate work. He met nurse Judith Boland and they were married August 22, 1970, and returned to Canada. In June 1972 they came to Huntsville with their six-week-old daughter, Sarah. Immediately, Dr. Morison found an office, which he shared with Dr. Ascah and Dr. Cloutier, and Michael and Judith purchased the stone cottage on Dairy Lane. Their son, Tom, was born in 1973.

Judith was active with the Muskoka Pioneer Village in the formative years of the early 1970s and for fifteen years worked part-time in Dr.

Morison's office. Michael enjoys woodworking and they both cross-country and downhill ski.

Judith is an avid, enthusiastic gardener who has transformed a small groomed lawn surrounded by raspberry canes into perennial gardens, a large vegetable garden and a Victorian herb garden.

Over the years there have been several changes to the interior of the house. In 1975 the closed staircase to the second floor was opened up and the original front door at the foot of the stairs was replaced with a window. In 1982 a partition dividing a small kitchen and dining room was removed to allow a larger, informal working kitchen. The front verandah was closed in to make a bright and comfortable sunroom overlooking Judith's gardens and the Muskoka River.

THE RANCH
17 ELM STREET, HUNTSVILLE
C. 1899

SEVERAL PROMINENT HUNTSVILLE FAMILIES have lived in this imposing two-storey red brick home situated on a large, well-treed lot that slopes gently to the Muskoka River. The roof has generous eaves and the wide band of wood trim that separates the brick from the eave emphasizes the strong gable shapes in the roof. The original, double-hung painted wood windows are intact and most have four lights.

In 1893, Archdeacon Thomas Llwyd purchased a three-acre parcel of land on Elm Street but it wasn't until November of 1899 that the family moved into their new home.

Thomas Llwyd was born in Manchester, England, in 1837 and was raised by his maternal grandfather, Jacob Derwert, squire of the manor of Thornhill, Derbyshire. He came to Canada in April 1874 with his wife, Emma Plummer, and seven children. After a short stay in Galt, Ontario, and a brief attempt at farming in Draper Township, Muskoka, the family moved to Gravenhurst where the two youngest of their nine children were born. Thomas was ordained as a priest by Algoma's Bishop Farquar

and from 1875 to 1884 served St. James Anglican Church in Gravenhurst. A year after Huntsville became a separate mission in 1883, Reverend Llwyd came to Huntsville. All Saints Anglican Church was built in 1896 during his tenure. He became the first archdeacon of Algoma and lived in this home until his death in 1903. Three of the six sons also went into the ministry: J.P. Derwent Llwyd became dean of Nova Scotia; Albert R. was archdeacon of Haiti and founder and dean of the theological college in Port-au-Prince; Hugh J. was in charge of the parish in Muskogee, Oklahoma. Captain Thomas T.D. Llwyd was with G. Goulding and Sons in Toronto for thirty-five years and occupied the bungalow at 11 Elm Street next door to The Ranch until his wife's death in 1913. Humphrey was a businessman in Toronto and Winnipeg and Charlwood, totally blind from childhood, was the popular and well-beloved organist at All Saints Anglican Church until his death in 1913.

Two of the three daughters kept their ties with Huntsville. Polly mar-

The Ranch, 17 Elm Street.

99

ried Mackie Kinton, and Emma wed John Ecclestone, both local men, while Elizabeth became the wife of W.B. Magnum, an Anglican minister in Denver, Colorado.

In 1911 Emma Llwyd sold the home to Polly but continued to live there with Polly's family until her death in 1922.

Polly Llwyd married Mackie on June 20, 1885. Mackie was born in London, England, February 27, 1862. His father was a lecturer at the Wesleyan Training College in England. At the age of sixteen Mackie came to Huntsville to join his older brother, Louis, who operated one of the early stores in the hamlet. In 1882 his father died and it was decided that his sister Florence should come to live with her brothers in Canada. Florence kept a diary, which was published by her sister Sarah Randelson in 1906. *One Blue Bonnet* recounts activities and scenery in the Huntsville area in the early 1880s.

Mackie continued at the store after Louis Kinton's death in 1890 until the store was destroyed in the great Main Street fire of 1894. He then opened an insurance and ocean ticket agency, which he carried on until 1933 when he sold the business to G.F. Hutcheson. Mackie and

The Ranch, 17 Elm Street.

Polly had five children; Derwent; Eva, who died in 1917; Clarence, who was killed in France in 1918; Mabel (Mass), who lived in Courtland, New York; and Christie, who married Arthur Trussler.

Mackie served on the school board and was long-time secretary of the Board of Trade. An active Mason, he was secretary of Unity Lodge for some years. When All Saints Church was built, he was on the building committee, serving as warden and chairman of the Cemetery Board for many years. Mackie Kinton died in 1936. On his casket as it was lowered into the grave was the simple wooden cross that had marked his son Clarence's grave when he was among the unidentified soldiers buried in France. Derwent identified the remains and brought the cross back to Canada.

In 1935 Arthur Hutcheson purchased the Mackie home. The house was in a state of disrepair and the grounds unkempt. The porches on three sides of the house facing the river were gradually removed and the grounds tidied. A partition with glass doors dividing the living room was removed and a fireplace added. The kitchen was enlarged and a dining nook built between the kitchen and dining room. The pantry was converted to a downstairs washroom.

Arthur was the youngest of the four children of Robert J. and Martha Wood Hutcheson. Throughout his working life he was in charge of the logging and sawmill operations of the Muskoka Wood Manufacturing Company and helped his father rebuild the company after the disastrous fire in 1922. This company served Huntsville until its takeover by Hay and Company in 1955. Arthur was mayor of Huntsville from 1941 to 1943. He was a great organizer and gave impetus to many organizations in Huntsville, including the Boy Scouts, Sea Cadets, Huntsville Ski Club, Huntsville Curling Club, Rotary Club, Huntsville and District Memorial Hospital and Muskoka Pioneer Village. Arthur married Edna Trusler, daughter of Absolom and Emma Scott Trusler, on October 25, 1922, and they had five children. Arthur and Edna, known as Teddy, a nickname given to her by her father as a small child, enjoyed a full and busy life together, travelling extensively and pursuing their interests. Teddy's first love was music (she played both the piano and the organ) and she was an avid bridge player and curler. Arthur and Edna lived at 17 Elm Street until their deaths in 1988 and 1995, respectively.

In late 1995 councillor Ken Oben and his wife, Kathryn, purchased this home and are now raising their family in this Huntsville heritage house.

SCOTT-KENDRICK-PEACOCK HOUSE
18 CENTRE STREET NORTH, HUNTSVILLE
C. 1893

LOT 186 ON CENTRE STREET IN HUNTSVILLE was originally part of the Allan Shay hundred-acre land grant under the Ontario Free Grants and Homestead Act of 1868. In 1893 Allan Shay sold Lot 186, an eighth of an acre, to Catherine Scott, wife of Abel Scott. Abel Scott was a carpenter of Dutch extraction who was living in Chaffey Township as early as 1879. In a Huntsville *Forester* of that year, he advertised "A.G. Scott, Carpenter and Joiner and General Carpenter, House Building and all kinds of work done to order. Huntsville, Ontario." So it is presumed that Abel Scott built the pretty house on Centre Street for himself and his family.

The house is set on a rough mortared fieldstone raised foundation. The exterior is clad in large horizontal siding, painted white. This two-storey home features a conventional gabled main roof and a steeper pitched front gable highlighting the main entrance. The windows, predominantly large, rectangular double-hung with wide wood trim, have been placed in a symmetrical pattern on each elevation and feature uniform full-height shutters painted in a dark contrasting colour, which match the asphalt roof shingles. Stone steps lead to the raised main entrance, highlighted by the use of a glazed transom above. The front door is bordered on each side by shutters consistent with those at the windows. There was originally a porch across the front of the house, and the side porch was not enclosed.

The Scotts had eight children. Unfortunately, Abel Scott died in 1902 while working in his carpentry shop at the rear of the house, at the

age of sixty-seven. Catherine stayed on in the home until 1912, when she sold it to Peter Boley. He was a foreman in the Anglo-Canadian Leather Company, which was situated across Centre Street and fronted on the Muskoka River. He was one of the many Italian workers at the tannery who formed a band, in which he played the horn. He rented out the house on Centre Street to another bandsman of Italian origin, Constango Pesando, and his family.

By 1917, the Anglo-Canadian Leather Company and its president, C.O. Shaw, were beginning to buy up houses in Huntsville in which to lodge their workers, many of whom were talented musicians. The Italian Band developed into the Anglo-Canadian Leather Company Band and

Above: Scott-Kendrick-Peacock House, 18 Centre Street. Right: Huntsville Downs Golf Club, c. 1930.

famous musician Herbert L. Clark was hired as its director. Other musicians were hired to work at the tannery as well as play in the band, which gained great musical recognition.

In 1917 the Anglo-Canadian Leather Company bought the house at 18 Centre Street. That year Ted Hazel, who was a tradesman at the tannery and played the baritone euphonium in the band, moved into the attractive house.

Seven years later another tannery employee and cornet player, Charles Cornell, and his wife were living there. Harold Bineman and his family were the next tenants. He was a clerk at the Anglo-Canadian Leather Company and also played the clarinet in the famous band.

By 1935 the Kendrick family were living in the Centre Street house and remained there until 1948. Stanley Kendrick was born in Markham, Ontario, in 1890 but moved to Huntsville at the age of five. He attended Huntsville Public School and then trained as a harness maker. He followed the trade to Woodstock, Ontario, where he met and married Nina Tomlinson. They had three daughters, Marjory, Jean and Betty. In 1916 they returned to Huntsville where Stanley worked as a saddlemaker and labourer at the tannery. He was also one of the members of the famous Anglo-Canadian Leather Company Band. He played the cornet. Nina Kendrick died in 1933.

Another talent of Stanley's was his ability to play baseball. He was one of the best baseball players that Huntsville ever produced. He died in 1951. He was survived by his three daughters, his brothers, Arley and Percy, and his parents, Mr. and Mrs. David Kendrick. David was a well-known local painter, and in 1952, on his ninetieth birthday, was proclaimed Huntsville's oldest citizen.

Harold Peacock, an accountant at the tannery, moved into 18 Centre Street in 1948. Harold's parents had moved to Huntsville in 1918. Besides Harold there were two daughters, Vera and Hilda. In 1945 Harold married Dorothy Fallis, a music teacher at Huntsville Public School. They met while they were both boarding at the Hart House on King Street. They had two daughters, Janet and Susan. During the Peacocks' time, the side porch was closed in, the front verandah was removed and new front steps

were built. When the tannery closed in 1962, Harold bought the pretty house on Centre Street.

Harold was involved in the Huntsville Downs Golf Club. After his job as the office manager of the tannery ended, he became the major shareholder in the golf course. He had the present clubhouse built. Around 1980 he sold the golf club to Mike Crighton.

Dorothy Peacock died in 1978, Harold in 1986. The house was sold to Douglas Fraser, who converted the house into three apartments. Mary Joan Kell, a local real estate agent, bought this house in 1988.

THE SHAW-LAWRENCE-WATSON HOUSE
25 LORNE STREET SOUTH, HUNTSVILLE
C. 1900

THE PROPERTY OF THIS ATTRACTIVE HOUSE on Lorne Street was originally part of Allan Shay's land grant from the Crown. In 1899 Lots 216 and 217 were purchased by Jackson Reid, who was a hotelkeeper (in 1902 he was in charge of the Vernon House, now the Bayview Hotel). In 1902 he sold the property and, it seems, the house to C.O. Shaw, the president of the Anglo-Canadian Leather Company. William Dickie purchased it in 1905. He was an accountant at the tannery. Mern Parker, who later owned the house, remembers it being called Bide-a-Wee and also the Dickie cottage.

One year later the house and property reverted back to C.O. Shaw. During his ownership from 1906 until 1927, many families who worked at the tannery lived there. In 1907 it was assistant general manager William J. Moore and his family. Bandsmen of the famous Anglo-Canadian Leather Company also lived in the house, including Schofield Schwartz and a Mr. Smith. For a few years in the 1920s the house stood empty.

The original building was square in shape, brick veneer, with a cottage-style roof. There were two bedrooms on the north side, a double parlour, or parlour and dining room, on the south side with a kitchen and washroom at the back.

During C.O. Shaw's tenure extensive renovations were made (he renovated several homes for the use of the bandsmen in his famous Anglo-Canadian Concert Band). The two bedrooms were made into a living room with a wood and tile fireplace at the west end. The former parlour became two bedrooms. The former kitchen became a dining room and kitchen with pantry and back porch. A small bedroom above was added on at the back.

A wing was added to the north side. This contained a bathroom separated into two parts, a bedroom and another room with a large closet and floor to ceiling cupboards. The additions were covered with red Insul brick. A verandah was built across three sides of the house. The foundation is a two-foot-thick stone wall.

Situated on an elevated, sloping site with a surround of mature trees, the entrance to this home is distinguished by the prominent exterior wooden flight of stairs to the dominant feature, the continuous open porch on the easterly and southerly exposures. The home itself, constructed in a low-profile bungalow style and L-shaped, features a cottage-style roof with slightly flared lower edges at the eaves. A consistent pattern of tapered, wooden columns support the eave edge and assist in defining the porch

Shaw-Lawrence-Watson House, 1900.

extent together with the continuous wooden railing and vertical balusters between. Horizontal wood siding, painted to match the railing balusters and window frames, provides enclosure for the space below the porch to grade. Large four-paned windows, opening onto the porch, assist in merging the enclosed home interior with the semi-enclosed exterior porch area. Two-tone brick provides the exterior cladding, besides the use of predominantly wood at the porch area. Brick soldier coursing is evident as an accent at window heads in combination with stone windowsills.

In 1927 the house was purchased by Mary Lawrence (nee Hares). She was the seventh of the thirteen children of Henry Hares and his wife, who settled in Stephenson Township. In fact, she was born in the Hares' log house now situated at the Muskoka Pioneer Village.

Mary Lawrence's first marriage was to Fred Parker, a lumberman. His family owned Parker Bros. Lumber Company, which had mills at Parkerville, Mary Lake and Deer Lake. Fred died in 1916, and Mary married Jack Lawrence, her childhood sweetheart.

The family moved into the Lorne Street house in 1927. Mern Parker, beloved schoolteacher at Huntsville Public School for over forty years, inherited the house when her mother died in 1956. She and a cousin lived there until sixteen years later when she sold the house to Murray Watson and his wife, who still reside there.

Murray worked at Muskoka Wood and later at a car dealership, the Hay Company and Weldwood. Mrs. Watson, nee Sword, came from Beatrice. The Watsons still live in the low, rambling bungalow up on the hill.

THE BRAES
23 MARY STREET, HUNTSVILLE
C. 1897

THIS TWO-STOREY, L-SHAPED BRICK HOME, with its steeply sloped roof and gables, features gingerbread trim on the uppermost sections of the peaks. The single hung windows are interesting with round-headed openings on the second floor. The windows at the front of the house

The Braes, 23 Mary Street, in 1897 and today.

are decorated with patterned transoms and coloured glass. Many of the original architectural interior features have been preserved: wainscot, passage doors and trim, baseboards, stairway newel post and balusters and ornate registers. The addition to the back of the house was made in 1908 and the addition to the east came later.

William B. Strachan, a prominent Huntsville businessman, had this house built in 1897, the year he married Sarah Elizabeth Marsh, daughter of Captain and Mrs. Frederick F. Marsh. He named it The Braes and here he and his wife raised six children.

William was born in Dundee, Scotland, where he apprenticed in the grocery trade before coming to Canada in 1886 to fill a position with James Stark, a general merchant in Ayr, Ontario. In 1889 he came to Huntsville to manage Goldie and Fisher's grocery department. Subsequently he worked at the Huntsville Lumber Company store where he met Harry Heath, the company bookkeeper. In 1895 William and Harry became partners as general merchants under the name of The Universal Store. Two years later, in 1897, the partnership was dissolved and William Strachan opened his own general store near the bridge. He operated there for a brief time before purchasing John Matthew's stock and Mr. Craddock's business near the Dominion Bank where William operated one of the largest general stores in Huntsville before he moved to Hamilton, Ontario, in 1919.

Absolom Trusler purchased The Braes in 1919. Absolom was born near Sarnia in 1872 and came as a small boy with his parents and siblings to settle in Brunel Township before 1881. His father died in 1886 and his mother in 1887, and by 1891 Absolom and his brother, John, were butchers in Huntsville. John died in 1912 and Absolom carried on as a butcher and cattle buyer throughout his working life. In 1898 he married Emma Scott, daughter of Abel and Catherine Pringle Scott and they had one daughter, Edna. Emma died in 1906 and Absolom married Lovella V. Hamley, with whom he had two children. From 1919 until his death in 1961, the Trusler family spent many happy times at 23 Mary Street.

From 1965 until 1972 Harris and Mary Congdon, who managed the popular Blue Skies Gift Shop on Brunel Road (where Quick Print is now) owned this house. Subsequent owners have been Reginald and Evelyn Lassetter, William and Evelyn Mattison and Peter and Bonnie Snell, who rented the home to young people.

In 1986 Susan and Ben Larsen, of Oakville, while vacationing in Algonquin Park discovered this house was for sale. Susan had always dreamed of owning a Victorian house, and with Ben nearing retirement, the dream became a reality.

THE FRANCIS HOUSE
87 MAIN STREET EAST, HUNTSVILLE
C. 1906

FREDERICK FRANCIS WAS BORN in 1844 at Seven Oaks, Kent, England, the ancestral home for several generations. His early manhood was spent in London, England, where he met and married Annie Newton in 1868. Shortly after their marriage they moved to Canada, settling in Hamilton and Barrie briefly before taking up Lot 29, Concession 11, Chaffey Township, as recorded in the Muskoka–Parry Sound Atlas of 1879. Early on, Frederick was recognized in the community, because in *The Forester* of October 22, 1877, an issue containing poems about local citizens, there is one about him:

Frederick Francis, Carpenter and Constable,
In Huntsville's view, is building new
Barn, shed and ample dwelling;
Schools, great and small, church and town hall,
Both shops and store for sell.
In architect, is all correct
In building town or city,
Of every kind that is designed
For owner or committee.
Is constable, does business well

And summer for collection
Jails every rogue with thieves in vogue
Is Huntsville's best protection
The best of board he will afford
His house he is enlarging
This card will tell he keeps it well
No double chalk or charging.

Although this poem is a little difficult to completely comprehend, it does tell us that Fred Francis was well occupied. As a carpenter he often worked with William Proudfoot, another well-known local builder. Together they won the contract to build the courthouse and lock-up on High Street. In 1880 twenty-three citizens petitioned the provincial government "for the erection of a jail in this place." The original building burned down but was rebuilt in 1882. It was a handsome Georgian-style clapboard building, with the jail on the lower floor and the courthouse above. It also served as Huntsville's town council chamber until our present town hall was built in 1926. Fred Francis was the caretaker of this building for many years. He boasted that he never lost a prisoner. He was also involved in building the public school on Caroline Street in 1888 and All Saints Church and its parish hall. His carpentry skill is also evident in two fine residences at 11 and 17 Elm Street — the Bungalow and the Ranch, as they were known as locally at that time.

Fred Francis was also an undertaker, as most carpenters were in those days — they could produce coffins of quality. A *Forester* of 1898 had this ad: "F. Francis, Undertaker and Funeral Director, Undertaking in all its branches, Funerals Furnished Complete. Caskets and Coffins. Various designs and prices always in stock. Coffins made at shortest notice. All orders promptly attended to. Charges moderate."

Fred and his wife had nine children, seven girls and two boys. Annie, the oldest, was a teacher at Huntsville Public School before her marriage to George Wilgress, a well-known local lawyer who had his offices where The Bookcase is situated now. Rose Agnes married Edwin Harrison Flaxman, whose father operated one of Huntsville's oldest businesses, a tailor shop. At one time they employed up to ten skillful tailors.

The Francis House, 87 Main Street East.

It was not until 1906 that Annie and George Wilgress sold part of Lot 15, Plan 1 Huntsville, to her mother Ann Francis, wife of Fred, who was then sixty-two years old. Plans for the large house situated high between All Saints Church and its parish hall were drawn by William Proudfoot.

Built overlooking the Main Street swing bridge and the Muskoka River, this two-storey red brick-clad home illustrates many design features common in late nineteenth-century construction. Prominently placed at the corner, a two-storey bay projection capped by a gabled roof pediment dominates the front facade. Casement windows on each bay faced with singular vertical and horizontal muntin bars provide an abundance of natural interior light. Flared brick soldier coursing and stone sills accent window locations. Large decorative brackets, moulding trim, diamond shaped wood shingles and an elongated circle head window are added features at the roof pediment. Balancing the bay projection at the first floor, a porch enclosure with a pretty trellis wraps the opposite corner and provides an exterior extension of the interior space on the river

elevation. Gabled dormers projecting from either side of the main cottage roof enclose windows to the interior space enclosed within the roof slope. It is a commodious house with four large bedrooms plus attic.

"Frederick Francis was the only resident charter member of the Unity Lodge, A.F & A.M. He was also charter member of Croydon Lodge, Sons of England. He served on the school board for many years. He was a man of firm conviction and the possessor of a personality that won him many friends. He had a keen sense of humour. In politics he was a life-long Liberal and in religion a long and faithful member of All Saints Church." So states his obituary of December 17, 1914, in the Huntsville *Forester*.

Ann Francis died in 1936, and in 1947 her daughter Maude sold the house to Laura and Franklin Moore. Laura (Moore) Cooper operated the house for many years as a tourist home known as the Red Chevron. Roy and Eva Boothby carried on this tradition until 1975. Ten years later the house became P.M's Restaurant.

Many structural changes were made to the main floor. The open verandah was extended and closed. ReMax Real Estate operated from the once lovely home in 1988.

In 1992 All Saints Anglican Church bought the building. The property and house, now renamed All Saints House, along with the parish hall and the church, will likely form the basis for a future parish and community complex. Undoubtedly Frederick Francis would approve.

THE HENWOOD HOUSE
MORGANS ROAD, HUNTSVILLE
C. 1897

WILLIAM HENWOOD built this one and one-half storey stone dwelling in 1897 with the assistance of local tradesmen. Located in a picturesque rural setting, it is a rustic example of the vernacular Ontario farmhouse. The exterior walls are constructed of fieldstone that has been tooled to look like more refined ashlar course work. Large pane windows placed symmetrically in each facade and under the front gable

The Henwood House, Morgans Road.

all have heavy timber sills, course stone lintels and wood shutters. Plain wood frieze boards outline the eaves and gables under the steep metal roof.

William first came to Muskoka in 1868 when, at the age of seventeen, he drove cattle from the Peterborough area to Hillside for Reverend Robert Norton Hill. He got lost in a blizzard for seven days and was forced to chew his snowshoe thongs when he ran out of food! William married Sarah Francey at Cavan, Ontario, in 1873 and they soon came to settle in the third concession of Chaffey Township. He had studied law but in the wooded areas of Muskoka he found a new field of endeavour and became a timber appraiser of note. Six of the couple's eleven children survived childhood — three died in January 1888 in a diphtheria epidemic. In 1889 William purchased Lot 34 in the second concession, across the East Road from his parents' home, from Esther Copeland, the widow of his half brother, James. In 1910 William dismantled his parents' frame home and shipped the material to Hershel, Saskatchewan, where he and Sarah lived until their deaths.

The stone house remained empty for some years until Theodore W.

Hutcheson purchased the house in 1919. Theodore was a druggist and the youngest son of George and Frances Ann Wilson. His father operated a mercantile business on Main Street before the 1894 fire but soon became a contractor, erecting several buildings on Main Street including the new Methodist church in 1897. Theodore and his wife, Mary McIntosh, had lived in Swift Current, Saskatchewan, but returned to Huntsville where Theodore operated the Rexall Drug Store at the northeast corner of Main and King Streets. Percy Fowler and his wife lived in the house during the winter months when the Hutchesons moved to town.

The stone fireplace in the parlour may have been built during this period. In 1924 the house was sold to Bessie Boother, and Theodore returned to the west about this time, settling in Penticton, British Columbia.

George Boother and his wife, Bessie Thomas, were married in England. In the 1890s George came to Canada with his brother-in-law, Frank Wilkinson, to work on the railroad at Scotia Junction. Bessie joined him later and when the Booth Railroad was built, they moved to a log home at Cashman's Creek near Ravensworth. At the beginning of World War I, George was active in organizing a Kearney Battalion but soon returned to England to join the British army. He left Bessie at Ravensworth where she was postmistress and operated a grocery store. George was killed in the war and Bessie moved to Toronto for a time before returning to Huntsville. She purchased the stone house, and her old friends from England, George Salter and his sister, lived with her. George was an artist who had been an illustrator with the publishers of the Eaton's Catalogue. In 1931 Bessie moved to Toronto to be near relatives.

The new owners were Mr. and Mrs. Brazier and their daughter. The Braziers had come from England before the war to settle in Berlin (Kitchener). Mr. Brazier was recalled to his British regiment and remained in England until May 1931 when he returned to Canada. The Braziers lived here until 1942 when they returned to England.

Retired businessman William Bombay and Mary Rennie Inshaw owned the house for the next nineteen years before selling it to Roger Simmons in 1960. Roger was the son of Bruce Simmons, a Huntsville entrepreneur who at one time was the owner of both the Dominion and

Kent hotels. The Kent house key was recently found and donated to the Muskoka Pioneer Village. It was from the period that Bruce Simmons owned the hotel. Roger, a forestry engineer who graduated from the University of New Brunswick, returned to Huntsville from Edmonton in 1960 with his family of five children.

There was no indoor plumbing, and water had to be carried from a nearby spring. Part of the kitchen was curtained off for the weekly bath in a galvanized wash tub. The Simmons always had chickens, ducks and geese and ponies that the boys would take to the local resort where they offered pony rides at twenty-five cents a ride. A large vegetable garden was divided into ten-by-ten-foot plots for the children. The plots were judged by Huntsville Fair officials and produce entered in competitions at the fair. Numerous apple trees on the property provided fruit for the table and for canning. The Simmons children spent many hours climbing and swinging on the old pine tree in the front yard. In 1966 the Simmons moved to Englehart where Roger taught school.

Stanley Meyers, a Toronto school principal, purchased the property in 1966 as an investment and retreat. He enjoyed skiing at Hidden Valley, and it was during this time that the property was divided.

Brian O'Donoghue, a land use planner with the Ministry of Natural Resources, and his wife, Deanne, purchased the house in 1977. The old stone-lined well was replaced with a drilled well and the original kitchen with its shed roof was replaced with a new rustic kitchen wing using beams from an old barn from the Rosseau area. The O'Donoghues have kept chickens, ducks, horses and sheep, and their three children have continued to enjoy swinging in the pine tree as did the Simmons children. Deanne manages the Stone House Gallery in an old log barn moved to the property from the Barkway area. Here she displays paintings by her sister-in-law, Trisha Romance, and invites you to visit by appointment during the summer months.

THE MORGAN HOUSE
MORGANS ROAD, HUNTSVILLE
C. 1902

FRANCIS (FRANK) MORGAN employed James Haysom, a stonemason from Dwight, to build this attractive stone house in 1902 on Lot 23, Concession 2, Chaffey Township. Members of the Morgan family lived here for the next fifty-nine years.

The attractive farmhouse of local stone is in the Ontario vernacular style, with a single peaked gable on the upper floor. The building is T-shaped, with an open porch across the front. The paned windows are arched with brick detailing. A gambrel-roofed barn with a small bell tower and a snake rail fence add charm to the setting.

Francis Morgan came to Canada from England in 1872 with his wife, Mary (Woods), and their infant son, James. After two years in London, Ontario, they settled in Chaffey Township east of Huntsville on the East

Morgan House, Morgans Road.

108

Road. Six more children were born in Canada. Francis soon began to take an active interest in the community, opening his home for Anglican church services before St. Paul's Anglican Church at Grassmere was built in 1881. His interest in public affairs culminated in his election to the municipal council, and after a number of years he was elected as reeve, a position he held for ten years, which earned him in his later years the title of "War Horse." He served as secretary-treasurer of Chaffey School Section 5 for twenty-five years.

Mary died in 1925 and Francis in 1927 and they are buried in the little Anglican churchyard at Grassmere. Their son Frank and his family continued to live here until 1961 when it was sold to Hidden Valley Developments.

From 1961 until 1993, the house was used as living accommodations for Hidden Valley Resort staff. During this time the kitchen was modernized — the paneling was covered with drywall and aluminum windows were installed.

In 1993 Pam Carnachan and James Honderich purchased the Morgan house with seventy-seven acres and with great care began to restore the property. All the outbuildings are new. The post-and-beam barn is constructed with material claimed from an old barn from the Burk's Falls area and provides shelter for several sheep.

The original interior vertical paneling, pine floors and window and door casings have been restored with some reproductions of detail. A fireplace has been added to the living room. The glass in the transoms over bedroom doors has been replaced and one of the five upstairs bedrooms has been converted to a modern bathroom.

Beautifully decorated in heritage colours and appropriate curtains and furniture, the lovely old stone house is now a charming bed and breakfast.

G.S. WILGRESS-KENNETH A. MAHAFFY
BARRISTERS AND SOLICITORS
THE BOOKCASE
93 MAIN STREET EAST, HUNTSVILLE
C. 1897

GEORGE SUTHERLAND WILGRESS was born in London, England, the son of a retired British army officer. The family came to Canada in 1873, settling originally in Cobourg, Ontario. Young George attended Upper Canada College, then studied law at the University of Toronto. In 1887 he was called to the bar and decided to practise law in Huntsville. He married a local girl in 1900, Annie Francis, eldest daughter of Frederick Francis, Huntsville carpenter, constable and undertaker.

In 1893 George bought part of Lot 15, Plan 1 of Huntsville, from John Scarlett, who had obtained the land from William Cann eighteen years earlier. After the disastrous fire of downtown Huntsville in 1894, the downtown core was rebuilt. George commissioned William Proudfoot to draw plans for a store and dwelling at 93 Main Street East. This building had George's law office on the main floor, with a lovely apartment above overlooking the Main Street Bridge and Muskoka River.

Two storeys high and clad in red brick veneer on a mortared fieldstone foundation, this building features uniformly spaced circle headed windows with arched hood moulding of brick soldier coursing accented by stepped, raised brick courses at the arch base, all common nineteenth-century design elements. Stone sills and stone keystones are additional consistent elements at all windows. A centrally located entrance, prominently positioned at the top of exterior stone steps also features the hood moulding and keystone as well as a complementary circle head glazed transom, glazed sidelight and half-glazed multiple-pane door.

George and Annie Wilgress also built a simple classical-style home for themselves at 40 Main Street West, which has been used as the office of local lumber companies for many years — originally the Muskoka Wood Company and later as the local office for Tembec Forest Products Inc. It was in this building that tragedy struck on May 1, 1924.

G. Sl Wilgress-Kenneth A. Mahaffy, Barristers & Solicitors, The Bookcase, 93 Main Street East.

The headlines in *The Forester* of that date state: "Huntsville Family Suffers Deep Loss: Mr. and Mrs. George S. Wilgress die within hours of each other." In "one of the saddest tragedies Huntsville has ever experienced," George, Annie and a Mr. Glascott, an adult living in the home, were stricken with pneumonia and "were in bed scarcely more than a week. Every medical and professional nursing attention was given them, but in each case complications arose which baffled the skill of the physicians. Mrs. Wilgress died Wednesday noon.... Mr. Wilgress at 9 A.M. Friday morning."

George had been a faithful member of All Saints Church, rendering the rector unselfish service in various official capacities. He was a cultured gentleman with a knowledge of ancient classics unequalled by any other citizen in town. Prior to her marriage, Annie, a woman of quiet disposition, had been on the teaching staff of Huntsville Public School.

It did not take long for the red brick office building at Main Street East to be occupied again, because on May 8, 1924, *The Forester* reports: "Opens Law Practice Here. Kenneth A. Mahaffy, B.A., son of His Honor Judge Arthur Arnold Mahaffy, of Bracebridge, has purchased the law practice of the late George Wilgress, B.A. — has taken charge this week. Mr. Mahaffy has for some years been a member of a prominent legal firm at Toronto, where he has been since his graduation from Osgoode Hall."

Colonel Kenneth Mahaffy was a lieutenant in the Twenty-third Simcoe Regiment and enlisted for active service on August 4, 1914. He was among the first Canadian troops to encounter action and served with distinction, rising to the rank of major. He was decorated several times, receiving the Military Cross and later the bar to the Military Cross, the Croix de Guerre and the Distinguished Order with bar.

He married Dorothy Edith Paget in 1931. She was the daughter of Arthur Paget of a well-known Huntsville family. They had three children, a daughter and two sons. The Mahaffys lived in the attractive apartment above the law office on Main Street East. They added the garage on the east side of the building, with an extra room above.

Kenneth Mahaffy re-entered military service when World War II broke out and served as lieutenant colonel, mainly at the North Bay army headquarters. In 1945 he became crown attorney for Muskoka, taking over those duties from Walter Clairmont.

Kenneth died in 1960 and his sons sold the building in 1969 to Bruce and Lenore Werry, who opened the Bookcase, a delightful store featuring books and local pottery. The Werrys converted the garage into another room for the store. The Bookcase has changed hands several times since its original opening, but it remains a very attractive and productive commercial building in downtown Huntsville, overlooking the bridge, the Muskoka River and town dock.

William E. Hutcheson House, 37 West Street.

WILLIAM E. HUTCHESON HOUSE
37 WEST STREET SOUTH, HUNTSVILLE
C. 1900

WILLIAM E. HUTCHESON was the eldest son of George Hutcheson, who was born in County Fermanagh, Northern Ireland, in 1837. When the potato famine hit Ireland, George, who was only ten at the time, immigrated to Canada with his family. His mother was killed on the great journey when she fell down a hatch on a barge that was taking their family up the Rideau Canal. In 1850 they settled on a farm in the township of Artemesia in Grey County, Ontario.

George learned the carpentry and building trade, serving as apprentice for four years with Mr. Thompson in Owen Sound. He saw a future in the lumber business and traded his farm for the Drinkwater Sawmill in Tara, Ontario. In 1859 he married Frances Ann Wilson, and they had eight more children after William, four boys and four girls. The family lived in a house on the mill site.

George purchased another sawmill, this time at Dee Bank on the Dee River between Three Mile Lake and Lake Rosseau in Muskoka in the late 1870s. The family moved to Gravenhurst. The mill at Tara was sold. Being a true entrepreneur, George heard of a good business opportunity in Huntsville in 1883 and purchased the dry goods business known as Smith and Culp, which became known as Hutcheson and Son, and later Hanna and Hutcheson. It was situated at 86 Main Street East and was later bought by Matthew Wardell. George built his family a prestigious home at 18 Main Street West, which is still standing and known as Flora Villa. This enterprising man went on to do contracting in Huntsville, building Trinity United Church on Main Street and the Huntsville Reservoir at the Huntsville height of land. He also purchased *The Forester* and built its permanent home at 72 Main Street East in 1901. After an extremely full life, George Hutcheson died in 1926 at the age of ninety.

His oldest son, William Edward Hutcheson, built the house pictured at 37 West Street South, Huntsville. He was born in Tara, Ontario, in 1860. After going to school there, he attended the Ontario Business College in Belleville, Ontario. When he came to Huntsville with the family, he became the office and store manager for Heath, Tait and Turnbull Lumber Co. (later Huntsville Lumber Company), where he worked for several years. He married Jennie Isabelle Forfar, of Waterdown, Ontario, a teacher in Deseronto and Tara. She was a devoted Christian and very active in church life, playing the organ for many years at the Methodist church in Huntsville. She was active in the Women's Christian Temperance Union, as well as Huntsville's Literary and Music Club. William and Jennie had four children: Harold, born in 1888; George Forfar, born 1891 (George published an excellent history of the family and Huntsville entitled *Heads and Tales* from which much of this information was taken); Eva, born in 1893; and William, born in 1900.

William and Jennie decided to build a house, so they purchased Lots 193, 194 and 195 on the west side of West Street in Huntsville, between Lansdowne and Duncan Streets, from Silas Jacobs in 1900. There was a frame house and stable on the property. William had the house moved. He proceeded to build his new solid brick house on the original foundation. It is constructed on a slightly raised site.

This home features a predominantly red brick facade, gable-roof style and two-sided porch enclosure typical of the turn of the century. Highlighting these basic elements is an abundance of decorative wood fretwork at the gable roof peak and porch area, popular during this period as well. Of note are the turned columns, cutout brackets and gingerbread eave and gable trim. A variety of window styles are evident: a large transomed picture window on the first floor, elongated curved-head windows at the second floor and a full semi-circular window at the attic loft level. Stone sills and brick soldier coursing accent the window and door locations. A bay projection to the south, with its abundance of windows on all faces, provides an extension of the interior space. The house had a typical smallish parlour with large dining room and kitchen, plus four bedrooms upstairs. Its total cost was about $1,500 at the time.

This was the first home William and Jennie owned, so it was a happy day for them when they moved in. There were many changes over the years — hot water heating, oak floors, improved electrical wiring and a second bathroom.

Their son George, who was nine when they moved into the house, remembers the family keeping chickens and a cow in the stable. It was his job to clean the stable, feed the cow and sometimes to milk her. In summer he had to walk the cow to the pasture before going to school or out to play. Over the years the pasture fields were in different locations: at Shay's property, the Reservoir Hill on the Point or at Elliott's in the west end of town.

William became involved in his father's mercantile business, Hanna and Hutcheson. Then when the family established the Muskoka Wood Manufacturing Company in 1902, he was actively engaged in that business until 1921. During the 1920s he established his own lumber business.

A strong interest in municipal affairs led to William's serving on the local school board and the Huntsville town council. He was mayor in 1917–1918 and again in 1921–1922. He was active in getting the town to acquire all the land where the Memorial Park and Lookout are situated. (The town previously owned only part of it.) In 1934 he purchased the property on Highway 11B North and donated it to the town as the Hutcheson Memorial Cemetery. Like his wife, he was active in Trinity Church, as superintendent of the Sunday school, Bible class teacher and church trustee for more than thirty years.

Jennie Forfar Hutcheson died in 1931. Three years later William married Margaret Vickers, of Owen Sound. She was a cousin of Jennie and the daughter of a prominent pioneer Owen Sound merchant.

Harold, the oldest son of William, became a United church minister. After his retirement in 1953, he bought the family home at 37 West Street South. The Hutcheson family lived in this house for more than seventy years. Harold's widow, Eva, sold it in 1971 to Robert and Joan Northey, who raised their family in the charming brick home with the gingerbread trim. In 1989 it was sold to Louis Liadis, who has made apartments in it.

WRIGHT-NYQUIST HOUSE
5 LORNE STREET NORTH, HUNTSVILLE
C. 1897

THIS HERITAGE HOUSE was built by one of Huntsville's most outstanding residents. William Wright, of Irish origin, was born in Egermont Township near Mount Forrest in October 1853, the eldest of the ten children of David and Susannah (Foster) Wright. He was a blacksmith in Fergus before coming to Huntsville in 1877. There was no railway beyond Gravenhurst and William came by stage with his bag of tools and a bag of blacksmith coal. The stage broke down some distance from the little hamlet in the woods and the young man had to walk with his tools on his back, returning the next day for the bag of coal!

On October 23, 1878, he married Mary Elizabeth Quirt and they had four children. William conducted a blacksmith and carriage-making business for many years, finally selling to Mr. Snyder in 1891. William Wright's brother Rheuben came to Huntsville in 1893 and was a blacksmith for many years. William entered the grocery and provisions business. In the early years he served as councillor and reeve of Chaffey Township. An active Methodist, William was the recording secretary of the Methodist church for more than twenty-five years and was an enthusiastic advocate for the construction of the new church in 1897.

William purchased two lots on the corner of Lorne and Caroline Streets and another across the road in 1897 and built a new home overlooking Hunters Bay. A small barn was built across the road for the family cow and a horse.

This attractive home, built on Lot 167, Plan 12, with its peaked front gable, is a relatively unadorned and eclectic interpretation of the Ontario vernacular farmhouse. Tall windows with heavy timber sills and gauged, flat brick arches are arranged symmetrically in the front facade and under

Wright-Nyquist House, 1897.

each end gable. A wide, moulded wood eave cornice and matching gable cornices accentuate the steep rooflines. The atypical verandah at the front of the house is supported by wood colonnettes resting on brick piers. The rear elevation features an octagonal, two-storey corner tower, an often-used element in Queen Anne-style architecture. A wide moulded eave cornice accentuates the flared roofline of the tower that is capped with metal cresting. The small verandah with the metal railing on the second floor above the front porch has been removed.

In 1904 William Wright received the Conservative nomination for the House of Commons, defeating Duncan Marshall, editor of the *Bracebridge Gazette*, with a substantial majority. In he was elected again in 1908 and 1911. In 1917, the year his wife died, he declined his nomination and moved to Toronto and then Thamesford where he conducted a grocery business. William Wright died in 1926 and was buried at the Lock's Cemetery beside his wife.

C.O. Shaw purchased this home in 1918, one of some ninety homes he purchased for tannery workers and members of his famous band, the Anglo-Canadian Leather Company Band. One of the three Collins brothers, all members of the band, lived here. In 1927, the year the band was disbanded, John "Jocko" Pesando purchased the house. Jocko, born January 26, 1897, in the town of Meanadi Sus, Italy, near the French border, came to Huntsville at the age of fifteen, along with several youths, to apprentice as a tanner with the Anglo-Canadian Leather Company. During his association with the tannery he became chief of maintenance, responsible not only for the tannery but for Bigwin Inn and the steamboats that serviced the vacation area. He played the french horn in the first Italian band, which later became the Anglo-Canadian Leather Company Band.

Jocko married Adele Calvo on July 28, 1919. Their only son, Mario, was an engineer with the Avro Arrow program and later with the NASA space program in the United States. Jocko lived here until 1967. He purchased the old bandstand on Susan Street, which he made into his home. A Mr. and Mrs. Toon owned the house briefly before Sven and Stina Nyquist purchased the house in 1968.

Sven and Stina and their two children came to Huntsville from California. Within a year Sven was made president of Wilk Hoeglund, now K.W.H. Pipe, manufacturers of the world's largest-diameter solid wall polyethylene pipe.

Other than general repairs and decorating, little was changed in the house until 1995 when the kitchen was renovated and a laundry area and the side porch added. Stina, a Masters graduate from UCLA in Theatre Arts, soon became involved with the North Muskoka Players in Huntsville and over the years has made a huge contribution to Huntsville. She has written many plays based on Muskoka history; currently she is preparing a play called *Shantyman's Daughter*, based on the story of Tom Thomson and Winnie Trainor.

DENTON-TAYLOR-SCOTT HOUSE
9 FAIRY AVENUE, HUNTSVILLE
C. 1898

Denton-Taylor-Scott House, 9 Fairy Avenue.

WHEN YOU PASS THE CORNER of Fairy Avenue and Mill Street in Huntsville, you will notice the pretty red brick house on the southwest corner.

Combining a flared mansard and flat roof construction, popular during the second empire period, this rectangular two-storey house is unique. The first floor exterior is clad predominantly in two-tone brick and in combination wood trim and siding at projections. Flared brick soldier coursing accents window heads and there are stone windowsills. A variety of exterior projections, such as the bay window, the enclosed porch with modified cottage roof and the projected flat canopy over the main entrance, add interest to the street facade. A variety of window shapes have been incorporated, ranging from multi-paned at the enclosed porch to single hung at the bay window and second floor. At the mansard-roofed second floor are symmetrically placed, full-height dormer windows that extend from the roof slope and feature a pediment gable roof style common to the period as well.

The property was part of the Hunt plan of Huntsville and Lot 6, Plan 3 was sold in 1874 to Samuel Smale, a tinsmith. In 1891 the property transferred to John S. Trusler, a local butcher. It appears that the house was built by Alfred and Mary Denton, who purchased the property in 1898.

Originally from Port Dalhousie, Ontario, Alfred Denton, a master mariner, became a prominent citizen in Huntsville. Alfred, along with engineer John Smiley and clerk John James Denton, incorporated themselves as Denton, Smiley and Co. They built the first steamboat on the northern Muskoka lakes. It was called the *Northern* and was in many ways similar to A.P. Cockburn's *Wenonah*, which sailed the southern lakes.

The steamboat was a double-decked side-wheeler with a twenty-five-horsepower high-pressure engine geared to the paddle shaft. Her hull was 74½ feet in length, and she was capable of carrying two hundred passengers, plus a lot of freight. Built at Port Syndey, by 1877 the *Northern* was launched and plying daily from Port Sydney to Huntsville and Lake

Vernon, a round trip of fifty-six miles with seven ports of call (the Brunel Locks on the Muskoka River were in use by then). The *Northern* also had a hinged smoke stack so that she could pass under the original Huntsville bridge as it was not a swing bridge. This steamer was very important to the early development of the Huntsville area, carrying settlers and freight into the newly opened up district.

In 1884 Captain Denton built another boat, the *Florence,* at Huntsville. With the arrival of the railway in 1885, the steamship connected with the local trains at the station on Hunters Bay. In 1888 the opening of the canal between Fairy Lake and Peninsula Lake meant the steamship could have an even longer route. The famous *Northern* lasted until 1893. Her remains are sunk near the site of the old Fairy Lake dock.

Captain Denton's wife died in 1905, and he eventually left Huntsville. He died in Taber, Alberta, in 1920 at the age of eighty-two. The house passed to the Dentons' son, Jordan, who was a merchant in Sprucedale. In 1907 the house was sold to a local lumberman, Alexander Speer and his wife, Agnes. They occupied the charming red brick house on the corner until 1913, when Mary Jane Taylor, widow of Hugh Taylor of Chaffey Township, bought it. Mary Jane was the eldest daughter of Reverend Robert Norton Hill — the founder of Hillside. Married in 1876, Mary Jane and Hugh Taylor lived in the big stone house on the canal (Concession 1, Lot 28, Chaffey Township) now owned by Deerhurst Resort. Hugh was clerk of Chaffey Township in 1901, and had been appointed a justice of the peace in 1888. He was a farmer, his favourite occupation. Both Hugh and Mary Jane were involved with the Hillside Mission of the Methodist church. After Hugh's death in 1912, Mary Jane moved into the Fairy Avenue house, where she remained, in failing health until her death in 1926.

In 1928 Robert Scott and his wife, Ethel, purchased the house. He had come from Penetang in Simcoe County in 1919 and worked as a sawyer for the Muskoka Wood Company for more than thirty-five years. Robert's young brother, Alfred, and his wife, Emma, lived with him. Alfred worked at various occupations over the years: the tannery, the Muskoka Wood Company and the Ministry of Transportation.

It was during the years of the Scott family's residence in the house that most of the renovations were done: the front porch was removed, the basement was renovated and made into a laundry and office, the kitchen was modernized and the old garage was demolished. However, the attractive interior details remained — the newel post, the stair railing, the transoms above the doors and the detailing on the door frames.

Robert Scott died in 1957. After Emma Scott's death in 1982, her son, John Robert, and his wife, Bernice, purchased the house. They now reside at 9 Fairy Avenue. John worked for the railroad, the Ministry of Transportation and Al's Taxi until he retired, and Bernice worked at the Huntsville Hospital. They cherish the delightful pioneer home that members of the Scott family have enjoyed for more than seventy years.

HUBBEL-COPE HOUSE
15 LAKE DRIVE, HUNTSVILLE
C. 1960

FRANK HUBBEL was a very prominent person in Huntsville. He was born in 1907 and spent his early life in Bancroft, Ontario, where his father, Urban, was involved in the lumber business. In 1937 the lumber company purchased the timber berths in McClintock, Livingstone and Franklin Townships. Two years later Urban moved to Huntsville. Frank and his wife, Betty, and their three children followed. The first Hubbel mill and logging camp was built on Long Lake at the western entrance to Algonquin Park. Many of the Bancroft employees and their families moved with the company. In the early 1960s this mill was sold, and the Fowler Mill on Highway 11B North was purchased. Bowling pins and parquet flooring were made there.

A great entrepreneur, in 1957 Frank purchased the hardware store at the southwest corner of Main Street East and Brunel Road in Huntsville. He also went into partnership with Sid Avery to form Huntsville Fuels. Another venture was a partnership with Walter Lindall selling prefabricated colonial homes.

Frank and Betty were very active in the community especially with Trinity United Church and the activities of the Fortnightly Club. They initiated the Shantyman's Supper, which was always a huge success. Frank served on the town council and in 1959–1960 Frank was mayor of Huntsville. He was president of the Rotary Club in 1953–1954, and also involved with the Masons. Huntsville lost an energetic and progressive citizen when Frank Hubbel died in 1968, only eight years after building his unique home on Lake Drive.

The property there had changed hands many times over the years. William G. Grierson, an architect from Toronto, was hired to design the Hubbel family's new home. William Grierson loved the secluded site, and drew the plans for the house to suit it. He believed in designing his projects to represent the style of the age he was living in. Two things that William remembers about the project: the Hubbel's son, Jack, could fly his airplane over the river at a lower elevation than the site of the house; and

Hubbel-Cope House, 15 Lake Drive, 1960.

Frank Hubbel had contrasting stone H's inserted in the stone walls between the garages.

Strong horizontal lines and the absence of historically referenced detailing characterize the unique 6,500-square-foot hillside home. The house is laid out in the shape of an inverted Y. The front has two granite-veneered two-bay garages framing a granite-paved entrance court leading to a glass curtained double-door entrance foyer. The horizontal line of the flat roof is strongly emphasized by smooth wooden-boxed eaves that contrast, both in colour and texture, with the granite walls.

The strong horizontal banding is continued down the hillside as the lower floor of the side elevations (emerging out of the hillside) is clad in coarse, darker granite while the upper is clad with smoother, lighter coloured, vertically grooved siding. The horizontal elements are also emphasized by a two-storey covered verandah wrapping around the rear wing of the house. Many large double-glazed windows look out onto the wooded hillside and Fairy Lake below.

Other exterior features include wrought-iron railings around the balconies on both levels, with concrete steps and railings leading to a concrete boat dock with cantilevered roof.

Some of the house's interior features include a laminated circular oak staircase connecting the two floors; extensive use of wood paneling, including the use of maple hardwood flooring for the ceiling in the entry, dining and living areas; a two-way stone fireplace separating the living and dining area; terrazzo flooring in the lower level; and an elevator and indoor swimming pool. It is reported that the bar on the lower floor was acquired from Mort Tepermann, who ran a Toronto wrecking business. He was a personal friend of Frank Hubbel's.

Bill and Beth Cope, longtime cottagers on Lake Vernon, purchased the house in 1968. They moved to Huntsville from Stamford, Connecticut, with their children, David, Catherine and Margaret, in June 1969. The Copes have been very active in the Huntsville community.

HUTCHINSON HOUSE, 38 LAKE DRIVE.

THE HUTCHINSON HOUSE
38 LAKE DRIVE, HUNTSVILLE
C. 1900

THIS STONE FARMHOUSE is a good example of how an old building can be fitted with modern conveniences while at the same time retaining much of its original character. The two-storey home, flanked by mature maples, sits on a generous lot overlooking Fairy Lake. The roof is gabled at one end and hipped at the other with a smaller gable framing it. The rough stone walls have wide mortar joints. The windows are new but care has been taken to select double-hung and fixed wood windows that fit into the original openings. The design of the new wood porch on the front and the brick addition at the rear has been chosen to blend the new with the old.

Although the house is almost one hundred years old, there have been only three occupants, the Hutchinsons, Agnes Eybers and Don and Mary Spring.

In 1900 George William Hutchinson, a stonemason, bought sixteen acres of land from Samuel Ware. Lot 16 was part of that purchase. George built a small four-room stone house, with two rooms downstairs and two upstairs. The walls were sixteen inches thick, and the outside was stone partially covered by cement. The windows, doorways and corners of the house were framed in red brick. Gingerbread woodwork outlined the roof.

The family operated the property as a farm. A barn was built as well as a chicken house, and two small buildings were used as workshops. There was also a root cellar, the remains of which can be found on the original acreage.

Mrs. Hutchinson loved flowers and kept a beautiful English country garden. The plants that grow wild in the field across from the house on Lake Drive are said to have come from her garden. The two large maples, the apple trees and the mountain ash were all planted by the Hutchinsons.

An addition was built in 1914. A wooden kitchen was added at the back and a glassed-in verandah was built on to the front. As well, a basement was dug under the living room, the walls of the living room and hallway were lined with strips of hardwood and painted dark brown and electric lights were installed.

In addition to farming, George continued to work as a stonemason. All Saints Parish Hall and All Saints Anglican Church are lasting examples of some of his craftsmanship.

There were four Hutchinson children, Walter, Charles, Mary and Lillian. Walter left home at an early age, while Charles and Mary stayed on the family farm and were later joined by Lillian, who had worked in Toronto for many years as a tailor. In 1964 Lillian, then the only surviving member of the family, sold the property to Douglas Bice and Frank Giaschi Jr. Douglas also bought an adjoining lot from Douglas Scott. These gentlemen developed the land, known as the Fairy Lake subdivision. In the transaction Lillian retained a life lease on the house and property, Lot 83.

In 1965 Agnes Eybers bought the property from Douglas Bice, but Lillian retained her life lease. As the developers began planning the subdivision, lots were sold, roads built, and water and sewer lines laid. The noise and confusion prompted Lillian to give up her life lease and move out of her house.

Agnes began her renovations in 1968. The whole interior of the house was torn out, the foundations were rebuilt, the front glass verandah taken off. The only thing left of the original interior of the house was the stairway. A red brick fireplace and interior wall were built using brick from the demolished old Huntsville Public School. Work on the house was completed in 1970 and Agnes lived there until 1986.

Agnes was born in Huntsville, the youngest of Andrew and Barbara Kellock's six children. Apart from a few years, she spent her life in Huntsville. Agnes loved Muskoka. At nearly ninety years old she recalled the happiness and excitement of growing up in this small town. She used to watch at the swing bridge when the big boats went through many times a day. There was the romance of dancing to live band music on the moonlight cruises, which were common in summer evenings. She also remembered the Anglo-Canadian Band concerts, which were held once a week and the year the Huntsville baseball team won the Ontario Championship. The Fall Fair was a big event in the life of the town. All the school children paraded down Main Street to the fair, located where the Fairvern Nursing Home is now.

Agnes, like Mrs. Hutchinson, had a beautiful flower garden appreciated by all her friends and neighbours. In 1986 Agnes sold the property to Don and Mary Spring.

The Spring family made a small house into a large one, adding a thousand square feet to the structure. They built a two-car garage adjoining the house with a side entrance hall and replaced an open porch on the west side, next to the kitchen, with a family room. They raised the roof over the kitchen to accommodate a master bedroom and ensuite bathroom. The exterior of the original farmhouse was left untouched.

Don and Mary, with their children, Erin and Jenny, have made 38 Lake Drive a focal point for the neighbourhood. In the front yard a rope ladder hanging from the branches of a large mature maple, planted by the Hutchinsons a century ago, entertains the children. On Halloween the children around Lake Drive have a parade to show off their costumes.

They frequently end up at the Springs' for hot chocolate. Victoria Day and winter skating parties are also times for community gatherings when the large lot of 38 Lake Drive offers everyone a place of warm welcome.

THE SHEARER HOUSE
19 FAIRY AVENUE, HUNTSVILLE
C. 1902

JAMES NORMAN SHEARER had a varied career. He was born in 1863 in Oakwood, Victoria County, Ontario, and had his early schooling there. His father, Thomas, died when James Norman was only five years old, which meant that James had to struggle valiantly to secure an education. After he successfully obtained his teaching certificate, one of his earliest teaching posts was in the Aspdin area of Huntsville during the 1880s. It was there that he met his wife, Julia Clarke, who succeeded him as a teacher at the Aspdin school. They were married in 1889, and had two sons, Beverly and Charles. Julia took charge of the original log school-

Shearer House, 19 Fairy Avenue.

118

house on Church Street (later incorporated into the Huntsville Fairgrounds site) and also was involved with the new public school on Caroline Street.

James Norman evidently decided to change occupations. A 1906 *Forester* reports that in 1903 he graduated from the Royal College of Dental Surgeons in Toronto. He practised dentistry in Huntsville until three years before his death in 1930.

In 1902 Dr. Shearer and his wife bought lots 10, 11 and 12, Plan 3, on Fairy Avenue near the river, to build a home. The land originally belonged to George and Sarah Hunt (part of their original hundred-acre land grant) and was successively owned by James Carter, J.T. and Matilda Burke and R.W. Godolphin before the Shearer purchase.

This home, pictured here in its early days, is bordered by a wooden picket fence. The brick house features a flared mansard roof with two-tone asphalt shingle laid in a horizontal accent and an extended parapet projection popular during the second empire period. Also predominant is the raised, continuous porch surround on all four sides, with a low sloped roof extending to below the mansard eave, supported by six equally spaced, turned ornamental wooden columns. Highlighting these base features is an abundance of decorative wood fretwork, popular during this period as well. Of note are the wide cutout railing pickets and brackets at the column heads. Symmetrical second-floor dormer window projections extend from the mansard slope capped by a pediment gable roof. The Shearers lived in this pretty house until their deaths.

In politics, Dr. Shearer was an active Liberal, a staunch supporter of Wilfrid Laurier, Prime Minister of Canada from 1896 to 1911. He did a good deal of active political campaigning in his day. He served on the Huntsville municipal council and school board, and was president of the Board of Trade. The Methodist church and the Literary Society were strong interests of the Shearers. Right Worshipful Brother J. Norman Shearer was elected to the office of district deputy grand master of the Masons' Georgian Bay District in 1899. He was a member of the Huntsville Unity Lodge for forty-one years. Another endeavour that Dr. Shearer became involved in was the Dodge Motor Car Sales dealership in

Huntsville in 1920; that was when the Dodge car first became available to the public.

Hunting and fishing were a big part of his life, as it is for most Muskoka men. For several years he headed up hunting parties to Marion Lake and maintained a hunting lodge on Ox Bow Lake.

After Julia's death the attractive house was sold to Ruby and Christian Wilson in 1943. C.H., as his friends knew him, came to Huntsville as manager of the Royal Bank of Canada. He was born in Kingston, Ontario, in 1871 and apprenticed as a teenager by his father as a clerk of the Bank of Montreal. He had an active career in banking for over forty-five years at various banks throughout Canada. While in Toronto he met his future wife, Ruby Stanhope Jallett, of Picton, Ontario. They were married in 1906. Their four children were born in Fleming, Saskatchewan, while C.H. was working for the Northern Crown Bank, which was later bought by the Royal Bank. Here they farmed a quarter section of land as true pioneers. When the children, Esther, Edward, Kathleen and Robert became teenagers, the family moved back to Ontario to better their education. While in Wallaceberg, Ontario, C.H. contracted tuberculosis and isolated himself in the Limberlost area of Muskoka for a year, where he was completely cured. After this absence, his final posting with the Royal Bank was Huntsville, where he retired in 1943.

He did the books for the McGregor Hardware at the corner of Brunel Road and Main Street. He bought the business in joint ownership with his sons-in-law, Fred Spencer and Maurice Cairns. C.H. also ran a small travel agency in the back corner of the store. Both C.H. and Ruby Wilson were active in public enterprises: the Horticultural Society, the Chamber of Commerce, the Board of Education, All Saints Anglican Church and the Literary Society. C.H also belonged to the Masonic Lodge.

Esther Wilson Spencer, eldest daughter of the Wilsons and a prominent Huntsville personage, remembers afternoon tea being served on the spacious lawns around the house — and a silver dish on the hall table for calling cards.

C.H. died in 1953, Ruby in 1955. The following year the lovely house was sold to Lorne Murray Caswell, a construction superintendent, and his wife. The outside bricks were painted, shutters added and the porch facing the Muskoka River closed in. The inside back stairs were also removed. The Caswell family enjoyed the house for nineteen years.

After Mrs. Caswell's death, the Henry family purchased the house in 1975. Many changes have been made to this 1902 heritage home, which is now owned by the Ankenmanns.

SILVERWOOD
124 HUNTERS BAY DRIVE, HUNTSVILLE
C. 1889

THE HANES WERE VERY EARLY PIONEERS in the Huntsville area. In fact they claimed to be the first white settlers north of Bracebridge. They were of Dutch origin and their name was originally Hans, according to Joe Cookson in his book *Roots in Muskoka*. They immigrated to the United States and later came to Canada as United Empire Loyalists. Fred Hanes, who became Huntsville's second postmaster, arrived in Muskoka with his family in the 1860s.

His oldest son, Allan, and his wife, Ellen, received Lot 11, Concession 11, in Chaffey Township under the Ontario Free Grants and Homestead Act of 1868. It was situated on the north shore of Hunters Bay.

They proceeded to build a large two-storey house overlooking the bay. Bricked over in 1908–1909, the house had verandahs on the front and west side, as well as a small one above the front porch. Beside the house there was a large barn, the foundation of which can still be seen.

Allan and Ellen were the grandparents of Edna Mayhew and Vivian Proudfoot, wife of Cecil, former well-known Huntsville residents. Allan died in 1932 at the age of ninety-one; Ellen had died twelve years earlier.

In 1929 Arthur Silverwood purchased the property. The Silverwoods were pioneer settlers in Chaffey Township. The farm on Hunters Bay was one of the most fertile in the area. Arthur had a fine herd of cows and sold milk to local citizens. He never married but lived with his sister, who was ill and blind. She died in 1966, followed by Arthur ten years later. He

Above: Silverwood, 124 Hunters Bay Drive. Left: Hunters Bay with farmhouse and barn in background, c. 1930.

left the property to the Salvation Army. The following year the proceeds from the sale of the estate went to fund the Salvation Army Children's Camp on Skeleton Lake.

Marion White (nee Martin) purchased the farmhouse in 1977. She was a Huntsville girl who worked at the Toronto National Drug Company for many years. She spent a year renovating the house.

Originally it had four small rooms in the front with a kitchen behind. The rooms were transformed into two large, elegant sitting rooms with a fireplace. The mantel was imported from England. The old kitchen was torn down — the sawdust insulation made a great bonfire in the field. A new kitchen-family room was added with a twenty-four-foot ceiling enhanced by barn beams. The front and side porches and the window frames were restored and the peaked gable above the small second-floor porch was repaired. Lanny Watt, a well-respected local craftsman, did much of the work.

Now the handsome house, beautifully restored, sits beside a magnificent old spruce tree overlooking Hunters Bay.

IVY GRANGE
THE TAYLOR-WINTER-JONES HOUSE
COOKSON BAY CRESCENT, HUNTSVILLE
C. 1903

IT IS SAD THAT THIS LARGE STONE FARMHOUSE with the pretty view overlooking the canal between Fairy Lake and Peninsula Lake now stands empty. Currently, it is owned by Deerhurst Resorts and its fate is unknown. However, it and the surrounding farmland have an interesting history.

Hugh Taylor built the house in 1903. The farm had originally belonged to his brother, John, and his wife, Christina, who received Lots 27 and 28, Concession 1, Chaffey Township, from the Crown.

John Taylor died in 1890. Nine years later Christina sold the lots, 115 acres and 133 acres, respectively, and all the portions of these lots lying on the south side of the canal to Hugh Taylor. According to the 1871 Census this 268-acre farm had a house, barn and pleasure boat, and produced two hundred bushels of turnips, two hundred bushels of potatoes and six bushels of carrots, and had three sheep. The Taylor family had come to Canada from Scotland where John was born. Hugh was born in Elgin County, Ontario.

Hugh was quite a landowner. Besides acquiring his brother's farm, he also owned Lot 29, Concession 1, Chaffey Township; Lot 32, Concession 8 in Brunel Township; and Lots 22, 23, 24 and 25, Concession 12, in Franklin Township.

Ivy Grange, Cookson Bay Crescent.

In 1876 he married Mary Jane Hill, the eldest daughter of Reverend Norton Hill, the founder of Hillside. Hugh worked under the supervision of Captain George Hunt on the building of the original East Road, now part of Highway 60. He was a prominent citizen of Chaffey Township. He became a justice of the peace in 1888, president of the Chaffey Township Agricultural Society in 1895 and in 1901 reeve of the township. He was also a well-known lay preacher. He and Mary Jane were involved in the Canal Church (no longer standing) which became part of the Hillside Mission of the Methodist church.

In 1902 the Taylors decided to retire from farming and to build themselves a house on the land Hugh had acquired from his brother. On October 31, 1902, *The Forester* reported that Hugh had sold his farm property at the canal and would "retire to some extent from the active and oft time arduous labours of farming. He has reserved 5 acres of the homestead on which it is intended to build a dwelling next spring." Two weeks later *The Forester* announced that Hugh had "commenced drawing stone for the erection of a stone house." The house, which the Taylors called Ivy Grange, was completed in 1903.

Squarish in shape, this two-storey home prominently displays mortared fieldstone wall construction featuring stone window sills, curved window lintels on the first floor and irregular corner quoining. Elongated rectangular, double-hung windows are set in a symmetrical configuration. The roof is a metal-clad cottage-style with a flat peak. The exterior of the house has had many changes over the years. Across the front, originally there was a porch with attractive turned posts. Now a metal-clad gabled canopy set on plain wood columns covers the entrance. At one time there was a chimney on the east side of the house. A large wooden two-storey addition across the back was removed and replaced with a small summer kitchen. This was torn down in 1973 and another huge addition with a fireplace was built across the back. The stone milkhouse was torn down and the interior of the house altered. The present log-and-frame building to the east of the house was originally a sugar shack and later a garage.

Hugh Taylor died in 1912 and his wife, in poor health, moved to Fairy Avenue in Huntsville. As the Taylors had no children they had adopted Ernest Winter, whose mother had died when he was four years old. Ernest was the son of Reuben Winter, an early settler in Sinclair Township. Ernest married Helen Coldwell and bought the farm after Hugh retired in 1902. The Winters had five children.

In 1910 Ernest Winter died. In the mid-1920s Helen married Henry Sproat. In 1923 she had conveyed to her the stone house and its five acres as well as some of the farmland. Some of the other farmlands were sold to John Pleace, William Callacott and John Turnbull. In 1928 Helen rented the large stone house and farm to Harry and Frances Jones, who had seven children. Besides working the farm, Harry worked at the tannery and in the bush. Frances worked for Dr. Hart in Huntsville. In 1948 Harry and Frances purchased the stone house and its five acres, plus eleven acres of Lot 28 and all of Lot 27.

Harry's son, Ken, was married to June Lupton in 1950 and they moved into the stone house. A smaller house was built for Harry on Lot 27 beside the original barn, which is still standing. Many of the waterfront lots on Fairy Lake were sold off to cottagers. When Frances and Harry moved into town, Ken and June moved into the smaller house and rented out the stone house. They ran the farm and June developed her home baking business.

In 1973 it was sold to Jack and Bobbi Welsh. Bobbi is a descendant of the original Hill family of Hillside. They built the big clapboard addition overlooking the canal, across the back of the stone farmhouse.

Two years later the house was sold to Donald and Jean Contant who lived there for thirteen years until they sold it to Deerhurst Resorts in 1988. Now the building stands forlorn and empty, awaiting its fate.

Deerhurst revived the sugar bush in 1993 as part of its spring maple syrup festival, and some of the beautiful farmland and wooded areas have become part of the award-winning Highlands Golf Course.

THE WATTSON HOUSE
26 FAIRY AVENUE, HUNTSVILLE
C. 1885

THE EARLY HISTORY OF THIS PRETTY BRICK HOUSE overlooking the Muskoka River is hard to ascertain. This area of early Huntsville belonged to George and Sarah Hunt, as part of their original land grant under the Ontario Free Grants and Homestead Act of 1868. In 1877 they sold Lot 25, Plan 3, to Robert Stinson for seventy dollars. Two years later it was sold to John W. McDonald, who was involved in a local mercantile business, Reece and McDonald Bros. The property changed hands again in 1879, when it was sold to Elizabeth Huggart, a spinster. It was probably during her ownership of the lot that the house was built, because in 1891 Charles A. Wattson, druggist, bought the property for $400.

This two-storey house with its T-shaped plan illustrates several different architectural features, as demonstrated in the predominantly masonry brick detailing, wood trim and roof styles. Accent detailing in the brick is

Wattson House, 26 Fairy Avenue.

evident in the form of projected windowsills, and flared soldier coursing at window heads. The roof style was originally a conventional gable, with an open porch along the river side of the house. Gabled porch roof projections on decorative wood brackets at the front and back doors complement the style and shape of the roof. A variety of window styles and shapes, generally multi-pane, complete the design features.

Charles Wattson, born in 1858, was a native of Bath, England and came to Canada at the age of eleven with his parents, who settled in Lambton County, Ontario. In 1882 he graduated from the Ontario College of Pharmacy. Three years later he purchased the Huntsville drugstore on Main Street East from A.J. Fisher. The drugstore burned down in the 1894 Main Street fire in Huntsville. Undaunted, Charles rebuilt his

store. A 1906 *Forester* describes the drugstore: "Many of the modern drug stores are emporiums of fancy goods, stationery and books, novelties, toilet articles, etc., and Mr. Wattson's store is no exception. In these days when physicians very largely fill their own prescriptions, drug stores must carry a varied stock of goods.... Mr. Wattson manufactures numerous preparations of his own, which are found to be most efficacious for the purposes intended. Amongst these might be named eureka lotion, cold cream, mosquito oil, blood purifiers, condition power, cough syrup, shoe polish, etc. Those who desire a protection against the attacks of mosquitoes will find his mosquito oil a friend."

Charles married Cecilia Gilhuly of Harriston, Ontario. They had five children, Daisy, Charles, Henry (Harry), Jessie and Helen.

In March 1908 young Harry Wattson was awarded the Royal Canadian Humane Society medal for courage for rescuing the three sons of Andrew Kellock from the frozen Muskoka River. It was the first medal the society awarded in Muskoka.

Later, Harry married Minnie Mulveney of Huntsville. She taught millinery and had a genuine interest in artistic crafts. She was the developer and designer of the Muskoka Tartan, which was registered at the Canadian Patent Office in the early 1960s. The first fine bolts of the tartan were produced on her loom in her Huntsville home.

Charles Wattson's sons, Charles and Harry, carried on in the drugstore until 1938, after the death of their father in 1931.

In 1939, the house at 26 Fairy Avenue was sold to Israel Ginsburg. He was one of the four Ginsburg brothers who came to Huntsville in the early part of the century and by 1923 were running the Huntsville Trading Company on Main Street East. Israel was mayor of Huntsville in 1930–31 and also 1949–50.

The property changed hands again when Norma Shearer bought it. She kept the lot on the river, Lot 26, and sold the attractive red brick house to Muriel Ethel Briggs, wife of Harold Briggs. The Briggs family had been jewelers in England since 1848. Harold immigrated to Canada and served in the Canadian Forces during World War I. He then opened his jewelry business in Huntsville on Main Street East. His two sons,

123

Harold (married to Hattie) and Edward-Ted (married to Muriel), continued on the business until 1979, when it was sold to Northey's (now Danton's). Ted and Muriel Briggs lived at 26 Fairy Avenue until 1966, when Walden Alder Fisher and his wife purchased the house. Walden was a retired bank manager and had been the manager of the Huntsville branch of the Dominion Bank from 1919 to 1923. After his death in 1971 the house was owned by H.K.N. MacKenzie, who still resides in Huntsville. Two years later, it changed hands again when Grace Rice, widow of Paul Rice, became the owner. Paul was the son of well-known Huntsville citizen H.E. Rice, former mayor and owner of the Huntsville *Forester* from 1912 to 1967. Grace Rice sold the house in 1984 to Patrick Reid and his wife, who in 1992 sold it to Tom Riach.

The house has not seen too many changes over the years. The original open porch along the river side of the building was screened in after 1920. Neighbours say that the addition behind the living room was put in about 1947. Some of the exterior trim had been removed.

The Riachs have restored the house to its appearance in earlier days, adding gingerbread detailing to the front of the house. The house, which has enhanced Fairy Avenue for over a hundred years, still retains its original charm.

THE WATERS-SWANN HOUSE
21 HANES STREET, HUNTSVILLE
C. 1911

THE WATERS FAMILY TRAVELLED EXTENSIVELY before they arrived in Muskoka in 1870 to take up land in Brunel Township on the south side of Fairy Lake. John Frederick Waters and his wife, Elizabeth, left their home in Tramore, Waterford County, Ireland, in the 1850s. John Frederick's father had been a British Navy surgeon and young John had also studied some medicine. He and his wife had thought of going to Australia, but decided the trip would be too long for their two young children. So they decided on Canada. Sadly, there was

an epidemic of scarlet fever on the ship that brought them over, and the two children died. Undaunted, they settled in Toronto, where the City Directory of 1864 states John Waters had a grocery store at 181 Queen Street West. Seven more children were born to the couple in Toronto. Beatrice Scovell in her book *The Muskoka Story* related that the store burned down when the building caught fire as the result of a Native smoking a pipe. After this tragedy, the family settled in northern New York State, where they had relatives. Two daughters — Eliza and Georgina — were born there.

In 1870 John and Elizabeth Waters and their nine children decided to return to Canada and applied for one hundred acres on Lot 19, Concession 13, Brunel Township, under the Ontario Free Grants and Homestead Act of 1868. Later the family acquired the two 100-acre lots to the west of them, formerly owned by John P. Fetterly — all along the south shore of Fairy Lake. There they built a log cabin, and in 1874, a frame family home. The Waters called their farm Bay Meadows, a pretty name the property still bears today. Here they also built one of the first cottages on Fairy Lake in 1906.

John died in 1899. The second youngest daughter, Eliza, who was a milliner and worked on Huntsville's Main Street, purchased lots 9, 10, and 11, Plan 7, on Hanes Street in Huntsville in 1902. This land had originally been owned by George and Sarah Hunt and changed hands a few times before the Waters family purchased it. Elizabeth Waters died in 1910, so the next year the remaining family decided to move into town and built a home on the Hanes Street property.

Combining a flared mansard and the flat roof construction popular during the second empire period, this two-storey red brick house stands apart from adjacent homes overlooking the Muskoka River and the Lookout. Unique rounded-edge asphalt shingles accent the lower flared roof edge in conjunction with regular rectangular shingles in the upper portion. Second-floor dormer window projections extend from the mansard slope capped by a pediment gable roof style. The first floor, clad predominantly in brick (reportedly from Burk's Falls) on a rough-mortared fieldstone foundation, features a porch projection clad in com-

124

Waters-Swann House, 21 Hanes Street.

plementary coloured horizontal wooden shingles overlooking the river. A shed-style porch roof on square wooden columns extends to the underside of the mansard roof above. To the east is a bay window. Punched double-hung windows, consistent with those at the second floor dormers, combine stone sills with brick soldier coursing at the heads. From this attractive family home Frederick, the eldest Waters' son,

went by boat back and forth daily to farm at Bay Meadows.

Georgina Waters, the youngest daughter, born in 1868, married Thomas Ware Jr. The Ware family had also been early settlers in Brunel Township on the south side of Fairy Lake. Thomas and his brother Louis were stonemasons and operated a brick yard at the east end of Huntsville (where the Brendale Square is now). They helped build All Saints

Anglican Church and supplied bricks to many of the new buildings on Main Street after the 1894 fire there.

Thomas and Georgina had two children, Leslie and Annie Georgina Patricia (known as Patty). Although Thomas died in 1914, Georgina lived to be a hundred years old. She taught school at the original log school in Brunel Township, S.S. No. 5, Brown's Road. When the centennial of that school was held in 1967, Georgina could still remember the names of the pupils she had taught eighty years before.

Leslie Ware died in 1962. Patty married Albert Swann after World War I. Albert was a Barnardo Home boy from England who came to live with the Waters family at Bay Meadows in 1904 when he was seven years old.

Dr. Thomas Barnardo in England became concerned for the homeless children in the 1870s and established homes with the motto "No Destitute Child Ever Refused." He developed the idea that these poor children, mostly from the streets of London, should be sent to Canada to serve on the land: Canada needed settlers. So in 1883 he launched a comprehensive program to send Barnardo children to Canada. The program was well organized and the children were sent out well equipped and clothed. Although the project was planned in good faith, some of the children did not fare well in their new homes across Canada. Most of the children who came to farms in Muskoka had never even seen a cow!

On October 4, 1895, *The Forester* quotes: "Another Cargo — A carload of Barnardo boys came into Muskoka last Friday to be distributed among Muskoka farmers. A number got off at this station." Dr. Barnardo paid farmers twenty-five dollars a month to board the children. Obviously Albert Swann fared well, as he married into the family! The last Barnardo children arrived in 1939.

The house on Hanes Street passed from Eliza Waters to her brother Stephen in 1924. He had never married and worked originally at his father's farm on Fairy Lake. Later he became one of the leading guides in Algonquin Park. His obituary in 1928 in the Huntsville *Forester* states that "he was esteemed by all." Those members of the Waters family left living in the house on Hanes Street were Fred, the Misses Swann, Eliza and Nellie (Ellen) Waters. Georgina Ware was living in Toronto, and Charlotte (Glenning) was in Buffalo. In his will in 1928 Stephen left the house for the use of all the remaining family during their lifetimes. After their deaths it passed to his niece, Patty Swann.

Albert Swann served with the Canadian army during World War I. After the war he worked in Toronto as a stationary engineer. He and Patty were married then and had two sons, Fred born in 1925 and Owen born in 1927. In 1938 they returned to Huntsville where Albert became the stationary engineer for the Muskoka Wood Company. Albert and Patty renovated the Hanes Street house before they moved into it with the remaining Waters family. The ceilings were lowered, cupboards added and a new heating system installed. A story is told that all the beds in the bedrooms had canopies and these were removed with a saw. In 1940 a fireplace was built in the living room.

In 1960 the house was changed into a duplex: the stairs were moved and the entrances altered. After her husband and her mother died in 1968, and with the remaining Waters all deceased, Patty lived alone in the lovely house by the river. In 1970 she deeded it to her son, Owen. He severed the lot on the waterfront from the original property and built himself a home. Patty died in 1990. The house was sold to Mr. and Mrs. Kenton Martin, who are happily restoring it to its original condition.

DYER MEMORIAL PARK, C. 1957
THE DYER CABIN, C. 1940
CONCESSION 7, LOTS 31–35, CHAFFEY
TOWNSHIP, HUNTSVILLE

THE STORY OF DYER MEMORIAL PARK, situated northeast of Huntsville, is a truly romantic one. Clifton G. Dyer who was born in rural Michigan in 1885, graduated from the University of Michigan as a lawyer. In 1916 he married Betsy Browne. Both being great lovers of the outdoors, they honeymooned on a canoe trip down the Big East River as it emerges from Algonquin Park. They were overwhelmed by the untouched beauty of the area, the river rapids, the cliffs, the rugged Canadian Shield terrain and especially the serenity.

In 1936 they returned to the spot for a second honeymoon. As they were canoeing down the Big East River, they had to debark at the head of Young's Rapids, which brought them out at the top of the hill almost exactly in front of the present site of the monument. The couple had been looking in eastern Kentucky and the Virginias for a secluded cabin site but found nothing to satisfy them. Clifton Dyer tells the story of the property purchase: "Walking down the hill to the little spring at the foot, we separated, Mrs. Dyer following the

Dyer Cabin, Williamsport Road, 1940.

127

spring to the river and I following the road between the stone ledge on the right and the precipitous descent to the river on the left. We were both intrigued with the spot and decided to have our guide see if he could purchase the site for us at that time."

Clifton Dyer purchased Lot 33, Concession 7, Chaffey Township (ninety-nine acres) from William Young in 1936. William was a well-known fire ranger throughout the area where the Bethune Lumber Company had timber rights. The Young cabin was on the site. With logs from the back of the property the Dyers were able to build their log

Dyer Memorial and park, 1959.

retreat on the bank of the Big East River for only $110 in 1940.

The cabin is built of chinked rounded logs and sits tucked into the surrounding heavily treed hillside. Rectangular in shape, the cottage features many early construction methods, wood-shake gable roof, wide wood window casings, wood window shutters and fieldstone fireplace and

128

Plaque on Dyer Memorial.

chimney with stone mantel and hearth. The Dyers used the cabin for more than twenty years in every season and enjoyed the place beyond measure.

In 1942 Clifton Dyer also acquired Lot 32 and the west half of Lot 31, Chaffey Township, which had been the homestead of the Alfred Ward family. George and Florence Adams had originally farmed on Lot 34, and Clifton acquired their ninety-eight acres also in 1942. Some of the stones from the Adams' barn were used in the building of the memorial.

Clifton Dyer became a very prominent Detroit attorney. He headed the firm known as Dyer, Meck, Ruegsegger and Bullard. Besides his legal practice, he was the director of both the Michigan-Wisconsin and American-Louisiana Pipe Line Companies. He was president of the Detroit Bar Association from 1929 to 1931 and a member of the Detroit Athletic Club, Lawyers' Club of Ann Arbor, Michigan, and the Bankers' Club of America.

When his beloved Betsy died in 1956, he decided to build a monument surrounded by ten acres of landscaped grounds, ponds and walkways as a tribute to her devotion. Located in the four-hundred-acre natural Muskoka property, the memorial is the focus of numerous cleared walk-

ways constructed of shaped fieldstone and rounded timber that meander through the natural pine woodlands. Built of natural fieldstone with mortared joints, the slightly tapered rectangular pylon, forty-two feet high, rises from its 4,200-square-foot stone terrace to its imposing height, capped with a stone slab. An urn at the top contains Betsy Dyer's ashes.

Clifton hired Roman Koolman, architect, of the Detroit firm Harley, Ellington and Day to design the simple, yet elegant monument. The stone work was done by Herbert McKenney, a well-known local stonemason. Edwin Kay, a Toronto landscape architect, was hired to create the beautiful botanical gardens of North American plants, shrubs and ponds fed by natural springs. The project cost $100,000.

When Clifton Dyer died three years later, his ashes were placed beside Betsy's in a second urn atop the spire. A bronze plate at the base is inscribed with these words: "Erected in fond memory of Betsy Browne Dyer (1884–1956) by her husband Clifton G. Dyer (1885–1959) as a permanent tribute to her for the never-failing aid, encouragement and inspiration which she contributed to their married career, and as a final resting place for her ashes. An affectionate loyal and understanding wife is life's greatest gift."

In his will, Clifton Dyer created a trust fund to maintain the beautiful property that surrounds the memorial "as a forest reserve and as a public recreation area, the income therefrom to be used to maintain such property and to provide for the care and maintenance of the monument and surrounding grounds in perpetuity, and particularly the perpetual care and maintenance of the monument and the surrounding grounds and approach as an attractively landscaped area."

The people of Muskoka are most fortunate to have had such an idyllic place left to them to enjoy forever — a place where love is enshrined. If you have not yet visited the tranquil retreat, drive north on Muskoka Road 3 (11B North) out of Huntsville, and turn right at the Williamsport Road and continue on until you see the arrows pointing to the Dyer Memorial. Cross the bridge over the scenic Big East River, past an old stone schoolhouse on the right. Turn right just past it and you will come to a parking lot on the dirt road. On the left will be the terraced stone steps to the monument and gardens. Enjoy!

PORT SYDNEY

AERIAL VIEW OF PORT SYDNEY
C. 1928

Aerial view of Port Sydney, 1928.

THIS 1930S POSTCARD OF PORT SYDNEY was probably printed from a picture done in 1928, the first time an aerial photograph was taken of the village. The road leading into the village, the Utterson Road, is now Muskoka Road 10 and runs eastward to the lake.

The building in the lower right corner of the picture, on the north side of the road, is the original Pine Lodge, built by Arthur Clarke for his sister-in-law, Elizabeth Clarke, widow of his brother Lewis. The lodge was taken over in 1946 by her youngest son, Bill and operated by him and his wife, Lilla, until 1979. The original structure was much enlarged by the Clarkes and again by the new owners, the Carters, in the 1980s.

Belleview Avenue can be seen leading north from the Utterson Road. The fourth house in the row was built for Mrs. Wright in 1910 and bought by Bill and Lilla Clarke in 1961. The first house, fronting on the main road, was the first pre-fab cottage built in Port Sydney for the Cathcart family in 1926.

At the bottom of the road, right beside the lake, is Cozy Corner, built in 1926 for Mr. Freeman, a piano tuner and organist. He used to spend the summer in Port Sydney and tune local pianos. His wife was a soprano who often sang for local tea parties.

The widest curve of the road marks the route used following the construction of the new bridge in 1926. The next curve is the former roadbed. The curve following the water's edge was the route taken by drivers who brought their horses down to drink in the creek, where the gravel bed at the lakeside offered easy access to water.

The large building past the curve of the road is the Port Sydney general store, which was built by the Ladells in the 1870s and, at the time of the picture, was owned and operated by Martin Hoth.

130

The large wing on the south side was The Balsams, which Elizabeth Clarke rented from the Hoths and operated as a tourist home before the days of Pine Lodge.

The town dock, the predecessor of the current dock, can be seen farther along. There is a freight shed at the end of the dock, used by the lake steamers that ran up through the locks to Huntsville and beyond. At the water's edge on the north side of the dock stood Hoths' boathouse. Before the parking lot was built there in 1956, there was a marshy area at the water's edge, a good place to catch frogs.

The first house clearly seen past the dock is that of William Clarke, the next is the McClure-Dubois home and beyond it is the former Anglican rectory.

The next building is the present Mary Lake Inn. It was originally Quigley's boarding house, which had provided room and board to the men who worked in the shingle mill. The mill, operated by the Utterson Lumber Company, stood on the patch of land jutting out into the lake opposite until 1895. Quigley's boathouse can be seen on one corner of the small point. After the mill closed Mrs. Quigley had a booth selling ice cream at the road side in the summertime and this practice was continued by George Cadieux when he bought the boarding house and converted it to the Mary Lake Inn. The boathouse became the first cabin on the property.

The large open space farther down the road is the playing field in front of the community hall, built in 1925, which is hidden by the trees on the right. To the north of the playing field is the Brown House, to the south is the house of Captain Casselman, a captain on the lake steamers. Mrs. Casselman was a daughter of the Jenners.

The next house belonged to Grandma Jenner and was built for her by her son Bob, who took over Clyffe House from his parents.

The small dock jutting out into the lake opposite belonged to Ballycroy; the boathouse is now part of the summer property of the Sisters of Saint John. The steeple of Christ Church can be seen through the trees behind it.

The three boathouses in the upper left corner belonged to a family compound of summer cottages built between 1911 and 1913. The lower one in the row is that of Lakewood, owned by C.E. Stockford, the second belonged to C.W. Moodie and the third to his sister, Jean Moodie. All three houses and boathouses are still there.

The smoke that can be seen in the centre of the upper edge of the photograph came from the sawdust dumped there from Albert Sydney Smith's mills, which once stood by the falls, just down river from the picture, and were closed following his death in 1925. The sawdust pile smouldered for many years. That land supports a house and boathouse. It is interesting that, while Port Sydney has changed and grown in the seventy years since this photograph was taken, all the buildings identified, with the exception of the Hoth boathouse, are still standing.

BUTCHER-RUMNEY HOUSE
745 MUSKOKA ROAD 10, PORT SYDNEY
C. 1878

ONE OF THE OLDEST HOUSES in the Huntsville area is the Butcher-Rumney house on Muskoka Road 10, near the corner of Fawcett Street, in Port Sydney. In the *Muskoka–Parry Sound Atlas*, published in 1879, is a drawing of the building looking very much as it does today. It is thought to have been built by Charles Geall, a local carpenter. It was purchased by George Charles Butcher and his first wife, Caroline, in 1885. George came to Canada from the isle of Jersey, England. In the 1881 census of Stephenson Township he is listed as a farmer, but by 1891 he was calling himself an insurance agent.

In 1902 the house was raised and put on a stone foundation. From 1904 to 1928 there was a store attached to the north side of the house. At that time there was also a porch across the front, which was removed in 1956. A fireplace was built in the main room, and new floors put over the old pine ones. Hydro was added in 1931.

The exterior of this small classical Revival dwelling has never been altered and the original horizontal clapboard siding with corner board

Butcher-Rumney House, 745 Muskoka Road 10, Port Sydney.

open gable ends, on which the original cedar shingles have been replaced with asphalt ones. The foundation is of rough stone. A red brick chimney is located at the peak of the south gable. This cottage-like dwelling is attractive architecturally in its simplicity and classical styling.

In 1887 George Butcher's first wife died and the next year he married Mary Caldwell, who was born in Huron County where her father had come from England to farm. Mary kept a diary of her daily life in Port Sydney from 1891 to 1904. Although the diary is only in note form, it records much about the daily life of the family and Port Sydney. From her descriptions we know that George, in addition to being an insurance agent, unloaded flour and wheat at Utterson, loaded tan bark, tended the Port Sydney mill, did roadwork and drove the stage. George also had time for hunting. The success of the deer hunts is always recorded. She mentioned many meetings concerning the cheese factory in Port Sydney.

Socially, the Butchers had a busy time. There were dances, magic lantern shows, concerts, debates and political meetings, as well as tea parties and oyster suppers. Picnics and picking huckleberries were favourite occupations. Football games between Utterson and Port Sydney, shooting matches, croquet, regattas, as well as fairs and barn raisings are mentioned. Moonlight excursions to Grunwald, a large castle-like hotel two miles up Mary Lake, built by the Gall family after 1900, were a highlight.

As transportation improved, the Butcher family progressed from walking to the Hays Store in Falkenburg (now the general store at the Muskoka Pioneer Village, Huntsville), to using the stage, to taking "Mr. Smith's pretty steamer to Huntsville" in 1895. On July 1, 1897, Mary recorded the launching of Mr. Sydney-Smith's boat the *Gem*. The church choir went on an excursion to Deerhurst Inn on Peninsula Lake for an outing. George Butcher went to Huntsville by train in 1893.

Mary also recorded more worldly events: the Main Street fire in Huntsville on April 18, 1894, and Queen Victoria's Diamond Jubilee in 1897, followed by her death in 1901. In February 1900 she wrote, "Good news from the war (Boer), Ladysmith relieved!" and on election day 1898, "Grits in again!"

trim is still intact. The front elevation is symmetrical about a double leaf, wood panel and glazed door. One double-hung window, with sixteen lights, is located on each side of the front door. Smaller double-hung windows, with eight lights, are located above these lights on the second floor. A simple casement window, with eight lights, is located above the door. The end elevations are plain with one double-hung window with twelve lights on the second floor. Two small windows are located on the first floor of the south elevation. The dwelling is T-shaped in plan with a summer kitchen wing at the back. It is clad with vertical board-and-batten siding and horizontal clapboard. There is a covered verandah on the north side of the summer kitchen. The medium-pitch roof of the house has

132

At the end of her diary this pioneer woman of Port Sydney was ready to open her store beside the house. Masons were putting in a foundation, Mr. Wingfield erected the chimney and goods were beginning to arrive. "Store fronts arrive at last," she wrote in October 1904. In November of that year her last entry is, "Busy moving into store." The store operated until 1924. Mary died in 1929. George Butcher had predeceased her in 1915.

This simple classic house is still used and enjoyed as a cottage by the descendants of George and Mary Butcher.

DUBOIS HOUSE
569 MUSKOKA ROAD 10, PORT SYDNEY
C. 1880

Dubois House, 569 Muskoka Road 10.

THE DUBOIS HOUSE STANDS ON THE MAIN ROAD in Port Sydney, looking north across Mary Lake. Built on land purchased from Herbert and Mary Anne Ladell, it is one of the older houses in the village.

Herbert and Mary Anne settled in Stephenson Township 1871 on Concessions 7 and 8, Lot 23. In 1874 they joined with Albert Sydney-Smith to unite the original settlement on Mary Lake with Albert's community centred on his mill on the river and to develop the Village of Port Sydney. Albert deeded a little over ten acres at the north end of his property to Mary Anne Ladell for $10.50. The Ladells retained approximately half of this land along the Mary Lake shore (Lot 25, Concession 6) at the northerly end as the site for their new house and store. The balance, lying along the lake, fronting on what is now Muskoka District Road 10 and stretching south as far as Gore Street, they divided into building lots. Six were on the road and the other six were in a second range immediately behind them. When the lots were sold, all the purchasers of front lots also bought the back lots. Two of these (Lots 2 and 11) were sold in 1879 to Edward Crown, who owned Crown Island. Edward built a small, two-storey frame structure on his land. At some

point the property reverted back to the Ladells and in 1903 was sold to Matthew McClure.

Matthew was born in Scarborough, York County, in 1862. Before coming to Port Sydney in 1893, he ran Halfway House, a hotel in Newmarket. After arriving in Stephenson Township, he worked for Herbert Ladell in his general store. In 1898 he married Bertha May Clarke and in 1905, on the death of Herbert Ladell, bought the general store from his widow and also became the Port Sydney postmaster. The McClures had six children, Herbert, Gordon, Donald, Edward, Beta and Bertha (who died when only a few months old).

In 1907 the McClures made major additions to their original small house. A large living room and two upstairs bedrooms were added along one side of the little house and a bay window was opened out of the din-

133

ing room on the opposite side. When Bertha inherited her parents' piano, it became a feature of the living room. The piano is now in Muskoka Pioneer Village.

The McClures added a porch on the first floor and across the front of the house on the second floor, with a small storage room above the upper porch. This room was reached by a ladder and also served as a summer bedroom for the boys.

At the back of the second-floor hall Matthew built a small closet containing an indoor toilet. He and Levi Stanworth, another Port Sydney resident, were in partnership as the firm of Stanworth and McClure "for the purpose of patenting and controlling the sale and manufacture of an earthenware Flusher and Closet." A red light outside the closet door came on when the light in the toilet was on, as a warning that the room was in use. The story was that the red light could be seen from the Port Sydney beach! The McClures lived in the house for the rest of their lives. Matthew died in 1943 and Bertha in 1944.

Their daughter, Beta, inherited the house and she and her husband, Walter Dubois, made some changes to the building. They added a fireplace in the living room in 1945, installed a full bathroom in one of the four bedrooms and replaced the original flat roof with the sloping one on the house today. In 1965 they replaced all the windows — upstairs because the wooden frames had rotted and downstairs because these no longer matched the upper windows. They removed the dining room's bay window because it made the room so cold. Also they removed the ground floor porch, minimized the second floor porch to let in more light (which did away with the small storage room) and replaced the wood furnace in the basement with electric heat. Beta Dubois died in 1990.

In 1993 Walter Dubois and his second wife, Mary, added space across the south side of the house: a sunny sitting room, a ground floor bedroom and bathroom.

While the house has been updated to make it warmer and more comfortable, some things remain the same. There is an elegant white-painted tin ceiling in the living room; the walls of the living room, dining room and staircase are panelled in tongue-and-groove pine, stained

dark walnut; and the front door, which opens into the centre hall, is the original wooden, decorated panel door with large square window. This house has stood on the Brunel Road for over a century, enjoyed by those who live in it and by those who pass by.

LAKEWOOD
24 MOODIE'S LANE, PORT SYDNEY
C. 1913

LAKEWOOD WAS BUILT IN PORT SYDNEY as a summer residence. The land on which it sits, part of Lot 26, Concession 6, at the mouth of the North Muskoka River, belonged to Albert Sydney-Smith, the man after whom Port Sydney was named. His mills stood down river at the falls, near the site of the present dam.

The property was purchased by Charles Stockford for $300 in 1912 with the two lots to the east, forming a family compound for the Moodie and Stockford families. William Moodie, Charles Stockford's son-in-law, had spent several summers exploring the majority of the Muskoka lakes before choosing Mary Lake for its combination of natural beauty and excellent fishing. The deed to the land stipulated that both the seller and the buyer were to maintain the significant stand of trees on the property.

While the Moodies came to Muskoka from Haliburton, Charles Stockford was a New Brunswicker who spent most of his working life in the United States. He employed a Connecticut firm of architects to prepare the plans for his summer home and it was built in 1913. Those plans are still in the possession of the owners of Lakewood. The three houses in the compound are reputed to have enjoyed the first indoor plumbing, telephone and electricity in the village.

The house is clad in one-by-eight-inch horizontal pine siding stained a dark blue-green and has white trim on windows and doors and white accents on the exterior rafters. There is a low-pitched hip roof with dormers on four sides. A deep verandah faces the lake.

Inside the house are twelve-foot ceilings, deep baseboard and wood trim throughout and glass transoms over the bedroom doors (there are

Lakewood, Mary Lake, 24 Moodie's Lane, Port Sydney.

four on the main floor). The most distinctive features of the interior are the beautifully carved ceiling in the dining room and the Italian oak dining room furniture. Charles saw the pieces being hand-carved by a craftsman during a trip to Italy and commissioned the full set for delivery to his summer home. The dining room has a bay window in order to accommodate the table, which extends eight leaves and can easily seat twelve people. When the house was built, the living room also had a carved ceiling. However, a fire in the mid-1980s destroyed it beyond repair. Some pieces of the dining room furniture remain water damaged from that fire.

The architect's drawings included maid's quarters, with a basin in the back bedroom to provide the maid with washing facilities. An electric bell system connected Lakewood with the house next door, where pre-dinner cocktails were often enjoyed. The bell alerted the staff to the imminent arrival of the family for a meal in the spacious dining room. A remnant of the bell's push button remains on the back porch.

The house remained in the possession of Charles Stockford's descendants until the late 1980s when it was bought by a great nephew of Albert Sydney-Smith. The new owners have restored the fire-damaged dining room and living room and carried out major renovations in the kitchen, incorporating a number of small food and china pantries into a single, larger room. A significant effort was made to maintain the "feel" of the original layout of the kitchen and, indeed, of the whole house. It is now a year-round residence of considerable charm and distinction.

THE STONE COTTAGE
105 ONTARIO STREET, PORT SYDNEY
C. 1937

THIS UNIQUE AND DELIGHTFUL STONE COTTAGE sits among the trees on a height of rock overlooking the dam on the Muskoka River as it flows out of Mary Lake.

In 1937 Dr. Albert Ley bought the property from Cyrilda M. Goodman. It is reported that Dr. Ley had been a commanding officer in the navy during World War I. He was also a medical doctor. Although he didn't have an official practice in Port Sydney, Daisy Hughes, an old time resident there, states he was available to see patients if a real need arose.

After he purchased the property Dr. Ley hired an architect to design his Muskoka retreat — William R. Webb, a member of the Ontario Association of Architects. He was involved in several partnerships in Toronto during his career and designed some substantial Toronto and area buildings.

The picturesque one-storey cottage is constructed of ashlar stone. Daisy Hughes remembers that the stonemasons were the Graham brothers of Port Sydney, who had originally come from Scotland. It is rumoured that the stone came from the construction site of Highway 11, which was a Depression project. The building is T-shaped, having a cedar shake roof

The Stone Cottage, 105 Ontario Street, Port Sydney. Right: The stained-glass windows represent Grimm's fairy tales.

with a stone chimney at each end. There is a recessed arch for the front door, which is rounded at the top, as is the door with a circular window.

The interior of the living room and dining room area is also of stone, with a wooden beamed ceiling. The fireplace has a carved wooden mantel and on either side are small windows of diamond shaped panes with small stained-glass designs in the centre. Windows of the same style, with stained-glass design insert, are also on the landing of the stairs and the front door. The stained glass is said to have come from Scotland (as is the carved mantel) where Dr. Ley saw the designs in a book of Grimm's fairy tales.

At one time the daughter-in-law of the architect came back to see the cottage and reminisce about the honeymoon she spent in its romantic atmosphere.

When Dr. Ley died he left the cottage to his unmarried sister, who in turn sold it in 1957 to Harry and Hilda Leavens of Niagara-on-the-Lake. Their grandson has many happy memories of his visits to the cottage at Port Sydney.

Three years later, after Hilda's death, Gladys and Howard Shaver of Huntsville purchased the property. Howard came to Huntsville in 1945 where he established the Howard Shaver Real Estate and Insurance Business. He also built the Shaver Building just west of the Capitol Theatre on Main Street West. Howard became very involved in the local Chamber of Commerce, serving as its secretary-manager from 1951 to 1966. He was responsible, along with Ed Parker, for initiating the Cavalcade of Colour, a period in the autumn when the fall colours were their most beautiful, set aside to encourage tourists to return to Muskoka. It was very successful. Howard was also involved in the Rotary Club, and both the Muskoka and Parry Sound real estate boards. He was an executive of all three organizations at various times.

The lovely cottage was sold again in 1977 to Rose and Ted Hamblin of Huntsville where they were in the furniture business.

Laura Harper of Oakville, the current owner, fell in love with the pretty place when she first saw it in 1982 and purchased it. Laura tells a story of two little children in raincoats coming to the door of the cottage on a misty, rainy day to ask if it was the place where the seven dwarfs lived! Such is the atmosphere of the spot.

Laura is involved in the "Sleeping Children Around the World" project and has travelled to many undeveloped countries delivering bed kits to needy children. In between her trips she enjoys the ambience of the charming stone cottage in all seasons.

THOMS FARMHOUSE
THOMS BAY ROAD, PORT SYDNEY
C. 1881

WILLIAM HENRY THOMS AND HIS WIFE, EMILY, with their two infant daughters, Ada and Clara, came to Muskoka in 1869 and took up land under the Ontario Free Grants and Homestead Act of 1868 on Concession 8, Stephenson Township, Lots 26, 27, 28 and 29. They had been married in Lambeth, England, in 1866. William was an educated man, a government clerk, who immigrated to Canada to provide for his growing family.

Their first home was the settler's log cabin, built in a clearing above the lake. The present handsome clapboard house was built in 1881 and was not only more spacious and comfortable, but was necessary to house their family of seven children. Clara died shortly after their arrival in Muskoka and was buried on the farm, since there was as yet no cemetery in the area.

Soon after the family moved into their new home, the great fire of October 1881 swept through Port Sydney and over the ridge of Buckhorn Point. It had started, typically, when one of the farmers in the village began burning a pile of dry brush. There was such a high wind that the sparks and burning branches from the spreading conflagration ignited the trees on islands in Mary Lake. Emily Thoms and her children escaped the fire in canoes, sheltered from the burning debris under dampened blankets, while her husband and other men tried to control the flames.

Thoms Farmhouse, Thoms Bay Road, c.1881.

The log cabin was destroyed completely but, fortunately, the fine new house escaped destruction.

William and Emily had eleven surviving children. Because there was as yet no school in the area, William taught his children at home. Only John and Richard, born in 1885 and 1886, went to the school built in Allensville, several miles away.

The Thoms property, while rugged, beautiful and, before the fire, covered with fine trees, included very little arable land. There was an excellent barn on the hill above the house, which still stands there, and a small shed, at the edge of the creek that ran beside the house, where the cream was separated and the milk and butter stored. But the land could not support such a large family. Relatives in England sent out boxes of clothing and William's uncle supported the family with five pounds every two months.

When they became old enough to find work, the five sons all worked out in the woods and in Sydney-Smith's mills in the village. Eventually

137

most of the Thoms children left the farm. Four went out West to Alberta and British Columbia, one to North Bay. Jack left in 1914 to join the army, was sent overseas in 1915 and came home at the end of World War I a captain. He married and lived in Huntsville, where his grandson is now a lawyer.

Dick Thoms was left to run the farm and care for his elderly parents, who died in 1917 and 1922, and his two spinster sisters, Louisa and Connie. He was a well-known and popular person in Port Sydney and area and much in demand as a caller at all the local square dances. He was also well loved by the summer people to whom he had sold lots on the property around the bay. He could build and make repairs, remove fallen trees, fill the icehouse in preparation for summer food storage and provide eggs, milk and fresh vegetables. A couple of generations of children and their parents visited with Dick and his sisters in the farm kitchen and enjoyed his stories, as well as his comments on events of the day.

In his later years Dick Thoms spent the winter in a house he had built in Port Sydney. In 1977 he left the farm permanently and sold the property to Horst Wiegenbroeker, who lovingly updated the house, refinishing the handsome staircase and pine banister in the front hall, restoring the pine tongue-and-groove walls and ceiling in the large kitchen, adding a fireplace in the living room and a tall brick chimney that reaches to the peak of the roof and, at the same time, by means of an addition at the rear of the building, installing bathrooms and a furnace and adding a garage. Later the Wiegenbroekers divided the property into five waterfront lots, of which the farmhouse section is the largest, and left the area.

The Thoms farmhouse is a well-proportioned building with twin windowed gables on the eastern side, fronting the lake, and a verandah running the full width of the house. The front door, with sidelights, is centred between two french doors opening from the original parlour and dining room. There are four large sash windows on each sidewall. On the south wall there are two in the living room and two directly above in each of two bedrooms. On the north wall the two lower windows illuminate the dining room in front and a small pantry (now a bathroom) between

it and the kitchen. The foundation is of fieldstone and was built by Dick Thoms and his brother in 1914 before Jack went off to war. The large kitchen is in a wing jutting out, L-shaped, from the west side of the house. The wood siding on the house, originally a creamy yellow, has been painted a dark grey since the renovation. An addition was put on over the kitchen and a new utility room and garage replaced a lean-to woodshed that used to stand behind the kitchen. The house has a splendid view out over Mary Lake.

The house is now owned by Val Bezic, whose family came as immigrants to Huntsville.

T.W. CLARKE HOUSE
65 BELLEVIEW AVENUE, PORT SYDNEY
C. 1912

MANY OF THE HOUSES AND COTTAGES in Port Sydney and around Mary Lake have been built by one of the Clarkes. The first Clarke to settle permanently in the area was William, who took up Lot 25, Concession 8 and 9, of Stephenson Township in 1869. His marriage to Emma Ladell in 1873 was the first to be solemnized in the newly built Christ Church. William Clarke was a skilled carpenter whose shop, built behind his house overlooking Mary Lake, provided most of the doors, windows and frames for houses in the area. He also designed and helped build Knox Presbyterian Church and the steamer Northern launched in Port Sydney in 1877.

William's son Arthur became a busy and well-known builder in Port Sydney, to be followed by his sons Victor and Mel and the present builder, Mel's son Richard.

William's son Lewis had a sawmill to the north of the village and lived in a house on the lake at the end of what is now Belleview Avenue. In 1912 he bought a steam-powered mill, which was shipped by rail to Utterson and then driven down the road toward the village and through

138

T.W. CLARKE'S HOUSE, 65 BELLEVIEW AVENUE, PORT SYDNEY.

the woods to the mill site. In order to raise money to pay for the mill, Lewis Clarke built a cottage to the south of his home and sold it to Reverend Smith.

The cottage was a two-storey structure, the living room lined with tongue-and-groove cedar, the kitchen, a plain, spare room to which water was carried from the pump in the yard. A staircase in the living room led to four small bedrooms with sloping ceilings, also cedar-lined, and a small porch under a gable facing east at the end of the hall. Off the living room

and overlooking the lake was a square verandah, which extended out under the upper porch. It was originally known as Maw-Wah (Beautiful View) Cottage, named by the Native people who camped in the next bay on Mary Lake every summer and sold their footwear and sweetgrass baskets to people in Port Sydney.

The cottage was later sold to Cyrus Dolph, owner of the Metal Shingle and Siding Company of Galt. Cyrus was a philanthropist and churchman who was instrumental in founding Pioneer Camp on Clearwater Lake. He improved the cottage by bringing water into the kitchen and it was he who furnished the living room with the solid wicker furniture that still stands there. He also added some fine stained-glass and leaded windows to the house.

Cyrus died in 1936, his wife a few years later, and the cottage was inherited by Mrs. Doph's sister. She used it intermittently until 1964, when she sold it to Terry Clarke, son of the builder, Lewis Clarke.

Terry and his wife, Audrey, lived in Toronto and used the house as a cottage until 1977, when Terry retired and they moved back to Muskoka. They transformed the basic cottage into a solid, year-round home with a modern kitchen and a bathroom and larger, more weatherproof windows. They incorporated some more leaded-glass windows into the building and built a ground floor bedroom on the north side of the house. On the south side of the house they added a carport. These renovations were carried out by Richard Clarke and Cyrle Somerset.

The present building is a handsome house covered in cedar shingles painted dark green with white trim on the windows, doors and exterior rafters and soffits and on the verandah and porch railings and trim. It sits on a rise above the lake and a wide lawn stretches down to a dock and boathouse at the water's edge.

139

GLENGYLE COTTAGE, C. 1900
ALLISON'S POINT, C. 1944
HIGHWAY 60, FAIRY LAKE, HUNTSVILLE
C. 1900

Glengyle Cottage, c. 1900.

THIS HUNDRED-ACRE CROWN LAND GRANT, Lot 22, Chaffey Township, with water frontage on Fairy Lake, was granted to James Bettes in 1885. He was a well-known and early settler in Huntsville. He moved to Bracebridge when he was appointed Muskoka's first sheriff in 1888.

The next year James sold the property to William Head. William had four boys and four girls and came from southern Ontario to Muskoka. The empty white and green farmhouse now standing empty on the north side of Highway 60 across from Allison's Point was the original house on that acreage. It later became known as the Skelding farm, after the next owners.

In 1900 William sold a portion of the property south of Highway 60 (then called the East Road) to a man with a very colourful name — Abraham Lincoln McCann. He came to Huntsville from Ottawa and became a well-known figure in the community. Abraham built the original buildings on the lakeside site and a house for himself back from the lake. Neighbours report there was also a barn. He also built the very picturesque old cottage on the point, which is still standing today. It was originally called Glengyle and is probably one of the oldest cottages on Fairy Lake.

A Hamilton couple, Professor Edward Zealand and his wife, Elizabeth, rented it for many years. As they had no children, their nieces — the Gibson family of six girls — joined them at the cottage during the years from 1915 to 1920. Dorothy Gibson kept a record of their fun family times on Fairy Lake and descendants of the Gibson family have heard many stories of the years the girls spent on the picturesque point. The family rented it for so many seasons they furnished the place with their own belongings.

140

Allison's Point, Fairy Lake, 1944.

lakefront property and modernized the original buildings. He and his wife opened their summer cottage resort, called Allison's Point. They lived in the original McCann house back on the hill and made many improvements to it. Summer cottage resorts were very popular in this era. June Dadswell, the Allisons' daughter, tells of having thirty-seven cottagers a night in the height of the season. There was a dock and boats and campfires on the sandy beach as well as a centre grassy area for children to play.

After John died in 1959, Grace married George Rowlings. The summer cottage business carried on, but at a less hectic pace. Grace sold the property to June Dadswell and her husband. They enlarged and modernized one of the cottages at the back of the property, close to the original house, where June still lives.

As tourists began to look for other types of accommodation, business slowed down. Lots were sold off the original property. In the summer of 1997 June held a grand, well-attended auction, selling all the old furniture and artifacts that belonged to the resort. An era has ended at Allisons Point.

Mounted on the wall in the living room was a moose head, known as Bruce the Moose, reported to have been shot by Abe McCann. The two-storey cottage of white clapboard was very simple, with a living room and kitchen on the main floor and four small bedrooms upstairs. There was a porch across the lakeside. Above it was a peaked gable in the roof. At one time servant quarters were added to the rear of the building.

Abe McCann also had a fishing and hunting camp on Oxtongue Lake, as well as boat business in Huntsville for twenty-six years. When he died in 1939, he left the property to his wife, Elizabeth. Five years later she sold the twelve-acre property on Fairy Lake to John Bradley Allison and his wife, Grace. Grace Allison was from the Hibberd family, early Huntsville settlers in the area of Highway 11 B North. (They called their farm Spruce Glen, after which the public school is named).

John and Grace met while working at Bigwin Inn and were married in 1922. They moved to Detroit for many years, but returned to Huntsville after World War II. John built the seven new cottages on the

FAIRYPORT
TIMBER BAY ROAD, FAIRY LAKE, HUNTSVILLE
C. 1890

IN 1876 FREDERICK MAY and his wife, Elizabeth Carter, homesteaded with their five children on the south shore of Fairy Lake. The 275 acres granted under the Ontario Free Grant and Homestead Act of 1868 were Lot 20, Concession 13 and 14, and Lot 21, Concession 13 and 14, in Brunel Township.

This beautiful land became home to six more children before the Mays sold in 1890 to John L. Baker, a son-in-law of the neighbouring Holinsheads. The Fairyport name was already established and a summer tourist home was flourishing. When John Baker's wife died in 1898, he sold Fairyport to Sarah and Henry Lye, who in turn sold to Helen Brooks Smith in 1908. Five or so acres of the westernmost lake frontage was purchased by Frank Stewart Mearns in 1904 and 1906. This site, known as Methven, remains with his heirs.

By early in the century, a three-storey hotel and eleven dwellings were on the property; five were two-storey cottages. An article in the Huntsville *Forester* of July 26, 1906, notes that Mr. T.H. Hungerford managed the summer resort, which offered croquet, row boats and canoes, excellent spring water and a piano for entertainment. The rate was seven dollars per week, with special terms for families. There were a number of owners at Fairyport after 1908, some with their own cottages on the waterfront. Between 1913 and 1916, Edwin John Ecclestone acquired all of the original land grant, except Methven.

Jack Ecclestone and his wife, Emma Llwyd, grew up in Huntsville and were married in All Saints Church in 1898. They moved with their infant daughter, Elaine, to Toronto where their son; Llwyd, was born in 1900. London, Ontario, was home until about 1917 when the family became year-round residents at Fairyport. In the fall of 1929 the hotel burned to the ground. Ann Brooks recalls that her late husband, Ross, told her that he and another man carried the piano out of the burning build-

ing. The piano was first owned by Letitia Ecclestone, Jack's only sister, and it survives in the McCaskill cottage, its mellow tone intact.

Ross and Ann spent many years caring for Fairyport. Most of the buildings and much of the furniture were his handiwork. The hotel was replaced in 1930 with an inn, four cabins and a home for the Ecclestones. The old farmhouse was expanded to accommodate a dozen guests, invariably teachers and librarians from Toronto.

After the Jack's death in 1932, Emma continued to manage Fairyport in the summer months. Although the rest of the year was spent with her daughter's family in Toronto and travelling, she loved her winter visits to her home in the north. Family and friends joined her on ski outings to Haverland and Puck's Lodge, and time spent at Limberlost was always a highlight.

Emma Ecclestone shone in her role as innkeeper. The little resort community looked forward each July and August to masquerades, Sunday walks, land and water sports days, bonfires on the beach, musicals, sing-alongs and all the popular card games. Boys and girls had their tree houses in the pine woods from which to make forays and great tall cornfields

Left: Cutting ice at Fairyport, 1930s. Right: Fairyport Inn and cottages, 1928.

142

in which to play hide-and-seek. Farmer Brown up the land let everyone jump in his hayloft and try to milk his patient cows. Somehow, everyone thrived on his unpasteurized milk!

By 1939 there were eighteen buildings on the site, as well as garages and workshops. In the woods was the Honeymoon Bungalow, a wee fairy-tale cottage. The Fairyport telephone company had been sold to Bell and water was piped in to the inn and many of the cottages. In those days guests always dressed "properly." On cold August days they bathed before dinner in the tub room attached to the outside of the inn. Since it was unheated, woolen clothing was quickly donned.

During the war years six British families from Hong Kong and Shanghai found summertime refuge at Fairyport. Everyone shared their concern for husbands and fathers interned in Japanese prisoner-of-war camps and their relief when the war was over. This international flavour, added to the mix of Canadian and American families, resulted in exciting vacations and lifelong friendships.

The inn was the hub of activity and the dining room the centre of conviviality. Forty guests could be seated at each meal. However, the number would swell to seventy-five for the Sunday midday meal and a second sitting would be required. All the cottagers and many townsfolk would come to savour the roast chicken and fresh vegetables from Holinshead's Farm. The hand-cranked ice cream was twice relished by those who were allowed to help turn the mixer. It was exciting, too, to be big enough to swing the mallet against the old circular saw blade hung on a post. The sound could be heard halfway to Huntsville! The half-hour between gongs was just enough time to run up the hill from the beach to change for lunch. Two icehouses held the summer supply of ice — lovely places to steal into on a hot summer day. The root cellar by the kitchen door was another fine cooling-off spot and no one minded being sent down to fetch a sack of potatoes.

Bessie Gurnon was the head cook at Fairyport for twenty-five years. After her death in 1950 and Emma Ecclestone's retirement the resort was renamed Timber Bay. Meals were no longer served, the cabins were removed and the trees began to reclaim the land.

Llwyd Ecclestone had inherited the property from his father and in 1962 gave lakefront lots to his nephew, John MacKay, and his niece, Joy McCaskill. Her son Kip and his wife, Sheila, own and live on part of this parcel and continue the old traditions of kitchen gardening, maple syrup making and wood lot management. John MacKay and his three children now own Timber Bay. Its six buildings, along with the MacKay and McCaskill cottages and Methven, grace a tranquil bay of Fairy Lake. The bustling resort of old has become a quiet retreat.

METHVEN VILLA
360 TIMBER BAY ROAD, FAIRY LAKE, HUNTSVILLE
C. 1906

FRANK STEWART MEARNS and his wife, Mima Angus, vacationed in the summers from 1903 to 1905 at Frogmore Cottage at Fairyport Resort on the south shore of Fairy Lake. In 1904 and 1906 he purchased two parcels of land at the west end of the resort from the owner, Sarah Francis Lye. This property was part of Lot 20, Concession 13 and 14, Brunel Township. A boathouse and dock were built in 1905 and a commodious cottage in 1906. The boathouse has remained in continuous use; however, the cottage burned to the ground in 1931 and was replaced the same year. The lumber for the cottage was milled by Mr. Cottrill at the locks and barged to the site.

The two-storey cottage features a wide front verandah; one end is screened and has always been known as The Monkey Coop. Frank Mearns cut a Dutch door between it and the dining room for easy access. The living room and dining room run the fifty-foot length of the cottage. The beautiful stone fireplace at one end was built by James McFarland, who fashioned the fireplaces for Bigwin Inn. At the dining room end, *National Geographics* dating back to 1912 line the shelves between the open studs. Mellow wood lines the walls from floor to ceiling. The family cherishes many of the original furnishings, including the piano bought by Frank Mearns in Toronto in 1899. It has pride of place and is still often played.

Methven, 360 Timber Bay Road, Fairy Lake.

A bedroom, the stairway and the kitchen are along the back of the cottage. An old-fashioned pantry stores crockery and foodstuffs. Down by the creek, a strong box set in a spring held butter and milk over the years. The spring provided excellent water, as does the present well.

There are five bedrooms upstairs; a bathroom was installed after electrification in the late 1960s. The well-maintained "Jinx" up the hill is still everybody's friend when the power goes off. With a lovely view out over Fairy Lake framed by Antler Island and the Twin Sisters, Methven is the ideal Muskoka cottage.

The name Methven derives from castle Methven near Perth in Scotland where Mima Mearn's grandfather, John James Angus, was head groundskeeper. Frank Mearns, a prominent Toronto barrister, had three children: Jean, Marjorie and Angus. Jean and Marjorie inherited Methven

in 1931. Now Barbara Firth Brown and William C. Firth, the children of Jean (who married Lorne M. Firth) continue to maintain and enjoy their historic summer home with their children and grandchildren.

GRANDVIEW INN AND CABINS
HIGHWAY 60, HUNTSVILLE
C. 1911

IN 1879, WHEN JOHN COOKSON received his Crown Grant for Lot 26, Chaffey Township on Fairy Lake, he was only nineteen years old. He had been an apprentice ironmonger in England, but decided opportunities were better in the New World. Four years later he married Minnie Pleace, who also came to Huntsville from England. She and her brother John were Barnardo children. Minnie was not too happy with her original placement and moved in with the Froats family who lived on the East Road, as Highway 60 was then called. It was there that she met her neighbour, John Cookson. Minnie and John had seven children: Nellie in 1884, Rose in 1886; Charlie in 1888, Leonard in 1892, Clara in 1894, Violet in 1896 and Archie in 1897. Later on they took into their family well-known local author Joe Cookson. He was a young child at the time.

John farmed the land and built a large farmhouse and barn near the road. He also built a stone fence facing the road, which was dismantled when Highway 60 was constructed in the 1940s.

Minnie Cookson was ambitious. She talked John into giving her five acres of his land along the lakefront to build an inn, to be called Grandview Inn and Cabins. In 1910 Minnie began her twenty-eight-room hotel — a three-storey wooden structure with a long, wide verandah facing the waterfront. The family moved into the living quarters above the big kitchen in the rear. The venture was a big success. Minnie was a wonderful cook and became famous for her raspberry pies. In her advertisements she added, "mother does the cooking." Originally the patrons came by boat, as Grandview had a dock for the steamers on the lake. Guests — often mothers with their children, while fathers worked

Rose, Minnie's second-oldest daughter, a teacher in Cobalt, returned to run Grandview. She continued many of her mother's traditions. It was Rose who coined the slogan "The Inn with the Million Dollar View."

Rose became a very colourful character. She had a very strong allegiance to

in the city — usually stayed two weeks. The rates were seven dollars a week for adults, four for children.

In his book *Tattle Tales of Muskoka* Joe Cookson describes the guest-rooms at the inn. Each bedroom was furnished with a white iron double bed, a dresser and washstand. On each washstand stood a large porcelain jug and basin, while hidden in its cupboard was the chamber pot.

It was young Joe's job to help haul the wash water from Fairy Lake. Horses were used to draw two barrels on a stone boat. All the family helped — the boys on the farm, and the girls in the inn.

John Cookson died in 1917, but Minnie carried on for twenty years until her death in 1937. The flag at Grandview flew at half-mast and her casket was draped with a Union Jack. At her funeral, her eight children were the pallbearers and her favourite hymns, "Shall We Gather at the River" and "Safe in the Arms of Jesus," were sung at her funeral. Her obituary states that she had many friends locally and across Canada and from the United States, guests who had enjoyed her hospitality at the inn.

things British and many of the cabins that were eventually built had British names such as Sir Winston Churchill and Monty. When Queen Elizabeth and King George were in Sudbury in 1939, Rose was there calling out "Queenie! Queenie!" as the procession passed. Local residents remember her for the many petticoats she wore, the folded bedspreads she used on the chairs and the layers of tablecloths she put on the tables in the dining room.

At the front entrance, off the lovely verandah, was a glass case, where the registration books were kept and stamps, candy bars and cigarettes were sold. Rose kept the money in a large mailbag beside the case. In fact, there is a story that when she went to Eaton's in Toronto to buy mattresses for the inn she had the cash with her in the mailbag. Rose introduced a five-cent slot machine to Grandview. There was a player piano for the enjoyment of the guests and, of course, there were all the usual resort and farm activities. Besides the farm animals, there were live peacocks, which were a big attraction.

Rose Cookson died in 1970. The inn hadn't been too active in her later years. Judy and Bruce Craik from Dundas, Ontario, bought the property that year. It consisted of sixty acres on the lake and forty across Highway 60. There were twenty-six buildings on the property — the inn and many cabins, two barns, an icehouse, creamery, woodshed, dance hall and boathouse. At the highway entrance there was another barn and tractor shed, and toward the bay stood a piggery.

The Craik family began extensive renovations over the next two years, changing the name to Grandview Farm. The original three-storey inn was converted to two storeys using the original foundation. The famous porch was removed and the building restructured and stuccoed. The original parlour and dining room were retained as were the front hall and staircase. A new fireplace was built in the parlour and a large mirror placed in front of the one in the dining room. Originally there were wall murals in both these rooms — "Fairy Lake by Day" in the one and "Fairy Lake by Night" in the other. The kitchen, which still had the original scullery, iceboxes and stove, was enlarged and modernized. The back stairs, which originally went up to the family quarters, were rebuilt and several bedrooms were made on the second floor.

The boathouse was converted into the present lakeside restaurant, and the beach and waterfront docks were refurbished. The barn near the inn was completely remodelled to make a bar, dining room, gift shops and offices. A new motel-type unit called Tree Tops was built to attract guests as well as business conferences and tennis courts were added. The barn at the roadside became a sales office. The Craiks had several horses as well as goats.

In 1987, after Grandview had been transformed into a sophisticated resort, the Craik family sold it to Bruce Evans of Bracebridge. He and his family came from Toronto and had bought Fowler Construction of Bracebridge in 1971. Bruce had spent the Depression years at Beatrice in Muskoka, where his parents had farmed.

Today the Cookson farm has been completely transformed. Beautiful condos, the Muskoka Room, an indoor sports centre, golf course and hiking and skiing trails have been added. A naturalist is on staff to teach city visitors more about nature in this very beautiful setting.

Haverland Resort. The Inn with farmhouse behind, c. 1925.

HAVERLAND RESORT, C. 1904
SWALLOWDALE CAMP, C. 1944
SWALLOWDALE ROAD, FAIRY LAKE, HUNTSVILLE

ETHELRED ROE, A HAT MAKER, emigrated from England as a young man and located on Lot 23, Concession 14, in Brunel Township, on the shore of Fairy Lake. George and Charlotte Roe followed their son shortly after and settled on a neighbouring lot.

In 1878 Ethelred's family constructed a home from materials readily available. The foundation consisted of flat stones, piled on top of the twelve-by-twelve pine beams that were used as footings. Pine clapboard was used to face the outer walls. Although darkened by age, the original two-inch tongue-and-groove pine siding still lines the inside walls of the farm kitchen. When some repair work to this house was required in 1978, the foundation was inspected and found to be as solid as it had been a hundred years earlier. The pine footings showed no sign of rot and the

146

piles of flat stones that formed the foundations were still in straight rows.

Anyone who has ever boated on Fairy Lake is familiar with the three-storey white house that sits on a hill on the southeast shore about half a mile west of the mouth of the canal. It was built in 1904 to accommodate summer guests. Ethelred called his resort Haverland, after a variety of strawberries. Haverland had fifteen guestrooms, allowing the resort to accommodate forty guests; rates were six to eight dollars per week.

The building sits on a stone foundation and the exterior walls are faced with pine clapboard siding. The steep pitch of the roof ensures that winter snow removal is never required. As you enter the building, the eye-catching feature is the beautiful wood on the floor and stair treads throughout. Also noticeable are the room numbers still inked on the doors.

The first floor had five bedrooms and a lounge, where the brick fireplace with its stone hearth enabled guests to enjoy a cozy atmosphere on many a cool evening. This lounge opened on to the covered verandahs on two sides of the building and provided a view of the lake and of the lawn bowling area alongside. The tennis court was only a little farther away. There were eight more bedrooms on the second floor. A door at the lake end provided access to the upper level covered balcony. The third floor had four rooms, accessed by a stairway so narrow you had to duck your head to round a corner. There were two dormer rooms, each just large enough for a three-quarter bed, and two larger rooms, one at each end.

Each room was furnished with a washstand, complete with basin, pitcher and chamber pot. Duties of the Roe girls (daughters and later the granddaughters) included delivering water to each room every morning.

Electricity was installed about 1935 but indoor plumbing was available long before that. In the enclosed porch at the end of the building, which faces the lilacs, there were separate men's and ladies' rooms with flush toilets and a separate room with a bathtub. Under the stairs on each of the first and second floors there was a sink. Wash water for the rooms could be obtained and emptied in these little service areas. Cleaning the cesspool was always a fall chore after the guests were gone — not a favourite job!

Haverland Resort. Original farmhouse and Dick Roe's house, 1943.

A gasoline engine pumped water from the lake to the shed behind the kitchen, where the water was heated in boiler tubs on the stove. This engine also pumped enough water for the laundry, which was washed by hand. Linens were immersed in a tub that had a curved washboard that moved back and forth and then wrung with a hand-operated wringer. A mangle was used to press the linens. In later years, the laundry was put on the steamboat and taken to the Bigwin laundry in Huntsville. A hand pump at the well just outside the cooking area supplied drinking water.

Some guests were accommodated in the main farmhouse. Tents accommodated staff and non-paying guests; the Roes acquired a lot of relatives!

Dick's House, the third-largest building on the property, was erected in 1921 for Ethelred's son Richard and his family. The two-storey building with its bay windows and covered verandah also had clapboard pine on its exterior. The building was razed in 1975.

Richard looked after the farming end of things and, if there wasn't extra help, he cut the grass, pumped the water and wheeled the guests' luggage to and from the dock. Grandfather tended the garden.

Haverland was known in the area for its vegetable garden. The Roes started seeds indoors, then moved the young plants to a cold frame before planting them in the large vegetable garden. Haverland gardens supplied the resort's needs and the excess was sold to Fairy Lake cottagers and often Boyd's Store in Huntsville. Neighbouring cottagers often made an outing of a rowboat trip to Haverland to purchase vegetables.

Haverland operated until the late 1930s. The number of guests had dwindled during the Depression and the resort closed after the outbreak of World War II.

Swallowdale Camp opened at Haverland in 1944. Mildred Targett and Simone Wallbank operated Waycroft, a boarding school in York Mills, Toronto, for children between the ages of three and fourteen. During the 1940s some of the boarders were wartime evacuees; others had fathers serving overseas and mothers working nights and long hours on the homefront in the war effort, and the school was asked to keep the children year round. Two summers were spent at the school in Hogg's Hollow, but conditions were far from ideal. For two seasons, a double cottage between Baysville and Bigwin Island on Lake of Bays was rented for a campsite. Haverland was purchased after the 1943 season. Mildred, or MT as she was affectionately called, passed away in 1960 and Swallowdale has remained in the Wallbank family ever since.

The name Swallowdale was taken from the series of children's books written by Arthur Ransome. These adventure stories, set in England's Lake District, were very popular with the Waycroft children. When the children arrived and saw the swallows that were always around, there was no question about what name the new camp would have.

In 1944 the old Roe homestead was extended to provide a dining room for Swallowdale campers. The old resort, now called The Big House, is used primarily as a staff house and campers live in cabins built into the well-treed hillside.

The highlight of the summer in the early years was the boat excursion. Early one day each summer, campers rode on the *Algonquin* to North Portage, then boarded the train to Lake of Bays, then travelled to Bigwin Island on the *Iroquois*. The children stayed on the island while the boat continued on its itinerary to Baysville and back. From the fire tower, the boat could be seen making its way toward the island on its homeward journey. This was the signal to return to the dock and travel the route in reverse, tired but happy.

Campers who lived in Toronto travelled to Huntsville by train until about 1970. Until it went out of service, the *Algonquin* brought the children from the railway station to camp. For the next few years a bus transported the children from the station. At first only the Lower Swallowdale Road (now called Roe Road) was open; the bus had to go up the steep hill backward to allow the gas to feed the engine and campers had to get off the bus and walk across the canal bridge.

One camper recently recalled the boat making an unscheduled stop once in the 1940s. There was great concern because the Union Jack could be seen from the lake flying upside down. All were relieved to learn that the counsellor responsible for raising the flag had made a mistake and was not signalling distress.

One pine tree that was not harvested in the 1800s is reported to be the largest tree in Muskoka. The trunk measures more than six feet in diameter and from the lake its top can be seen towering over the surrounding pines.

Ethelred's granddaughter and her husband still live on part of the original property overlooking Fairy Lake.

HEOROT COTTAGE
FAIRY LAKE
C. 1939

THIS SUMMER HOME WAS BUILT IN 1939 for Walker and Francis Lautz, a retired couple from Buffalo, New York. Walker first came to Huntsville when he was nineteen and returned many times to the area to camp. In 1938 he purchased the lakefront property that was part of the Skelding farm. The cottage, situated on a point on the north shore of Fairy Lake, has excellent views of the lake from the large screened porch.

It was called Heorot after a dwelling so named in the old English epic poem "Beowulf."

The builder, Erik Skat Petersen, was known in the area for his unusual architectural embellishments. Heorot has squirrels on the roof and dragon's heads at the gable ends. Inside he built a large trestle table with benches, which are there to stay because of their size and weight.

The Lautzes enjoyed their retirement years at Heorot. Walker was an avid fisherman and Frances loved to paint in oils. Grandchildren visited, their annual growth recorded in pencil on the tool-shed door. They made root beer in a special crock with extract obtained from Braund's drugstore.

Cottagers were well served in those days. Milk was delivered by Huntsville Dairy. Bakery products, too, were delivered, and Mr. Fowler supplied fresh eggs and produce.

Walker built several rock gardens with the help of his two sons. Many of the original plants have spread all over the point and, with the profusion of wild flowers, is a naturalist's delight.

Heorot Cottage.

When the elderly couple moved to Florida and found the annual trip to Huntsville difficult, it was time to sell the cottage. George M. Foster of Toronto bought it in 1961. George made some improvements including the addition of a deck on the west side. Because they liked the area and had made friends here, the Fosters decided to move to Huntsville when George retired in 1978. They bought a house in town and kept the cottage, which is still enjoyed by the family in the summer.

MCINTOSH-VINCENT COTTAGE
COOKSON BAY CRESCENT, FAIRY LAKE, HUNTSVILLE
C. 1934

HARRY JONES SOLD A WATERFRONT LOT from his farm property, part of Lot 27, Concession 1, Chaffey Township, to Alexander McIntosh and his wife in 1934. They proceeded to have Walter Knight build a two-storey log cottage with red trim on the point on the east side of Cookson Bay on Fairy Lake. Harry's son, Ken, recalls that they cut the logs for the cottage in minus sixty-degree Fahrenheit weather!

Alexander McIntosh was editor-in-chief of the *Globe and Mail* from 1936 to 1948 and was a distinguished journalist for more than forty years. He was born in Simcoe County but attended schools at Woodstock and Strathroy, where he formed a lifelong friendship with Sir Authur Currie, commander of the Canadian Corps in World War II. He obtained a teacher's certificate at seventeen and taught in a rural school in St. Mary's, Ontario. After attending Queen's University for a year, he went to fine arts college in Syracuse, New York, and joined the Syracuse *Post* as a reporter.

From then on, he was a newspaperman, except for the period from 1918 to 1928 when he was an industrial relations consultant. In 1910 Alexander left Syracuse and was appointed city editor of the *Globe*. He then progressed to assistant editor and in 1936 to editor-in-chief. He was a crusading editor who championed many causes, including penitentiary and mental hospital reform. Believing strongly in the importance of the

Left Above: McIntosh-Vincent Cottage, Fairy Lake.
Right: Patio at McIntosh Vincent cottage.

British connection to Canada, he also tried to stimulate immigration to western Canada from the British Isles.

He was in poor health for the last few years of his life and died in 1950. His wife, whom he met in St. Mary's, predeceased him by a year.

Bertha Vincent, who was living in Montreal at the time, rented the cottage for a couple of years before purchasing it in 1955. She embellished the site by having the beautiful stone patio and railing built along the lakefront. Bertha was a keen gardener and covered the patio with an abun-

dance of flowers, a very pretty sight for boaters passing by. Herb McKenny, a well-known local stonemason, who also constructed the stone foundation and chimney of the cottage, did the stone work for the patio.

Jack Vincent, a pediatrician from London, Ontario, and his wife bought the cottage from his mother. In 1987 the property was purchased by the third generation of the Vincent family, John and Susan and their young children. For nearly forty-five years members of the Vincent family have enjoyed the beauty of Fairy Lake in Huntsville.

150

CAMP ONAWAW, C. 1925–69
CAMP WABANAKI, 1969–
ASPDIN ROAD, LAKE VERNON, HUNTSVILLE

EDWARD AND SUSANNAH TURKINGTON started Camp Onawaw on part of Lot 32, Concession 2, Stisted Township, in 1925. Margaret Govan, who was a counsellor at the camp starting in 1927, wrote that Edward Turkington was a Presbyterian minister but had become a United church member and had retired from the active ministry. Susannah had worked at the YMCA as a girl's work secretary and had connections with Western University before her marriage. Both Edward and Susannah had been so interested in Glen

Camp Onawaw, later. Camp Wabanaki, Lake Vernon.

Bernard Camp, run by Susannah's niece Mary Edgar in Sundridge, that they thought it would be a wonderful opportunity to work in a similar camp. After searching for many years, they located a cottage and five acres of land on the south shore of Lake Vernon. The spot seemed ideal for a camp and so Camp Onawaw, which means spirit of the dawn, was begun.

In 1927, Margaret Govan reported, there were eleven cabins. "I found myself in a wooden cabin with a room of my own, almost, for the partition only went up to the slope of the roof." There were four girls, aged fifteen and sixteen, in the cabin and it contained "metal cots, an orange crate for each girl and a basin and bowl on a corner shelf. The cabin had a solid back and the rest was only wooden for about two feet. It was well screened and had a screen door for the campers and one for me…. We all brought our own blankets and sheets and pillows."

The lodge was perched on the highest point of the area. It had been the Turkingtons' cottage and had been built by two sons of the previous owner. It consisted of a living room, kitchen, two bedrooms and a large room upstairs, and a large verandah to the west, north and east sides. The Turkingtons removed the partitions, making one large room on the ground floor, and built a kitchen and utility room behind. The east and west verandahs were now a dining room, served through windows from the kitchen.

"It was an attractive and natural looking building," writes Margaret. "The eating verandahs had heavy curtains to give protection from wind and wet. The dishes were a conglomeration of various patterns but quite ample for our needs. There was a dock and a boathouse and a small swimming area with a boardwalk around three sides where non-swimmers would be taught." On the north side of the point, the water was fourteen feet deep and there was a diving board, as well as cedar canoes and a couple of rowboats. The camp also had a clay tennis court and a games field, and there was a stable — "decidedly a summer stable" — in the hollow behind the camp. There was a utility room behind the kitchen, a storage house, icehouse for the ice that was cut during the winter, a woodshed, a room for trip equipment and a small shelter with running water — and privies around the camp. Candles lighted the cabins; the lodge had a Coleman lamp and a telephone. "There was an elderly and uncertain car for emergencies. There was the remains of a corduroy road which lumbermen had left. The hired man had a motor boat which he took to town daily for mail, groceries, etc."

A small motor boat took the girls and counsellors from the Huntsville train station to camp.

Margaret returned to the camp again in 1930 and was head counsellor for nine years. A great deal happened in that period, she wrote. "In many ways it was not easy because the Depression was upon us and we were all very much aware of it. It certainly did not allow us the equipment which most of us would have liked to have." However, Susannah Turkington must have managed reasonably well for there were many additions. She bought the acreage behind the camp — a steep and rocky piece of land that was about to be cleared of timber — and an eighteen-acre island from the same farmer. She added a glassed-in dining room to the east of the lodge, with a storage room above it. It had square tables, painted an attractive green, with a camp scene in black at each corner and finished with varnish. Each table seated eight people. The opposite end of the verandah was also glassed in and served as a library. She put a roof shelter up for the canoes and decked the whole area. A small swimming area for junior campers was located at the point. She had a beautiful chapel with a great stone pulpit built on the water's edge, with the hill used for its seating. It was one of the loveliest spots in the camp.

Delco power was installed in the main building. It was "an asset but it didn't always work. There was a better motor boat and the car had been given up altogether. It was now possible to get a taxi in an emergency. We all washed in the lake, did our teeth in the lake, washed hair and did some of our personal laundry in the lake. It was pure water so nobody worried"

Susannah's health deteriorated over the years until, by 1937, she was no longer able to carry on and asked Margaret Govan to become director. Margaret bought the camp in the fall of that year.

The camp ran through the war years, and sometime after 1945 Margaret writes that she had hydro installed, and "flood lights at the water's edge and at the playing field. The cook decided she would like an electric stove. Gradually we added better kitchen equipment." Margaret installed a couple of prefabricated cabins and a sewage lagoon for the effluent. She also built a recreation hall, "a marvelous building, designed by a man who knew what he wanted, and how to produce it. We called it The Ark since the two long outer walls slanted outward. I don't know what it was about that building but it gave a free and easy feeling to everybody, and a happiness about indoor games. I think the sloping sides made it possible to use uprights at the sides, and thus not interfere with game space." There was a stage at one end, and two dressing rooms, one with a toilet. Benches of varying heights were installed so that the lack of slope did not prevent anyone from enjoying operettas, Sunday service on wet days and skit nights.

Margaret changed the icehouse to a walk-in refrigerator. She made a small dock for the wooden sailboats beside the island, on the lake side of the bridge, and bought a tiny, one-acre island for an over-night camping spot and installed a toilet and small dock.

The lodge was becoming overcrowded and had structural problems caused by shifting during winter frost. Margaret decided to construct a new main building, at the exterior of the property so that deliveries could be made easily. It would mean moving the stable, which she "thought would be a good idea anyway because of flies." The architect wanted to make it a split-level building, which would reduce heat for the kitchen staff, with a dumbwaiter up to the dining room on the second floor. (The dumbwaiter would have cost $2,200, so someone suggested using an electric hoist, which they did.)

It was a beautiful building — "costly too — with very few faults." The new stable was built out of "lodge wood" and as they had a number of windows left over from the lodge, they built a little museum for their nature library. "We were going to use one end of the new building for crafts with tables outside. This didn't work. We kept our supplies there but built a crafts house and an open air shelter down near the water. Eventually I decided to move up to the cabin, which had been serving as Infirmary since it had now become the centre of camp. I built a new infirmary with two good rooms for patients, and a toilet room with a basin and a wash tub with running water to serve as a foot bath — since most cuts seemed to be in the feet."

She decided to create a "magical ambience" at the nondenominational camp (which never grew beyond 115 campers). Margaret became known as Robin and her counsellors were her Merrie Men with each choosing a male pseudonym.

At a 1994 reunion campers held at Camp Wabanaki, a longtime camper and counsellor, Huntsville resident Martha (Briggs) Watson, recalls: "The magic manifested itself once a week with a special gathering on a nearby island. We walked over the bridge to the island and gathered around a huge fire in an area known as Shining Glen. The fire was lit with great reverence by one member during a small ceremony, the atmosphere was almost spiritual, and then we would sing songs and Robin would tell her stories, one usually a Robin Hood legend, another about camp or a fictional fun story….Robin was very special to us, she truly believed in each of us as individuals and we have never forgotten that."

Margaret Govan operated the camp through the summer of 1969 when, at the age of sixty-six, she sold it to the Kitchener-Waterloo YMCA with the stipulation that it would always remain a camp for children.

The new owners changed the name to Camp Wabanaki and it can house over two hundred campers. Many campers share wonderful memories of Lake Vernon.

LAKE VERNON LODGE
RAVENSCLIFFE ROAD, LAKE VERNON, HUNTSVILLE
C. 1927

IN 1927 ROBERT KENT bought part of Lot 1, Concession 6, Chaffey Township, from James Blackley. There was a building on the property, which the Kents called Lake Vernon Lodge. Their daughter, Doris Troth, wrote in 1992 that they bought the lodge in 1925 or 1926. Her dad and brother lived there for two years fixing it up "before we opened the lodge. We did not have electricity or plumbing. We used well and lake water. I remember we advertised spring-filled mattresses on all beds. Each bedroom had a bowl and jug and slop pail. People took soap to the beach." The lodge had seven small bedrooms and one double one upstairs; four bedrooms, living room, dining room, kitchen and pantry downstairs. Later Robert Kent took one bedroom off downstairs to enlarge the living room. He built a new stone fireplace and put bark around the bottom of the walls in the front and dining rooms. The lodge could accommodate

Lake Vernon Lodge, Ravenscliffe Road.

153

thirty to thirty-five guests. The kids slept on cots. The rates went up to fifteen dollars a week.

The lodge was open mostly in July and August, with the odd person coming in September, and people came from Detroit, Buffalo, Niagara and Toronto, mostly by car but some by train. The Kents did not have a car so they used the launch to go to Huntsville, seven miles away. The return ride was twenty-five cents. Doris writes: "Mother cooked all the meals and was up at 4:00 A.M. some mornings baking. You see, we had wood stoves — fresh biscuits and fruit pies and cakes every day. The menu was plain but very good (no fast foods)." Breakfast was a piece of fruit, cereal, bacon and eggs or eggs and toast; dinner was roasts, steaks or pork chops, potatoes, gravy, vegetables and fresh pie; and supper was usually cold salads, meats or fresh fish and chips, fruits and cakes. "Mother seemed to know the special dressing for each meat or fowl and sauces…There was always seconds. (Supper was held for the fishermen till after dark.) Always a catch in those days (even cat fish!)."

The Kents also built cottages on their property for summer tourists. They sold their property in 1948 to Sydney Bernard Voyce and his wife, Ivy Doris. In 1958 the Voyces sold the property to Vincent Barton and his wife, Hazel Rita.

In 1966 it was sold again, to Helen and John Podkowa, and in 1989 it passed into the hands of Helen's daughter, Hanna Urszula Zmuda, who is the present owner. In 1992 there were four cottages on the property. One, a log cottage, where the owners spent the winters, was built in the 1930s. The other three cottages were built in the 1940s and were used as guest cottages. There was an icehouse and water tower on the property. The water tower is still standing but only the foundation of the icehouse exists. There is still a large formal dining room. Although the building has had some changes, the dining room and living room still are original. The furniture, oil lamps, etc. are still in the lodge. In 1993 extensive renovations were done on the interior and vinyl siding was applied to the exterior of the house. However, it is enjoyed by all who visit this site on lovely Lake Vernon."

GANDIER COTTAGE
SKYHILLS ROAD, LAKE VERNON, HUNTSVILLE
C. 1923

IN 1916 REVEREND ALFRED GANDIER purchased land in Concession 3, Lot 4, Chaffey Township, on the shore of Lake Vernon, from William and Sarah Hopkins. Seven years later the Gandiers proceeded to build a large cottage overlooking the lake. The builder was Oliver May of Ravenscliffe. The area was known as Mount Vernon, due to the height of land behind the cottage.

The cottage is a large two-storey clapboard building with a semi-enclosed porch on the front and side of the main floor. On the side section is a delightful rope swing. The cottage has large paned windows and an attractive double front door. Inside, the interior walls are panelled, as are the doors. The living room has an imposing stone fireplace made by James McFarland, a well-known Huntsville stonemason. Above the mantel is an interesting square design of stone. There is also a wood stove in the living room.

The kitchen, with an attractive welcome sign above the door, has a propane stove. Coal oil lamps are used. There is a forty-gallon reservoir for plumbing on the upper floor, where there are four bedrooms. One-third of this floor is a large sitting room overlooking the lake.

Dr. Alfred Gandier's father was a minister; his sister was the wife of Sir Robert Falconer, who had a cottage nearby. Alfred attended Queen's University, where he was a gold medallist in philosophy, English and history. He was a leader for over half a century in the Presbyterian and United churches as principal of Knox College and later Emmanual Theological College in Toronto. When he died in 1932, the Toronto conference of the United church was in session, and all members stood for several minutes of silent prayer.

In 1952, the Gandier family left the cottage and property to the United Church of Canada for missionaries and ministers to use as a summer retreat. One such missionary from Japan, the Reverend Frank Carey, and his wife and six children visited the cottage in 1980. His memories

Gandier Cottage, Skyhill Road, Lake Vernon.

were of happy times. He writes, "We decided to have a family reunion and the cottage was available. As it turned out, the cottage was ideally suited and ideally located for such an occassion. There was plenty of bed space for several families, with spillover space for bedrolls on the floor! And the large living room was ideal for evenings of singing together. Outside, the children found lots of room to roam and play. The neighbouring meadow abounded in wild strawberries which some of the kids got a kick out of picking. Canoeing and swimming provided another outlet for the energetic ones, while the less energetic could sit on the rocks and watch. One of the odd memories that we have of the cottage was of the old, wooden, hand-operated washing machine that stood on the verandah. It surely must have dated back to the time when the cottage was acquired! Fortunately, our washing did not depend on it. Another memory, less pleasant, was of the mosquitoes. They seemed to have the ability to bite right through one's jeans! Fortunately, this minus was far outweighed by the real pluses of the vacation, so that the memory of that

reunion and of the cottage where it took place is one that we all recall with pleasure."

Another missionary who enjoyed the cottage at Mount Vernon was Reverend Paul Webb and family, who was serving in Hong Kong. The United church personnel continued to use the property until 1985, when it was rented to the Moxley family.

Mr. and Mrs. Peter McBirnie from Thorndale, Ontario, now own the cottage and seventy-two of the surrounding acres. A new road has been built into the property and this beautiful site overlooking Lake Vernon is now being subdivided.

MAPLEWOOD
SKYHILLS ROAD, LAKE VERNON, HUNTSVILLE
C. 1916

MAPLEWOOD, the cottage of Sir Robert and Lady Falconer on the shores of Lake Vernon was built in 1916. The Falconers discovered the property while visiting Lady Falconer's brother, Reverend Alfred Gandier, who owned Part Lot 3, Concession 4, Chaffey Township.

After purchasing the lakefront property, the Falconers proceeded to have their large three-storey cottage built. Oliver May of Ravenscliffe was the builder, and his son, Frank, and family looked after the property over the years — doing repairs and the yearly opening and closing of the cottage. The building materials for the cottage came by both boat and wagon from Huntsville.

The exterior of the cottage was cove siding, which has since been covered with vinyl. There was a large enclosed, screened verandah on the second floor, as well as an open porch on the main floor. There were french doors at the front and the windows were paned. Six bedrooms (one for the maid) in the cottage accommodated all the visitors that the Falconer family entertained. The interior walls were v-joint partitions of dressed lumber. The original kitchen has been replaced and the former dining room is now the kitchen. Prior to the installation of hydro in 1939, a Delco plant provided power. The original boathouse was replaced in 1935.

Robert Falconer was born in Charlottetown in 1867, but spent his youth in Trinidad, where his Presbyterian clergyman father was posted. He was educated at London and Edinburgh universities, concentrating on classics and philosophy, and pursued postgraduate work at Leipzig, Berlin and Marburg, Germany. In 1892 he was ordained a minister in the Presbyterian Church of Canada and took up a lectureship in New Testament Greek at Pine Hill College, Halifax, becoming a professor there in 1895. He was appointed principal in 1904.

Robert is remembered chiefly, however, for his twenty-five-year tenure as president of the University of Toronto, from 1907 to 1932. In 1906 a royal commission appointed to investigate all aspects of the university had found administrative chaos and low morale. It recommended a complete constitutional reorganization and implicitly a new president.

To the surprise of many, the forty-year-old Falconer was asked to replace James Loudon. Much of Falconer's time and energy for the next two decades was given to executing the recommendations of the 1906 commission. He inherited a collection of colleges; he left behind him an integrated university that led the country in industrial and scientific, as well as humanistic research.

An unemotional and cerebral scholar, Falconer was much in demand as a public speaker, particularly on the importance of maintaining the British imperial connection, the nurturing of "idealism in national character" (the title of his 1920 collection of wartime addresses) and the integrity and place of the humanities in an increasingly scientific and practical university environment.

Active in the Presbyterian church, Falconer sought to bring his denomination into union with Canada's Methodists and Congregationalists in the 1920s. Such was his reputation within the British Empire that in 1929 Edinburgh University broke with tradition to offer him its principalship, a position he declined.

He married on May 12, 1897, Sophie Gandier, daughter of Reverend J. Gandier of Newburgh, Ontario, and sister of Reverend Dr. Alfred

Maplewood, Sky Hills Road, Lake Vernon.

Gandier, principal of Knox College, Toronto, and later of Emmanual Theological College, Toronto.

After Dr. Falconer's death in 1943 at the age of seventy-six, the cottage passed to his son Gilbert Falconer. In 1930 a very formal wedding with three bridesmaids took place at the cottage when Gilbert married Dorothy Patrick. Their only child was Margaret Falconer (Allan).

In the November 19, 1932, edition of the *Toronto Star Weekly*, there is an article by Sir Robert telling of the joys of his granddaughter Margaret. "This summer when we were up in Muskoka, my tiny dark-eyed granddaughter, Margaret, aged three, used to come into my room and waken me every morning with, 'Please tell me a story, grandfather.' Then the day would begin with delight. I would tell her tales of my sea voyages and other travels. I hope some day she will enjoy these things as I have."

Margaret Allan relates that in its heyday, the cottage would be overflowing with visitors — the young men often slept in cots on the third floor, not by any means a cool spot during a heat wave. Sir Robert often

156

entertained English and European visitors — professors and government ministers, particularly from England. Professor E.G. Coulter, the greatest living mediaeval scholar of English history at the time, was in delicate health and must have added to his problems by falling all the way down the stairway into the living room, much to the consternation of the Falconer family. Sir Robert was always very proud to show lovely Lake Vernon to his foreign guests.

Another memory of Margaret Allan concerns Camp Tawingo canoe trips. Twice she remembers evening visits from distraught counsellors in search of help for ailing canoe trippers, once during a terrible storm. The counsellor followed the hydro lines to locate the cottage. Eventually "Gorgie" from Camp Tawingo arrived from the camp and carried a very ill camper up the very steep path with no assistance — a real feat in a bad storm.

Three generations of Falconers have loved the large family cottage on Lake Vernon for more than eighty years. At the time of writing, unfortunately it had just been sold.

THE MERRY MANSE
TYRER-KEEVIL HOUSE
ETWELL ROAD, LAKE VERNON, HUNTSVILLE
C. 1908

IN 1888 GEORGE WALLINGTON acquired Lot 26, Concession 5, and other adjacent lands in Stisted Township. He evidently built a house and barn on the part of the property across the creek from the present house. In 1908 he sold fifty acres of land to Alfred Henry Tyrer, who had a very interesting career.

In her book *Chronicles of Stisted Township*, published by the Herald-Gazette Press, Bracebridge, in 1976, Marjorie Demaine tells the story of the Tyrers' colourful life.

Alfred, who was born in England, came to Canada in 1885 at the age of fifteen. His parents, Mr. and Mrs. William Tyrer, a brother, William Jr., and a sister, Mrs. Garside, came a short time later. Their home was many miles from a school in the sparsely settled District of Muskoka, and Alfred gained most of his education from books brought from England by his father.

Alfred became a teacher at the age of eighteen and first taught school at Hoodstown, then a village on Lake Vernon. He later attended Model School (teachers' college) in Bracebridge. While he continued to teach, he studied for the ministry. On Christmas Day in 1894, Alfred married Mary Adelaide Golden, of Orangeville. They had one son, Elliott Golden, who in later years lived with his wife in Vancouver.

Alfred and Mary went to Oklahoma in the United States where he became a preacher, and later, in Nebraska, was ordained as an Anglican priest. After spending some time there they returned to Stisted Township. In 1908, they built their home on the west end of Lake Vernon at Etwell on Lot 26, Concession 5, Stisted Township. They also built a hall on the property where church services were conducted (since demolished). They lived there from about 1909 until 1926.

Reverend Tyrer established an interdenominational mission, which he maintained for fifteen years. Services were also conducted in the little

Tryer home and hall, Etwell Road, c. 1920.

157

Presbyterian church at Etwell, which had been moved sometime in the 1890s from Hoodstown. He was an Anglican clergyman for almost fifty years, and in later years, a specialist on social problems and marriage relationships. He was an ardent advocate of birth control and published several pamphlets advocating it. His book *Sex, Marriage and Birth Control* sold well and was praised by prominent clergymen for its outspoken attitude on sexual problems. He also wrote *And a New Earth*, which prophesizes a world revolution in which old systems based on motives of profit and inherited wealth are to pass, and in which many other reforms will be made possible.

Alfred was interested in photography and took a number of pictures of the homes and people in the local area. These he made into three-by-three-inch lantern slides. Using a battery-powered projector, these slides were shown in Stisted Township Hall about March 1915. Almost everyone in the neighbourhood came out to see himself or herself on the screen.

Another hobby was oil painting. He did a many paintings of Lake Vernon and surrounding area. One is in the museum at Pioneer Village in Huntsville.

A farewell party for Alfred and Mary was reported in the Huntsville *Forester* under "Ashworth News" on October, 1924: " Between 40 and 50 people assembled at the home of Mr. and Mrs. A. H. Tyrer on Vernon Lake, Wednesday evening last. The entrance of so many guests came as a great surprise to them, but they made everyone welcome and soon all were enjoying themselves with music and games, and looking through Mr. Tyrer's large telescope at the moon."

Guests were served tea, speeches were made and Alfred was presented with an engraved fountain pen and Mary, with an engraved gold pencil, both wrapped in a gift of bills from the congregation of Knox Church in Etwell. The guests left at midnight "after a most enjoyable evening."

The Tyrers took a church in Florida for the winter and made their home for the last few years in Toronto where they both died, she in 1929 and he in 1942. They are buried in Mount Pleasant Cemetery.

After Mary's death, the house and property was sold to Charles Paget of Huntsville. Unfortunately, he died that same year, and his widow sold

The Merry Manse, Tryer Keevil House, 1908.

it to Harold Gallaher, who was a businessman. He used the property as a hunting camp, until Dr. Ralph Keevil and his family from Toronto purchased the house and large acreage on the shores of Lake Vernon in 1966.

Mrs. Keevil's brother had originally come to the Lake Vernon area, and Dr. and Mrs. Keevil followed by renting cottages around the lake, including the property they purchased in 1966. Ralph, a radiologist, practised at Sunnybrook Hospital in Toronto, as well as at Oakville and Orangeville, but he spent the bulk of his career in Chatham, Ontario, from 1950 to 1977. He even did a short stint at the Huntsville Hospital in his later years.

The Keevils called the house on Lake Vernon the Merry Manse, a wonderful name. Mrs. Keevil states that when they purchased the house, there was no water or electricity. They used coal oil lamps and a propane fridge and stove. The floors were linoleum.

The Keevil family loved the place and acquired more property. They modernized the large three-storey clapboard house by installing electric-

158

ity and running water, and added a mudroom, washroom and large closets. The living room has an attractive brick fireplace with interesting brickwork above the mantel. The furnishings and property were all very attractive and well cared for.

Ralph Keevil died in 1985. Mrs. Keevil lives at Rowanwood Retirement Home in Huntsville. The Keevil family still uses the old substantial house beside Tryer Creek with its beautiful view of Lake Vernon.

TIPPER HOUSE
RAVENSCLIFFE POST OFFICE, GRAY'S STORE
1557 RAVENSCLIFFE ROAD, HUNTSVILLE
C. 1887

GEORGE TIPPER ARRIVED WITH HIS FAMILY from Kingsley, Staffordshire, England, in the spring of 1871. They settled in the area north of Lake Vernon known as Ravenscliffe.

The family brought with them building skills, particularly the building of homes using fieldstone. Near the corner of Ravenscliffe and Line Hill roads the family acquired land, Lot 5, Concession 6, Chaffey Township, from a man named Spencer Thomas Quaife. There they built the distinctive stone, one-and-a-half-storey home that was to become the Ravenscliffe post office, and in later years, Gray's Store.

George, John and Edmund Tipper were master builders in their homeland. Not only did they construct buildings, they also built furniture. The home was eventually occupied by Lydia Tipper, the first teacher at the Ravenscliffe School, which was situated next to St. John the Baptist Anglican Church (still standing today).

Although a teacher by training, Lydia became better known as the post mistress of the Ravenscliffe. She took over the position from a man named John Piper and held it for forty-five years until she passed away in December of 1931. Miss Tipper was never married and shared the home with her brother Edmund, once a reeve of Chaffey Township, for a number of years. John also lived at the home in his elder years.

Tipper House, Post Office, Gray's Store, 1557 Ravenscliffe Road.

During that time, the home also took in boarders, often teachers who worked across the road at the one-room school. One of them was a young teacher named Bertha Mawhiney who eventually married Order of Canada member, William Sinclair, of the Sinclair farm about three miles

159

toward town from the Tipper house. William also operated the Ravenscliffe Telephone Company and the Tipper house was the first on the road with telephone and hydro.

In February 1946 the house changed hands from a Fred Sanford to Howard Clinton Gray. Howard built a large porch on the front of the building and established a store. It was a popular stopping place for many years, particularly in the summer tourist season, until subsequent owner realtor Ross F. Davis closed it down, in the early 1970s. The building also stopped housing the post office in the mid-1960s.

The land around the Tipper house was known for its unique ability to grow fruit. As many as fifty apple trees once graced the property, as did pear and plum trees, quite unusual for this northern climate

In May 1977 the house was purchased by longtime, award-winning editor and columnist of the Huntsville *Forester* Ev Van Duuren (now in private business) and his wife Barbara, a registered nurse and diabetes educator in Huntsville. Although the fieldstone was lovely to look at, the Van Duurens decided to insulate and cover it, bending to the demands of modern energy conservation.

Ross Davis built a large addition on to the back of the house, which eliminated the summer kitchen. The interior still has some of the hardwood and ten-foot-high ceilings of the original construction.

WAB-NA-KEE
RAVENSCLIFFE ROAD, LAKE VERNON, HUNTSVILLE
C. 1926

IN 1918 FARMER ROBERT MAY of Ravenscliffe, bought Lot 33, Concession 7, Stisted Township, from Edward Malken, who had received it in 1882 under the Ontario Free Grants and Homestead Act of 1868. Eight years later Robert sold three acres on Lake Vernon to Norman Ross Telfer of Toronto.

When this piece of land was purchased, there was a log cabin and barn still standing on the property. The barn was torn down in 1926 and

Wab-na-Kee, Ravenscliffe Road, Lake Vernon.

the log cabin was used as a summer cottage. An icehouse that was on the property was moved and attached to the end of the cottage and made into a bedroom. The lean-to on the other end of the cottage that at one time had served as a blacksmith shop by Robert May was converted into the kitchen. When Ross Telfer bought the cabin, the walls were covered with many layers of newspaper. In 1932 the Telfers decided that they would like a fireplace in the building. Ollie May of Ravenscliffe examined the cabin and found that the logs were not sound, so in the spring of 1933 he tore down the log structure and built a frame cottage on the same site. Later in the same year Ollie May and Wilson Cairns built a stone fireplace in the cottage.

The cottage was twenty-eight by thirty-four feet. It had a cedar-shingled hipped roof. Cove siding was used on the outside walls. The inside partitions were of dressed, unpainted lumber. There were two bedrooms, a kitchen with ice box and coal oil stove, a dining room with french doors leading to a living room with stone fireplace and a verandah

160

across the front. Also on the property were an icehouse, outhouse and a pump house with a bark-covered roof. The pump produced cold spring water. The cottage was painted a cream colour with "cottage" green trim. It was called Wab-na-Kee, which means home of happiness. Electricity reached Ravenscliffe about 1945. As a result people stopped cutting ice in Lake Vernon so in 1948 the cottage was electrified. However the backhouse stayed until 1962 when a bathroom and pumping system were added. The verandah was never screened as Mr. Telfer liked the uninhibited view and the children enjoyed sitting on the wide rail.

When the three acres were purchased it was an open field and Bob May used to take the hay off. All the large evergreens on the property were planted by the Telfers. Ross was a commercial artist and was able to spend six weeks each summer in Muskoka and eventually eight weeks. When the family first started coming to the cottage from Toronto, they used to stop at Sparrow Lake overnight. They had a Model T Ford and the Big East River hill was quite a challenge. They pulled a trailer and one time they had to take the trailer off and pull it up separately. The Ravenscliffe hill could be especially daunting after a heavy rainfall.

Ross came to Muskoka to sketch and fish. During the World War II,

when gas for boats was unavailable, he made a sail for the cedar strip Peterborough boat to get around the lake. He knew where the bass were in the lake (under logs in the days before waterskis). He also knew there were lake trout as he had caught them in the spring when they were close to the surface. However, he didn't know where they went in the summer months. So he and a relative spent a good part of the summer sounding the lake to find the deepest spot. It turned out to be at the mouth of the Big East River.

A few days later they brought home several beautiful large lake trout. They were quite proud of themselves for finding this spot. And as any fisherman will know, it was to be a deep-dark secret. A few days after this momentous event, while talking about lake trout, one of the local people said, "Oh, we know where they are — they're all down at the mouth of the Big East River in the summer. We just never have time to go and fish for them!"

All the produce used at Wab-na-Kee was purchased from the Bob May farm, along with milk, eggs, butter and chicken. The Telfers spent many happy years on Lake Vernon. The cottage was sold in 1974 to Gerald L. Gatto.

BIBLIOGRAPHY

Boyer, Robert. *A Good Town Grew Here.* Bracebridge, Ontario: Herald Gazette Press, 1975.

Cookson, Joe. *Tattle Tales of Muskoka.* Bracebridge, Ontario: Herald Gazette Press, 1976.

——— *Roots in Muskoka.* Bracebridge, Ontario: Herald Gazette Press, 1978.

——— *Early Footsteps in Muskoka.* Sprucedale, Ontario: Olympic Printing, 1984.

Denniss, Gary. *Brief History of Schools in Muskoka.* Bracebridge, Ontario: Herald Gazette Press, 1972.

——— *Brief History of Churches in Muskoka.* Bracebridge, Ontario: Herald Gazette Press, 1996.

Demaine, Marjorie. *Stories of Early Muskoka Days.* Bracebridge, Ontario: Herald Gazette Press, 1971.

——— *Chronicles of Stisted Township.* Bracebridge, Ontario: Herald Gazette Press, 1976.

Hamilton, W.E. *Guide Book and Atlas of Muskoka and Parry Sound.* Toronto, Ontario: H.R. Page, 1879.

Hillside Pioneer Memorial Church. Bay Press, Huntsville, 1992.

Huntsville Old Home Week Association. Huntsville Old Home Week, 1926, souvenir book.

Hutcheson, George. *Heads and Tales.* Bracebridge, Ontario: Herald Gazette Press, 1972.

Johnson, George H. *Port Sydney Past.* Cheltenham, Ontario: Boston Mills Press, 1980.

Laycock, Jack. *A Brief History of Trinity United Church,* 1977.

Scovell, Beatrice. *The Muskoka Story.*

Terziano, Edward. *The Little Band that Grew and Grew.* Bracebridge, Ontario: Forester Press, 1986.

DOCUMENTS

Archives of Ontario, Toronto, Ontario

Heritage Huntsville Records

Huntsville Assessment Rolls 1896–1950

Huntsville *Forester* 1878–1980

Huntsville Public Library, Huntsville, Ontario

Metro Toronto Reference Library, Toronto, Ontario

Muskoka Land Registry Office, Bracebridge, Ontario

Muskoka Pioneer Village Records

Toronto *Mail* 1892

View from the Lookout, Huntsville, of Huntsville's Red Cross Hospital. Mountview Avenue is in the foreground, Church Street to the right, 1948.